CHRISTIAN ART

ERIC NEWTON AND WILLIAM NEIL

219 illustrations 17 color plates

HARPER & ROW · NEW YORK

DESIGNED BY GEORGE A. ADAMS

© 1966 THAMES AND HUDSON LTD LONDON

PRINTED AND BOUND IN YUGOSLAVIA FOR
HARPER & ROW, PUBLISHERS, INCORPORATED

FOR INFORMATION ADDRESS HARPER & ROW, PUBLISHERS,
INCORPORATED, 49 EAST 33RD STREET, NEW YORK, N. Y. 10016

LIBRARY OF CONGRESS CATALOG NUMBER: 66-10230

I The Virgin and Child:
late 3rd-c. fresco in the Catacomb of Priscilla, Rome

THE AUTHORS

Eric Newton was widely recognized as one of the foremost art critics of our time. As art critic to the *Guardian* for many years he provided a running commentary on past and present trends in sculpture and painting and not only stimulated public interest in this field but also greatly influenced public taste. He was a man of profound religious convictions. Although the discerning reader might have gathered this from his published work it is not until now that a book specifically on Christian art has appeared under his name. This was his last work before his sudden death in 1965. He welcomed the opportunity to select a rich variety of the great masterpieces of painting and sculpture in which Christian artists have expressed their faith from Byzantine times up to the present day.

The many publications of Eric Newton, some of them now standard works, have established his reputation as a master of sound judgment combined with sensitive appreciation.

William Neil is Warden of Hugh Stewart Hall and Reader in Biblical Studies at Nottingham University. Born in Glasgow in 1909, he was educated at Glasgow Academy and at Glasgow and Heidelberg Universities. During the war he was an Army Chaplain and from 1946–1953 was Head of the Department of Biblical Studies in the University of Aberdeen. Among his other books is the famous *William Neil's One Volume Bible Commentary*. He is editor of the *Knowing Christianity* series of paperbacks for thinking laymen.

William Neil, as an eminent theologian, provides a sketch of the historical developments, tensions and conflicts within Christianity itself, and shows the effect that the theological climate at different stages in the history of the Church has had on the output, quantity and expression of Christian art.

2000 YEARS OF CHRISTIAN ART

2000 YEARS OF

Contents

Preface

It is a matter of deep personal regret to me that this preface is not a joint introduction by the late Eric Newton and myself to a book to which he has contributed so much. His sudden death so soon after he had completed his part of this project has left a gap in the ranks of art critics which will not easily be filled. Those of us who knew him as a man will cherish also the memory of a kindly and generous scholar who loved his subject and spent himself in its service.

This book was the first venture in which Newton had collaborated with a theologian or I with an artist. For me at any rate it has been an enriching and enlightening experience. Neither of us could or would have undertaken such a joint assignment unless we had both been sympathetically interested in each other's fields. Newton was a man whose deep religious convictions combined with his profound knowledge of painting made him an ideal choice for a work on Christian art. With no more than an interested layman's understanding of art appreciation I could add nothing to his expertise in this province.

We decided at the outset, therefore, that in any attempt to sketch an outline of Christian art covering the past two thousand years there must be three elements. *First,* the illustrations, and as Newton himself said, the book stands or falls by them. The text contributed by both of us is merely an obbligato to the great masterpieces of Christian painting and sculpture which are reproduced here. For this selection Newton was solely responsible and his choice was made with the care and insight which marked all his work.

Second, there must be a running commentary on the illustrations by way of explanation and exposition. Newton's earlier books have taught us to expect the sensitive judgment and shrewd appraisal, coupled with an engaging enthusiasm, which we find displayed in his contribution here. But since this was to be a book on *Christian* art we felt that there ought to be a *third* element which would draw attention, not so much to the religious significance of individual painters or paintings, but which would sketch with a broad brush the historical and theological developments in the two thousand years of the Church's story, since we both believed that it is to these movements and events that the variety of artistic expression can ultimately be traced.

My own contribution has therefore been designed to complement Newton's critical appraisal of the works of Christian artists by trying to show why at certain points in the history of the Church over the last two thousand years there has been a veritable outburst of creative Christian art, while at other stages there has either been a complete dearth of artistic output or merely mediocre achievements. Why, for example, should Christian art of the Byzantine period be so different in character from that of the Renaissance, or why should Catholic art after the Reformation express itself in the flamboyant Baroque style of Rubens or Bernini while Protestant art adopted the restrained and sober treatment exemplified by the seventeenth-century Dutch masters?

Throughout the centuries it would appear that the output, quality and character of Christian art depend in the last resort on the theological climate and that therefore a book which attempts to assess the merits of Christian masterpieces must try to explain at the same time the underlying causes of the diversity of their form and content. The interaction between the historical development of the Church and the expression of Christian art in any given period was felt by both Newton and myself to be fundamental to any proper understanding of the subject. Although for practical reasons therefore this book is by two hands, it has only one purpose, to appraise and account for the rich variety of Christian art and to demonstrate at the same time its basic unity, which derives from the Christian faith of the artists.

WILLIAM NEIL

8

I

Faith and symbol

ERIC NEWTON

It is arguable - and, indeed, as little as fifteen years ago it would have been fashionable to argue - that to consider the visual arts from the point of view of their subject-matter was to misunderstand the nature and purpose of art itself: that a work of visual art, whether a building, a mosaic, a painting or even a necklace or a saucepan, was an expression of its maker's temperament, his sense of form or colour, his preference for complexity or simplicity, modified a little by the natural behaviour of his chosen medium, and modified still further, in the case of objects with a function, by the purpose to be served, but none the less, primarily a communication of the artist's own visual discoveries. And that what was essential, whether the picture were of an apple or a goddess, the building a church or a bank, the statue a saint or a politician, was that the artist should be true to his own personal vision. In a word, that an artist's worth was not to be judged by his subject-matter.

I am convinced that such an argument, though it contains a half-truth, is essentially untenable. If I believed it I would certainly not regard it as reasonable to think of 'Christian Art' as a valid category, for it is a category that imposes on the artist not a 'subject' but a state of mind and a set of emotional attitudes that are of primary importance and must govern the whole of his creative processes. The category 'Christian' (and I am not using the word as a loose equivalent for 'religious') is far more decisive, both for the theologian and for the art historian and the art critic, than such categories as 'Classic', 'Romantic' or 'Realist', which belong to the literature of aesthetics rather than to the nature of human experience. Doubtless an apple and a god, a saint and a politician have certain common factors and it is part of the artist's task to discover what they are. But the frame of mind in

10

which a sculptor carves his politician is emphatically not that in which he envisages a saint. And that frame of mind is the centre of the problem. To the theologian or to the mystic the two statues are different in meaning. To the art historian or the art critic they are - they *must* be - different in shape. For it is only by the invention of shape that the visual artist can make a precise statement about his meaning.

My own task, therefore, in writing this account of twenty centuries of Christian art, is to trace the long sequence of attempts to make the shape of the Christian work of art a precise equivalent of the meaning, or the many meanings, of the word 'Christianity'. I emphasize the word 'precise' because I believe that the visual language used by the artist is as capable of infinite subtleties as the language of words, even though it cannot be described in a dictionary or reduced to a grammar or a syntax, and that his use of that language has very little connection with his technical skill or his control of his medium. There have been decades when the greatest masters have been incapable of producing what I hope to define as 'Christian' art. One can be forgiven, for example, for not guessing whether an admirably painted family group by Rubens should be entitled 'Holy Family' or 'Portrait of the artist with his wife and child'. And one knows that no French Impressionist in the last quarter of the nineteenth century could have attempted a 'Crucifixion' or a 'Supper at Emmaus' with any hope of persuading the spectator that he had understood the meaning of what he had to convey: for his purpose as a creative artist did not include the communication of such meanings.

On the other hand, certain Byzantine icons or Romanesque ivories are so fully charged with an intensity of Christian feeling that no such misunderstanding or doubt could possibly arise. There is no question that a 'Madonna and Child' icon of the Moscow School could have been intended as a portrait. Nor could it be argued that the icon painter had attempted to produce a picture of a particular woman holding a particular child but had failed owing to lack of skill. Nor could one account for Rubens' failure by saying that he lacked sincerity or that he was incapable of genuine Christian experience.

11

It would be absurd to attribute Rubens' failure to insincerity or the icon painter's success to a lack of painterly competence. The explanation lies much deeper than that. If certain human emotions give rise to certain harmonies of colour and shape which exactly correspond to them, then we can only examine what the theologian would call 'variations in religious intensity' and art critics would describe as 'shifts in period style' by surveying the history of emotional experience in its complex journey from the art of the catacombs to the art of the twentieth century.

And here one is faced with the awkward fact that the only evidence on which one could base a history of emotional experience is the work of art itself - the carving, the painting, the melody, even the gesture that expresses it. Cause and effect, in fact, are so closely interwoven that only by studying the effect can we guess at the cause, yet only when we have guessed at the nature of the cause can we hope to understand the meaning of the effect.

This admission that one is forced to argue in a circle about relationships between subject-matter and style, is a disheartening beginning to a book on Christian art. If our historical survey were concerned with the painting of still-life we should find ourselves in a safer position, for we should start with a fixed set of reference points. We know, for our optical experience has told us and our visual memories have confirmed, the images of the apple, the jug, the bunch of flowers which have been the painter's starting point. We can compare our own photographically remembered image of a jug with the images of similar jugs presented to us by van Huysum, Cézanne or van Gogh. They differ from each other and each of them differs from our own image. But these differences are exactly what will make the history of still-life painting interesting and intelligible. For it is always delightful to compare one man's image with another's. Each extracts a portion of truth and presents it to us as though it were the whole truth. We know that it is *not* the whole truth, yet the fragment of truth about jugs extracted and presented to us by Cézanne has an intensity, despite its incompleteness, that no photograph could capture.

But that possibility of comparing photographic truth with an artist's interpretation of it cannot occur in the case of Christian art. For Christian faith, unlike a jug, has no visual existence. When man comes to consider his relationship to his God or his gods, he has left behind the world in which such phrases as 'visual existence' or 'physical appearance' have any meaning and he has entered the world of the supernatural. For the artist, in such a world, only symbolism will serve. And whoever undertakes to write the history of Christian art and to illustrate what he writes with chosen examples, must first make up his mind as to the nature and purpose of symbolism.]

In its simplest form, symbolism is not difficult to understand. Like a metaphor, it is a short cut. It works by association, by comparing the unfamiliar or the abstract with the concrete, thereby making the unfamiliar easier to grasp either with the eye or the mind. For the writer, metaphor is far commoner than most of us suppose. We can hardly escape from it. When we read about 'eradicating' a habit or publishing an 'anthology' we need not even think of pulling anything up by physical roots or gathering real flowers. The metaphor makes no demands on us: it merely simplifies an abstract idea by comparing it with a visible action.

But visual symbolism does make demands both on the artist and the spectator, and in the case of Christianity those demands become acute. Even the simple convention of a halo to indicate holiness or divinity only becomes meaningful by repetition, and we know that by the time that the interpretation of Christianity had established itself as the artist's most normal preoccupation, the glossary of Christian symbolism had grown to formidable proportions.

And yet symbolism, however elaborate, can never be a mere agreed system of 'equivalents'. There is, of course, a kind of symbolism based on a meaning, agreed and established between the artist and his public. The anchor that 'means' hope and the pair of scales that 'means' justice shed no light on the nature of hope and justice, any more than the signs $+$ or $-$ shed light on the nature of addition and subtraction, or the sign 2 explains the truth about duality. Even though such signs make the invisible visible, they do not make vivid

13

for us the essence of the invisible. And there are plenty of accepted symbols for Christian concepts - the fish that 'means' Jesus Christ, the nimbus or halo that indicates divinity or holiness, even the gesture of extended arms or the act of kneeling which makes it clear that we are concerned with prayer - these are conventions only distantly related to the emotion or the fact that the artist wishes to communicate. They are dead, or, at best, moribund symbols. They are useful but they do not illuminate.

The illuminating symbol, which each artist must discover for himself without relying on an accepted glossary of symbolism, is of another kind. When an artist wishes to tell us that there is a difference between the execution of a criminal and the Crucifixion of the Son of God and that despite the obligation, imposed on him by the very nature of painting or sculpture, to depict the event with a fairly close reference to visual truth, his first problem is to make it clear that he is less concerned with visual truth than with the meaning behind it: and that, in fact, the more he sacrifices meaning to appearance the less he can expect to succeed in producing a work of Christian art.

It follows, therefore, that symbolism of the kind that lies outside and beyond what I have called the accepted glossary, is forced upon him. The more he is obsessed by the material world of phenomena the more he will have to resist the temptation to refer to it in his work of art and to make it his task to interpret rather than to describe if he is to be a Christian artist in the sense that I propose to use the term in this book. One of the most familiar discoveries in the art historian's survey of the development of 'style' is to note the slowly increasing power of the painter and the sculptor to describe the world of phenomena that began in Italy in the fourteenth century and steadily increased until, by the middle of the seventeenth, the painter could solve, in his picture, almost any problem in the portrayal of weight, volume, structure, space or the impact of light. It would be absurd to suggest that this increasing power to describe the phenomena that surround him in life has any connection with his genius as an artist or with his power to make us consider him a 'good' artist. Indeed, I

14

have already suggested that the reverse might be the case. What I am confident of is that his equipment as a recorder of appearances is certain to interfere with his capacity to depict, in visual terms, the essence of Christianity, and that a Rembrandt, who had the fullest equipment of any artist known to us as a 'describer' of the tangible, has to rise far beyond that equipment if he is to make us aware of the difference between the material and the spiritual experience: to make it clear, for example, that a painting of the Nativity of Christ is not a representation of the birth of a Dutch baby in a barn near seventeenth-century Amsterdam.

We know that this is precisely what Rembrandt *did* achieve, despite and not because of his grasp of the material world: we know that hardly any of his contemporaries wished to attempt so hazardous a distinction and would have been powerless to do so had they wished: and we know that to Giotto, despite his lack of interest in space and light and the laws of perspective, the task of doing what Pieter de Hooch, or even Velazquez either failed to do or were not required to do, was comparatively easy: and we know well enough that Giotto's success was mainly due to his genius but that he succeeded more easily because nothing in his equipment as an artist interfered with his vision as a Christian.

We can be sure then that the impact of a work of Christian art depends to a certain extent on the artist's command of his own visual language, but to an even greater extent on his power of using that language in the service of Christianity: and as we survey our sequence of such works from the age of Constantine to the present day, we become more and more convinced that Christianity had no need to use more than a fragment of that language for its most intense expression. No deficiency on the part of the painter of a mediaeval illuminated manuscript, in the art of telling the truth about human anatomy or the fall of light on a solid object, rendered him one whit less capable of expressing the truth of spiritual experience in symbols of his own devising.

This book, therefore, will be concerned with attempts to communicate the spiritual rather than the material, and consequently the mediaeval world will occupy a greater part

15

in it than the civilization of the Italian Renaissance which had begun to discover the enchantment of the human body and the beauty of the world's surface. Still less important will be the Baroque age with its command of rhetoric and its determination to be impressive. After the Baroque the spiritual temperature steadily dropped until the end of the nineteenth century, and at last, at the beginning of the twentieth century, a revolution occurred as a consequence of which the pursuit of representational truth slackened and a new kind of symbolism began to replace it. This may not have been what Christianity most needed, but it was, at least, a symbolism that Christianity could use. The passionate statements of a Rouault, the modern tapestry and the stained glass of Coventry Cathedral, could not have occurred in the nineteenth century. This new art is important, and only a revolution in the language at the artist's disposal could have brought it about. In this brief general introduction it should be noted that the birth of a new religion and its emergence and recognition under the Emperor Constantine in the fourth century from being an underground movement, often persecuted, never triumphant, brought with it an immense new opportunity to develop a new iconography and imposed on the artist, the architect and the craftsman-designer, a set of tasks of a far wider range than they had ever enjoyed before. To evolve a new iconography, however plentiful and varied the material at the artist's disposal may be, is not easy, and to conceive of that iconographical material in terms of symbolism imposes a new kind of strain on the artist's imagination. The religious art of Egypt, of the Babylonians and the Greeks, however admirable, was of little use as a starting point for Christian artists or iconographers.

Egypt had been concerned with religion as a part of the impressive state machine. Dignity and ceremonial, kingship and the machinery of government were its main concerns. And when Egypt attempted to envisage the future life, it was no more than an exact replica of life on earth. In Mesopotamia symbols of physical power of a rather ruthless kind were the artist's main concern. And in Greece a conception of the gods and goddesses made in man's image had produced

16

an art based on physical perfection that was again to dominate the whole of Europe from the Renaissance until the end of the nineteenth century.

It was the task of the first Christian artists not merely to ignore but to destroy these potent images of power, efficiency and physical perfection, and to replace them by - what? The simple answer is 'by a new emphasis on the soul and a comparative disregard of the body: by a new way of symbolizing the relationship between God and man, made possible by the incarnation of God *as* man, in the person of Jesus Christ: by the ritualistic symbolism that makes this relationship possible in the Sacraments: and by illustrating the events in the life of Christ as recounted in the four Gospels'.

Obviously the programme was immense. It could only be developed slowly for there were two kinds of difficulty to overcome. One was to adapt traditional styles that were already in use for non-Christian or pre-Christian purposes. The other was to select out of the new and always growing material that early Christianity brought with it, whatever was most suitable for translation into visual terms. In brief, a style had to be evolved by modifying the existing style: and a range or ranges of subject-matter had to be decided on which would be self-explanatory with a minimum assistance from labels or inscriptions.

The style, of course, especially along the shores of the Eastern Mediterranean, was ready to hand. The Hellenic art that had spread from Greece both eastwards to Constantinople and westwards to the Italian peninsula was suave and graceful. It consisted largely of sculpture though a certain amount of Hellenistic painting was familiar to the early Christian artists. It was based on the Greek theory that the visual arts, if they were to be something more meaningful than mere decoration, must be an imitation of nature and that there was nothing in nature more worth imitating than the human figure, although these figures were, in turn, idealized.

But it soon became apparent that such a style was, by its very nature, unsuited for the expression of Christian or Jewish themes. Pagan art was concerned with the physical, and at its best it evolved types of physical beauty which have never

17

been surpassed. To express what is implied by our use of the word 'soul' was never part of the pagan artist's programme. Christian art, on the other hand, had hardly any other purpose whether it was concerned with pure symbolism, the presentation of semi-symbolic images, or narrative. It is an art that has no other preoccupation than the supernatural, the nature of man's relationship with God. That relationship had been explored and explained in Jewish literature. Yet little art had been inspired by the Old Testament, for Jewish law forbade the making of religious images lest the confusion between the representation and what was represented should lead to idolatry. It is not very easy for us, who have no such fear, to realize the Jewish attitude which will not allow the visible, tangible image to interfere with the power of the invisible and intangible idea. Especially as this fear of imagery is difficult to understand when we read, in the Old Testament, of the many interchanges between Jehovah and his Chosen People.

But from the moment when God sent his only begotten Son to dwell on earth, born of a mortal woman, to preach, to perform miracles, to suffer death at the hands of the Jews and to be resurrected, the situation for the artist changed, for the new religion contained within itself the fact of the invisible made visible, the Deity made human, the supernatural made physically manifest. At last there was no reason to forbid imagery, for if God Himself became incarnate there could be no possibility of the artist's images of Him leading to idolatry.

Perhaps this argument approaches too closely to theology for it to be appropriate to an art historian's account of the origin and development of Christian art. Yet it is important to note how the spreading power of Christianity itself, in the first three centuries after the Crucifixion, made a new kind of iconography not only possible but essential. If imagery is forbidden, the artist cannot serve religion either as an interpreter or a propagandist. He becomes impotent - a mere decorator of surfaces and filler of spaces. The gradual release of the painter and sculptor, his increasing freedom to use the whole of his creative faculties on the invention of new images for new meanings, gave rise to a period in art history more varied and more intense than any previous period.

18

Bronze crucifix made for the Abbey of Werden in Germany, c. 1070

In the end, though inventiveness continued, intensity faded. The mystery of the supernatural was ousted by the rediscovery of the material world, but not before, during a few precious decades at the beginning of the sixteenth century, art had managed to balance the two without sacrificing either.

Meanwhile, in AD 313, the Emperor Constantine had established the Christian Church as the state religion and by the end of the sixteenth century Pope Gregory the Great had made a pronouncement to the effect that since painting can do for the illiterate what writing can do for those who can read, the way was clear for the artist. The whole of the Old and New Testaments was there to provide him with material, from the Creation of the world to the Revelation of St John. All that he needed was wall-space, a certain amount of guidance from ecclesiastical authority and the kind of visual imagination that could adapt an old style to new subject-matter.

From the end of the fourth century all three were available. Along the north coast of the Mediterranean from Rome to Ravenna in the West, across the Balkans, Macedonia and Thessaly to Constantinople in the East and along the Eastern border from Antioch to Jerusalem and then as far South as Alexandria the new Gospel was spreading. And with it spread the need for the kind of art that would interpret it, making it vivid and meaningful to the growing mass of converts to Christianity.

Christianity and the arts

WILLIAM NEIL

The Christian Church is bound by its title deeds - the Bible - to be both a patron and a promoter of the arts. The God of the Creation story in Genesis 1 is an artist who 'saw everything that he had made, and behold, it was very good'. The Church is thus committed to the belief that the Creator delights in the beauty of the world as an expression of the beauty that is in Himself. The glory of a sunset, the marvel of a flower, the song of a blackbird, the comeliness of the human body are for the Christian no accidents of nature but the handiwork of God.

By the same token the skills of the artist and the craftsman are regarded in the Bible as the gift of God. It is the Creator Himself who 'hath filled him with the spirit of God, in wisdom, in understanding, and in knowledge, and in all manner of workmanship: and to devise cunning works, to work in gold, and in silver, and in brass, and in cutting of stones for setting, and in carving of wood, to work in all manner of cunning workmanship' (*Exodus* 35: 31-33).

The sense of the beauty of the human body is deeply rooted in the Scriptures, whether it be the youthful beauty of a Rachel or an Absalom, or the venerable beauty of a 'hoary head' *(Proverbs* 20:29). The Jesus who saw in the 'lilies of the field' a loveliness which surpassed the magnificence of the ostentatious Solomon, reveals His delight in the countryside and its creatures in story and parable. Moreover the author of the Sermon on the Mount was not only a master of the spiritual life but of the artistic life as well. 'The soul of the poet in Jesus blossomed on His lips'. St Paul, too, in his famous catalogue of the kind of things we ought to keep in the forefront of our minds includes, together with all that is true and honourable and just and pure, also 'whatsoever things are lovely' *(Philippians* 4:8).

21

But of course for the Christian it is above all the fact of the Incarnation that proclaims the intrinsic value of the arts and their status as an essential part of the human scene and an enrichment of the human mind. We live on a visited planet. The Son of God came among men as a craftsman and a teacher making the common things of life holy and secular things sacred. The gulf has been bridged between God and man, for Christ made the earth the forecourt of heaven. The world around us reflects the glory of God and the Christian artist, whether he works with words or harmonies, with canvas, wood or stone, interprets his vision of God's glory for the enrichment of men's minds and the beautification of their environment in obedience to the declared purpose of God in Christ to transform and renew the whole life of man, beginning here and now.

This book is concerned with the Christian practice of the arts. It is the more surprising therefore, in view of Christianity's origins and its dependence on its Hebrew heritage, that the people of the Old Testament handed on so small a legacy of artistic achievement in this specific field, namely, painting, sculpture and architecture. Their reputation as musicians was considerable (*cf. Psalm* 137:1-3) and the evidence of their skill as lyric poets is manifest in the Psalter, the Song of Songs, and elsewhere in the Old Testament. We might add to that their excellence as *littérateurs*, whether it be exemplified in vivid narrative, such as the Story of Joseph (*Genesis* 37-50) and the Court History of David (*II Samuel* 9-20), or in the philosophical drama of Job.

But when we look to Israel for anything comparable with the palaces, temples and artistic treasures of ancient Mesopotamia, or the royal tombs and wall-paintings of ancient Egypt, we draw almost a complete blank. Such evidence as archaeologists have uncovered in Palestine suggests fairly primitive architecture, inferior pottery, and apart from the engraving of gems for seals and signets, and the carving of ivory, in both of which arts the Hebrews appear to have excelled, there is no decorative work of any great distinction. On top of this is the almost complete absence of representational art, either painting or sculpture.

The Ark of the Covenant (here, a 6th-c. mosaic) was the only image of God possible to the Hebrew artist

22

Solomon's great Temple in Jerusalem - completely destroyed in 587 BC - was the work not of Hebrew but of Phoenician craftsmen

Much of this negative result is rooted in Israel's history. The Hebrews were basically a nomadic people who became settled agriculturalists only after a prolonged period of struggle for a foothold in the Levant. For about a century of their chequered history they had an independent kingdom and a measure of prosperity. For most of the rest of the time they were economically the poor relations of their wealthier neighbours, harassed by civil war and foreign oppressors, hard put to it to scrape together the bare means of existence, far less indulge in artistic adventure.

When in their one brief period of affluence through King Solomon's development of the copper industry and active cultivation of foreign trade, they were in a position to enrich and beautify their capital city of Jerusalem with a Temple, a royal residence and other public buildings, they had to import Phoenician craftsmen to carry out the work. All of this was destroyed in the sack of Jerusalem by Nebuchadnezzar of Babylon in 587 BC and when Herod the Great at the time of Christ outshone Solomon's Temple with a reconstructed sanctuary which was one of the wonders of the world, it was again not the product of native Jewish art but a building in the Graeco-Roman style which dominated the Hellenistic world.

23

The absence of painting and sculpture, however, was due to more than poverty and war. The second of the Ten Commandments is categorically explicit: 'Thou shalt not make unto thee a graven image, nor the likeness of any form that is in heaven above, or that is in the earth beneath, or that is in the water under the earth.' No representational likeness of any being, divine, human or animal was permitted by the Law which governed the total life of the people. It is safe to say that although this edict is attributed to Moses it was either not fully formulated or not rigidly enforced until the latter stages of Israel's history. Images were made and idol worship had to be denounced as long as Israel was a monarchy. Solomon's Temple had its golden cherubim, composite winged creatures, which guarded the symbolic dwelling place of God in the Holy of Holies.

But in the few centuries before the coming of Christianity, the period from which any artistic productions would have been most likely to survive, the Law was paramount and the distinctive nature of Israel's monotheistic faith was rigorously upheld. It has been said that properly speaking there is only one character in the Old Testament, namely God. Whatever polytheistic background lies behind Hebrew religion it is certain that from the time of Moses the monotheistic principle progressively dominated Hebrew thought. When we recognize that Israel was surrounded by peoples each of whom had its pantheon of gods and goddesses, sun-god, moon-god, storm-god and so on, often represented as animals, and worshipped in innumerable shrines and temples through idol and image, it is not surprising that prophet and priest alike fought to the utmost to root out anything that might adulterate Israel's austere faith.

They did this on practical as well as on doctrinal grounds. Most of the Near Eastern religions were nature-cults, with temple prostitutes as part of their stock-in-trade. Without the absolute authority of a monotheistic faith ethics of any kind became a casualty. But above all prophet and priest fought against the idolatry that polytheism involved because they believed that Israel had been given a unique revelation of the truth about God, man and the universe, and that she had a mission to stand fast for that truth herself and to communicate it to the rest of mankind.

The God of the Old Testament is transcendent, invisible, and undepictable and to preserve this conception the Hebrews forbade the making of any image or likeness of anything in heaven or on earth which might become a substitute for the truth. We may regret that the result was a dearth of creative art but we can at least understand the cause. Israel left no memorials of empire like the Assyrians and the Egyptians. Her history is of no importance in terms of political or economic achievement. Her artistic bequest to mankind is equally unimpressive. Her contribution was made exclusively in the field of religion and ethics. It is no small legacy.

The first Christians were Jews for whom the Old Testament was the voice of God. They were the new Israel, acknowledging Abraham as the founding father of the faith. The twelve apostles represented the twelve tribes and Jesus was the Messiah whom prophet and psalmist had foretold. How then did this Jewish community so far forget its past that it grew into a Church which fostered not only the traditionally Jewish arts of music and poetry but opened its doors to painter and sculptor, covering its walls with likenesses human and divine, filling its niches with imagery and its windows with the figures of heavenly beings?

The basic reason was of course that the invisible God had become visible and His undepictable Majesty had been expressed in a human life. It was not that these devout Jewish Christians substituted belief in Christ for belief in God. With one accord they proclaimed their conviction that the Unknowable had now made Himself known. What Jesus did and said, God was doing and saying through Him. When men came face to face with Christ they came face to face with God. All that men needed to know of the nature and purpose of God they could learn from Christ. God had come down to man's level to lift man up to His. The Second Commandment had been designed to prevent the worship of false gods. To encourage the worship of the true God by depicting Him as He had now revealed Himself in a Man, teaching, healing, forgiving,

25

One of the oldest
Biblical texts in
existence - a fragment
of Isaiah, from the
Dead Sea Scrolls

blessing, suffering death and overcoming it, was clearly wholly in line with the spirit of the Commandment.

There was in addition the fact that while the Christian Church was Jewish in origin it quickly showed itself to be equally at home in Gentile surroundings. While the Gospels and epistles of the New Testament were written almost entirely by Jews, they were written in Greek, the lingua franca of the Roman Empire, for Christian communities in Italy, Greece and Asia Minor. The Roman-Jewish war of AD 66-73 involved the destruction of Jerusalem and the virtual disappearance of Jewish Christianity. But long before that the detachment of the new faith from its Palestinian setting had begun.

Only for a few years was it possible to disguise the fact that the Gospel was an explosive mixture which could not be contained in the narrow nationalistic confines of orthodox Jewry. To begin with the new movement was regarded as a harmless Jewish sect and the conservatism of the earliest followers of Jesus succeeded in establishing a satisfactory compromise between the faith of the Temple and that of the Nazarene meeting-house. The radical thinking of St Stephen and St Paul - both of them Jews but both deeply conscious of the implications of the new faith in terms of a world mission - ensured that Christianity was soon seen in its true colours as Good News about God not only for Jews but for all men.

Persecution by the Jewish religious authorities, among them ironically enough Rabbi Saul of Tarsus, first drove the Nazarenes from Jerusalem and planted cells of the new faith outside the confines of Judaism. The conversion of St Paul to discipleship of the Christ whose name he had tried to erase from the pages of history was the greatest single factor in ensuring that the link which bound Christianity to its Palestinian origins was decisively broken. With his brilliant mind and tireless energy he not only re-interpreted the faith so that it became meaningful for the Gentile world but himself planted it firmly throughout the Mediterranean world.

By the time of his death about thirty years after the Crucifixion the Gospel had spread like wildfire and centres of Christian activity had been established throughout Asia Minor, Greece and in the imperial capital itself, Rome. The Church

The first great missionary was St Paul, here disputing with the Greeks

of Jerusalem had become progressively a backwater, soon to be virtually obliterated, and the future of Christianity lay in the See of St Peter. A Church which was predominantly Gentile while it treasured its Old Testament heritage of psalms and prophecy set little store on the shibboleths of Jewish law and custom from which it reckoned Christ had set it free. Jewish inhibitions in respect of pictorial art meant little to men and women whose chief interest in the Old Testament was that it spoke to them of Christ.

Just as St Paul and other New Testament writers had used Greek poetry and philosophy to illuminate their message for the benefit of those to whom such ideas were more familiar than Hebrew thought, and to whom a metaphor drawn from the athletic games in the stadium was more meaningful than allusions to the lives of the kings of Israel, so the first Gentile Christians availed themselves of the art forms of the pagan world, and used them in the service of the Gospel as visual aids to the deeper understanding of the faith and as an expression of their inmost convictions.

They had indeed a wealth of material at their disposal in the Bible. For them the Gospel Story was rightly the centre-piece, to which the Old Testament was the prelude and pointer,

27

while the rest of the New Testament was its sequel. So in early Christian art Jesus Himself must obviously take pride of place as Saviour and Lord, together with such incidents in the Gospels as illustrated the cardinal doctrines of the Faith - the Virgin Birth, the Last Supper, the Resurrection. The apostles - and above all St Peter - as not only the first followers of Jesus but as the founders and guarantors of the Faith were also an obvious choice.

But the Old Testament with its incredible galaxy of vivid incidents and memorable personalities likewise offered a rich quarry for instruction and inspiration. Obvious parallels with the New Testament story would at once suggest themselves, such as the sacrifice of Isaac (*Genesis* 22) through its association in the liturgy with Good Friday. This type of illustration of Gospel themes by Old Testament narratives would tend to have a stronger appeal than the mere representation of colourful or exciting incidents from Hebrew history for their own sake.

The Sacrifice of Isaac: 6th-c. mosaic in Beth-Alpha Synagogue

There was, however, a rich store of motifs available for painters in the imagery and symbolism of the Bible. The Hebrews were never afraid of thinking and speaking of God in anthropomorphic terms. It was not so much that they recognized speculatively that if we are to talk of God at all without getting lost in philosophical abstractions we are bound to speak of Him in terms of the highest category we know, that of personality. It was much more that God was for the people of the Old Testament a living God, a God who acts, who is known by what He does.

Thus He is described as father, shepherd, judge and king. He is the husband who has been saddled with a faithless bride, Israel, or He is the husbandman who is plagued with an unproductive vineyard, again Israel. In such homely imagery taken from everyday experience Hebrew thought did not for a moment suggest that this was all that there was to be said about God or that these images did more than suggest and reflect aspects of His character and activity. There is a similar robust anthropomorphism in the language of Jesus. When He tells the parable of the Prodigal Son He is obviously not asking us to believe that God is an old man who runs to meet the penitent sinner. He is encouraging us to think

'Thou art Peter, and upon this rock I will build my Church': 3rd-c. fresco in the Catacomb of Peter and Marcellinus

imaginatively about God and to see religious truth in a simple human tale. When Christian artists used the imagery of bread or wine, a lamp or a vine, to convey a message of profound theological significance they were being completely faithful to the Biblical way of thinking.

Some Biblical symbols are of course undepictable. The symbol of the covenant, for example, the relationship between God and His people, which binds the Old and New Testaments together, and is indeed the same word as testament, could perhaps be suggested by a portrayal of the Ark of the Covenant

29

Symbolizing the relationship between Christ and the Church, vines were from the earliest times natural subjects for the catacomb painters

which contained the tables of the Law, or in the case of the New Covenant, by the eucharistic bread and wine, symbolizing the new relationship to God made possible through Christ. But there were plenty of powerful and evocative symbols by which the Christian artist could convey the unfathomable mysteries which only the poet or the painter can communicate.

How better to express the truth of a Trinitarian faith than by the Biblical symbols of a divine Father, supreme, omnipotent, transcendent, a Son who gives Himself for men that they too might become sons, and a Dove as the symbol of the gentle Spirit of God which hovers over the created world? But God's Spirit does more than hover over us, it energizes, stimulates and propels us. So the Spirit is also depictable as Wind. Yet it also cleanses, purifies and judges us, so the Bible sees it also in terms of Fire. The humility of our Lord and His self-sacrifice are summed up in the symbol of the Lamb. He is the Good Shepherd who knows each one of His sheep, lays down His life for them and seeks to bring other sheep into the one fold with one Shepherd.

The Vine was for Jesus a symbol of the union between Himself and His people. The parent stock gives life to the branches: unfruitful branches are fit for nothing but destruction. Like other Biblical images the Vine becomes a pregnant motif in Christian art. The sacramental symbols of Baptism as the beginning of the new life of the Christian, and of the Eucharist as a dramatization of the Passion and Resurrection, are summed up by the quasi-Biblical imagery of the Fish which features so largely in early Christian painting. The letters of the Greek word for fish, *ichthus*, were ingeniously seen to be the initial letters of the Greek words 'Jesus Christ, Son of God, Saviour' and to the Christians of the second century no symbol said so much. It stood for Incarnation, Redemption, Resurrection - the whole scheme of Christian salvation. But it was historically linked with the miracle of the Loaves and Fishes and the apostolic vocation to become 'fishers of men'.

Another quasi-Biblical symbol was the Ship, again reminiscent of the Galilean scene, but linking the second-century Church with the Ark which bore Noah and his family across the waters to safety, foreshadowing the salvation now offered

The fish of Christ and the anchor of faith, on an early funeral stele

31

to all through the water of Baptism. But most moving of all symbols was the Cross, which has persisted through the centuries as the universally acknowledged token of the Death which meant new life for all. Symbolism in Christian art and architecture became more elaborate as time went on but its basis and justification are to be found in the Bible itself in the rich imaginative texture of the Hebrew-Christian records of God's dealings with men.

Religious art in any civilization is bound to be concerned with the representation of the divine being or beings, with the after-life, with man in his various interests and aspirations as they are related to the supernatural order. Christian art no less than any other shares these characteristics. But in the world in which Christianity grew up there were as St Paul said 'gods many and lords many'. Every city had its plethora of shrines and temples with gods and goddesses from every corner of the vast amalgam of races and traditions that made up the Roman Empire.

For Christians, however, there was, as St Paul continued, only 'one God, the Father, from whom all being comes, towards whom we move; and there is one Lord, Jesus Christ, through whom all things came to be, and we through him' (*I Corinthians* 8:5-6). It was not only that Christians claimed to worship the only true God, revealed to man through Christ, they also maintained that the moral and religious aspirations of all other faiths and philosophies were summed up and fulfilled in Christianity. This was at long last God's final word to man, embracing all partial apprehensions of the truth about life, and the world in which it has to be lived.

Christianity was therefore not presented as one among many rival faiths competing for men's attention but as the sole answer to the questions that men had always asked about the meaning and purpose of existence. Men had always been oppressed by the sense of their own mortality. Standards of behaviour had always been a matter of dispute. Various religions offered varying solutions to the problem of pain and the suffering of the innocent. The Christian missionaries maintained that these and all such concerns were now no longer enigmas.

32

'I am Alpha and Omega, the beginning and the end':
a 5th-c. cross incorporates this idea,
together with the monogram of Christ

Their claim was stark and uncompromising. 'When in former times God spoke to our forefathers, He spoke in fragmentary and varied fashion through the prophets. But in this final age He has spoken to us in the Son whom He has made heir to the whole universe, and through whom He created all orders of existence: the Son who is the effulgence of God's splendour and the stamp of God's very being, and sustains the universe by His word of power. When He had brought about the purgation of sins, He took his seat at the right hand of Majesty on high ... so Christ was offered once to bear the burden of men's sins, and will appear a second time ... to bring salvation to those who are watching for Him' (*Hebrews* I : 1-3; 9 : 28).

These words were written to a group of Christians in Rome by an unknown missionary probably just before the Emperor Nero's madness provoked him into the first bloody persecution of the Church by the Roman authorities. What did they mean to men and women who stood face to face with death? Simply this, that God's eternal Son had come among men, living with them and dying for them, that through committing their lives to Him their past failures were blotted out, that they had been admitted into a fellowship in which death had no power over them, that their lives were 'hid with Christ in God', that if they died for Christ's sake they would share His glory, and if they lived they would see Him come again.

It was this sense of living in a new dimension, of being pilgrims on this earth with heaven as their goal, that gave the first Christians that indifference to the changes and chances of life that the New Testament so faithfully records. They were the men of whom St Paul could write: 'Honour and dishonour, praise and blame, are alike our lot ... dying, we still live on: disciplined by suffering, we are not done to death; in our sorrows we have always cause for joy; poor ourselves, we bring wealth to many; penniless, we own the world' (*II Corinthians* 6 : 8-10). It was in such a spirit that the first Christian artists expressed their faith on the walls of the catacombs of Rome where they worshipped God in secret under sentence of death.

The forms of the otherworldly

ERIC NEWTON

It was over a geographical area in which the pattern of government was Roman and the tradition of culture and religious belief largely Hellenic that the Apostles first began to spread the new religion. Long before it had begun to assert itself as a competitor with the other religions that coexisted within the boundaries of the Roman Empire, the belief in Christ as the Son of God, the story of His birth, life, death and resurrection had been spreading among the Jews and the Gentiles alike. To the Jewish converts it must have seemed that Christianity was an extension and a climax to the Jewish faith. To the Gentiles it must have been rather different, a new conception of religion not specifically linked with Judaism even though its birthplace was Jerusalem.

The Old Testament was well known as the official repository of Jewish history and Mosaic law. To the Jews, scattered over the whole area, the choice was between the acceptance or rejection of the belief that Jesus was the awaited Messiah. If He were, in reality, the Son of God, then the new Christian Gospels were an integral part of the old Jewish religion and the New Testament an inevitable sequel to the Old. If not, a false prophet had arisen and had been justifiably done to death by the very people that He had served, taught and inspired.

In the Acts of the Apostles one can read the story of the conversion of both the Jews and Gentiles, the gradual formation of Christian communities, united by faith and encouraged by teaching, scattered over the shores and the hinterland of the Eastern Mediterranean from Rome to Antioch. That they should have been feared and often persecuted by the Roman government even though they never exercised political power and never attempted to interfere with the Roman machinery of government, is for the political historian to explain rather

36

than the recorder of the history of art. But certainly 'He who is not with me is against me' is not a creed likely to endear a dedicated minority to a powerful government.

Meanwhile the creed enrolled more and more adherents and it was not surprising that when in the year 313 the Emperor Constantine officially approved of what had been a secret sect with no official headquarters and no recognized places of worship, the effect of the release was immediate. It is true that tentative attempts at Christian imagery exist which date back a century before Constantine. They are artistically unimportant: what is significant is that they exist at all as a proof that small assemblages of Christians were not only meeting secretly to assert their faith, but that they wished to record their adherence to the worship of Jesus by producing visible records of it - however primitive they might be.

But once they were released from the fear of persecution the only obstruction between the artist and his full opportunity to express himself and his religious beliefs was simply the lack of space to work on and in, and only the architect could supply him with what he required.

What the architect himself had to do was to invent a building that would appropriately serve an entirely new pattern of worship. The pagan temple had housed the sculptured image of the god; his devotees remained, for the most part, outside it. The Christian Church, on the other hand, was required to house a mass of worshippers: the statue was supplanted by an altar for sacrifice, and the god himself could only be referred to in works of art, reminders, as it were, of his essence. Objects of religious use were also needed, the chalice, the episcopal throne, the vestment worn by the priest, the missal and the reliquary.

Just as in art the stylistic traditions of paganism had to be adapted to the new iconography, so in architecture the prototype of the Christian Church had to be found in whatever pagan building seemed most appropriate to the new ritual. And the only prototype that would serve Christian purposes was the Roman basilica, the enclosed market place or the public law court which had been specially designed for public assembly, often with a semi-circular dais at one end in which the chairman

37

or judge could be seated, which now became the proper place for the altar with a space round it for the choir. Carvings decorated the capitals of the columns, but sculpture of the kind associated with the pagan temple did not appear till centuries later. But from the sixth century onwards the walls of the nave and the semi-dome of the apse behind the altar proved admirable places for the development of Christian imagery; the former were often used for symbolic narrative drawn from the Gospels; the latter for a more generalized and more hieratic kind of symbolism whose purpose was not to tell a story but to implant a spiritual idea in visible form on the mind and memory of the beholder.

Naturally these experiments in a new kind of iconography developed slowly. The centre in which they rose to their most impressive heights is Ravenna, once a seaport facing the Adriatic and the headquarters of the Roman fleet. The sea coast has retreated and today the city is five or six miles inland. But four of the churches, three within the city walls and a fourth outside it, sum up the supreme achievement of Christian art in Italy between the fifth and sixth centuries. It is in the churches of Ravenna that we can most easily study the beginnings of Christian art - not because in them we find the earliest examples of Christian iconography but because nothing so complete in its cumulative effect or more varied in its detail exists elsewhere. In Ravenna too, one finds not only the meeting point of Eastern and Western Christianity but also a fusion between the two both in architecture and imagery.

For that reason it is convenient to abandon the chronological sequence and to describe the whole of the splendid series of decorations as a single unit even though it is true that they were spread over a period of about a hundred years - from the middle of the fifth century to the year 547 when Bishop Maximian consecrated the church of San Vitale in the presence of the Emperor Justinian and his Empress Theodora.

What characterizes the whole of the Ravenna cycle is the consistent use of mosaic with a new sense of its decorative and iconographical possibilities. The medium was not, of course, a new one. The Romans had used it, but largely to cover floor spaces or, if it were used on walls, it was to protect

Miracle of the loaves and fishes: early 6th-c. mosaic in S. Apollinare Nuovo, Ravenna

the curved insides of fountain niches, or surfaces where paint would have been destroyed by moisture.

The employment of mosaic in early Christian art - not only in Ravenna but in Rome, Constantinople, Daphni in Greece, and, later, in Sicily and Venice - is one of the two most daring and successful experiments in the exploration of the effective uses of a medium in the whole history of art. The other is the development of stained glass in a later century and in Northern Europe. Both were the result of the opportunistic use of an architectural context.

In the South and South-East of Europe it was inevitable that the fierce glare of the sun should compel architects to reduce window areas to a minimum and the resultant spread of wall surfaces could not fail to attract the artist. In the North, the development of what had started as Romanesque architecture and then gradually became fully-established Gothic,

39

the exact opposite occurred, and equally inevitably. The sun, throughout Northern France, Germany, and the British Isles, was not felt as an inconvenience, and as the Gothic style, with its dynamic upward thrust of vaulted roofs supported on piers, enlarged its scope, the architect discovered that the wall was no longer a necessity, either as a defence against light or as a support for the weight of the roof.

Consequently the Mediterranean basin developed the habit of using the wall for its most splendid effects while the Gothic North concentrated its most telling imagery within the ever increasing area of the window. The fact that the period in which the Byzantine style dominated Christian iconography preceded that in which Gothic art made its most daring experiments by seven or eight centuries is no more than a by-product of the direction in which the Christian religion spread across Europe. Had Jesus been born in Rouen or Winchester the history of architecture, painting, and sculpture would have followed a different pattern.

But even within a context where the wall rather than the window provided the artist with his fullest opportunity, he still had the choice between fresco and mosaic, and it was the choice of mosaic and his intelligent use of it that makes the Ravenna churches among the most colourful and impressive of all decorated interiors.

Mosaic has certain characteristics which produce effects beyond the reach of fresco. It is composed of small tesserae of coloured glass or marble embedded in cement which is not merely adhering to the wall following its curvature; it *is* the wall. The mosaic covering is therefore an integral part of the structure.

The rich colour of the tesserae and the fact that pure gold was available - gold leaf fused between layers of transparent glass - gave it an intensity denied to any form of pigment. In addition, the fact that each of the tesserae is embedded at a slightly different angle to its neighbours gives it a vibrating texture and hence a richness of surface unobtainable by any other means. Mosaic is a stubborn material. It cannot achieve the flexibility of paint and for that reason it is incapable of detailed or naturalistic effects. The mosaicist is compelled, by the nature of his medium, to aim at breadth of pattern. What he does is intended to be seen at a distance. He covers large areas and his decorative or iconographical effects have no limit except those imposed by the shape and extent of the wall itself.

Mosaic is, within reasonable limits, permanent. The tesserae which compose it are not coloured: they are composed of unalterable colour. This is equally true of the gold which, in darkish interiors, lit by small windows, shines with a mysterious glow that can be deliberately controlled by slight alterations of the angle of the tesserae.

The technical problems offered by such an intractable medium can easily be described. The effect of the interior whose walls are encrusted with it is indescribable. Nor can any photograph convey the combination of brilliance and mystery, remoteness and decorative magnificence. A good reproduction of a painting by Titian or Rembrandt can bring the spectator within reasonable distance of the work of art itself. No photographic short cut will bring one near to the experience of entering the mausoleum of Galla Placidia or the Sanctuary of San Vitale in Ravenna.

The little cruciform building - no larger than a moderately roomy cottage - called the Mausoleum of Galla Placidia (the name is traditional but the evidence that connects the building with the daughter of the Emperor Theodosius, sister of the Emperor Honorius, is slender) - is possibly the earliest major example of Christian art in Italy. It belongs to the middle of the fifth century. The barrel-vaulted ceiling is thickly patterned with rosettes in pink, green and gold on a blue ground and the effect is oriental in its opulence. Two of the semi-circular ends of the interior are filled with mosaic panels depicting two harts drinking from a spring against a background of acanthus scrolls. The other two show, on one side, St Lawrence and the instrument of his martyrdom, the flaming gridiron: on the other is the famous panel of the Good Shepherd, Christ, seated in a rocky landscape, surrounded by six sheep. He is beardless, and although He wears a gold nimbus as a symbol of His divine nature, He is evidently based on a Hellenistic Apollo and He is richly clad as though to suggest a Roman Emperor.

41

St Lawrence: mid-5th-c. mosaic in the Mausoleum of Galla Placidia, Ravenna

This is, in fact, our first large-scale glimpse of the tentative beginnings of the Byzantine style - that fusion of oriental decoration, Hellenistic naturalism with echoes of pagan subject-matter, and Christian symbolism. The stiff hieratic solemnity of later centuries has not yet appeared. There is an ease and a pastoral elegance in this Good Shepherd that is still more than half-pagan. The notion of an aloof, awe-inspiring Saviour has not yet emerged.

Of the remaining three churches in Ravenna that use the medium of mosaic in order to make their meaning clear, two are of the basilica type, with immense corridor-like naves leading to the climax of the High Altar and the semi-dome behind it. The earlier of the two, Sant'Apollinare Nuovo, was built under Theodoric, King of the Ostrogoths from 493 to 526, and has one of the completest mosaic ensembles in existence. The other, Sant'Apollinare in Classe (Classis, the old Roman harbour, lies a mile or two outside the city), contains a simpler scheme in which the mosaics are iconographically less ambitious and are confined to the semi-dome, the walls of the apse, and the triumphal arch. This belongs to the reign of Justinian (526-561).

The mosaics in the nave of Sant'Apollinare Nuovo (the apse mosaics have disappeared) are in three zones. The upper zone, between the roof and the windows below them, contains a series of twenty-six squarish panels, narrative in content, telling the story of the life of Christ, with miracles and parables on the left and scenes from the Passion on the right. Below, in the spaces between the windows are single figures of prophets and authors of the Bible, tall, static and solemn, dressed in white robes under ornamental, umbrella-shaped canopies.

Beneath the windows, and above the row of arches that separate the nave from the aisles, are two processions of hypnotic solemnity. On the left, twenty-two virgin Saints move slowly from the town of Classis towards the altar, where, headed by the three Magi, they are received by the enthroned Virgin and Child, flanked on either side by four angels. On the right, a similar procession of male martyrs moves in the same rhythmical manner from the palace of Theodoric

Mosaics on the north wall of S. Apollinare Nuovo, Ravenna. The two upper rows are Early Christian (*c.* 510), the procession below, Byzantine (*c.* 550)

Christ hands the martyr's crown to S. Vitale in the presence of Bishop Ecclesius, who holds a model of the church he founded (showing its polygonal shape): mosaic of the mid-6th c. in the apse of S. Vitale, Ravenna

to the enthroned Christ, similarly guarded by four standing angels.

If, as is possible, the whole of this elaborate scheme has been conceived by the same mind and executed by the same craftsmen, the interior is one of the most remarkable tributes in existence to the flexibility of early Christian iconography. The narrative panels on the upper walls are so dramatically imagined, so simple in composition yet so clear in narrative content, that each tells its own story with a minimum of reference to the Gospels. It is worth noting that the Christ of the Miracles is beardless while the Christ of the Passion is bearded, though there is no indication that a different set of artists was responsible. The single figures, so motionless yet so varied, compel the eye to pause and accept their authority. The two processions never hurry but never rest in their slow progress as the eye follows them to the splendid throned figures who await their arrival.

The fourth of the Ravenna churches, San Vitale, is utterly different in conception and therefore in its emotional impact. Justinian built it and he and the Empress Theodora were present at its consecration on 19 April 547. Here, in this octagonal interior, an elongated choir surmounted by a vault leading on to a semi-dome contains the mosaics. There is no steady processional progress from west to east as in Sant'Apollinare Nuovo. The eye is not tempted to travel towards the prepared climax. Rather, the whole of the Sanctuary mosaics forms a single, complicated unit, and one stands, amazed, as though an illuminated manuscript had enlarged itself and had engulfed its reader, making him dazed with the elaboration based on gold and green that surrounds him on either side, vibrates above his head and looks down on him from the semi-dome where a beardless Christ, seated on a blue globe, extends His right hand to offer a crown to

Abraham entertains the angels and prepares to sacrifice Isaac; around the lunette are Jeremiah and Moses, and a group of Israelites with Aaron: mid-6th-c. mosaic in the chancel of S. Vitale, Ravenna

San Vitale himself and holds in His left hand the Book of the Seven Seals. The Saint is dressed in a rich brocade: he is balanced by Bishop Ecclesius who offers a model of the Church. Beneath their feet are rocks and flowers. Overhead on the vault of the Sanctuary is the richest possible scrollwork. Four bands of fruit and flowers, each with a peacock with spread tail at its base, support a medallion containing the Holy Lamb. On the walls beneath the vault, the Four Evangelists, seated among rocks, beneath the four creatures who are their symbols, write their gospels. Further west, Abel and Melchisidek sacrifice on a white altar, and on the opposite wall Abraham is seen with the three angels. Above them are Moses, Isaiah, and Jeremiah, in romantic rocky landscapes. Below, on either side, on eye level are the two famous groups of Justinian with his courtiers and deacons faced by Theodora accompanied by her ladies-in-waiting. If the whole resembles an illuminated book, these two secular panels seem to form the title page.

It is worthwhile to describe this interior in some detail, for probably nowhere else in Europe does there exist a scheme that, in sheer decorative opulence, is so rich without seeming overcrowded or fussy, and in symbolic or iconographical content, so clear and so satisfying. Here, and perhaps nowhere else, do gorgeousness and solemnity combine, each enhancing the other. Yet a description fails to suggest the total effect, for to describe is to examine piecemeal. And this, in San Vitale, one cannot do, for the effect, despite the density of pattern and imagery, is cumulative. Of all the interiors that Christianity has inspired, San Vitale is the one which must be visited to be understood. Michelangelo's Sistine Chapel, Giotto's Arena Chapel in Padua and the great cycle of frescoes by Piero in Arezzo will yield up at least some of their secrets to the photographer. The Sanctuary of San Vitale will not. Even a detail showing the Empress wearing a crown loaded with jewels has the wrong impact for it fails to suggest the context, the human worshipper in supernatural surroundings - proud yet dwarfed by the presence of the Son of God attended by angels and prophets.

The pre-eminence of Ravenna as the centre of the most important group of Christian mosaics cannot be doubted, and

Led by Maximian, Archbishop of Ravenna, Justinian and members of his court move in procession to offer a gold paten to the church: mid-6th-c. mosaic in the chancel of S. Vitale, Ravenna

it is in Ravenna that one realizes the effect of Justinian's influence as the greatest early patron of Christian art. But before Justinian's reign began, and even before the little mausoleum of Galla Placidia had been filled with mosaics, Christian imagery had already appeared in Rome and elsewhere. A spirited little wall painting representing the three men in the fiery furnace described in the Book of Daniel has been found in the Priscilla Catacomb, in a style based on the Hellenistic frescoes in Pompeii and probably done in the third century; and the earliest known representation in sculpture of Christ himself, between Ss. Peter and Paul, forms the centrepiece of a Roman sarcophagus, entirely Hellenistic in style, in which Christ, a graceful and by no means awe-inspiring figure, is derived, like the Good Shepherd of Galla Placidia, from an Apollo-like prototype.

These are among the earliest relics of Christian art, but they are forerunners of a good deal of fine craftsmanship in the form of ivory reliefs (including one of the most ambitious

47

The three men in the fiery furnace: early 4th-c. fresco in the Catacomb of Priscilla

of all carved ivories, the throne of Archbishop Maximian of Ravenna which dates from the middle of the sixth century), icons (painted panels on a wood base), illuminated manuscripts in sumptuously jewelled covers, silver dishes, silver flasks in which pilgrims to Palestine could take home Holy Water from the Jordan, and covers for reliquaries.

We are apt to draw a distinction between works of fine art and good specimens of craftsmanship made for religious purposes. But the distinction is probably not one that would have occurred to the artists of the period between the reign of Justinian and the great outburst of mosaics, illuminated books and ivories in Venice and Sicily in the eleventh and twelfth centuries.

Constantinople was, of course, the centre from which all this creative energy radiated, but the Byzantine style was not necessarily evolved in Byzantium. Imperial patronage was certainly not local, nor can one regard everything that was produced outside the capital of the Byzantine Empire as provincial in style or inferior in craftsmanship. The productive centres were rather the monasteries than the cities, and what we call

48

Ivory throne of the Archbishop Maximian, carved with Biblical scenes and figures of the prophets set in a frame of inhabited vines: Ravenna, mid-6th c.

the Byzantine style varies little between one centre and another, or even from one period to another during the gradual spread of Christianity in the first eight or nine centuries after the Apostles set out on their journeys.

It is a baffling period for the art historian, who always finds himself a little uncomfortable when he has no names to conjure with, no personalities to whom he can ascribe the origin of a style, not even a describable sequence of stylistic developments. Instead of being faced with a series of outstanding works of genius that can be linked together to form an historical chain, he is confronted with an assemblage of objects whose undeniable beauty and religious intensity is rooted in a tradition that makes the most insistent demands on craftsmanship but rejects the contributions of personality. In the ivory plaques that compose the great archiepiscopal throne at Ravenna, it is evident that at least three hands have been at work, yet we do not know the names of the artists responsible, nor can we tell whether they came from Constantinople, Alexandria, or Ravenna itself. Several scenes from the life of St Joseph suggest an Egyptian origin, but to make guesses on the grounds of subject-matter is hardly satisfactory.

Yet the phenomenon of a style that, despite its flexibility, absorbs and dominates the personality of the artist, and turns him into a mere tool in the service of a cause bigger than himself, is surely the most impressive feature in the history of Christian art. After Justinian, most of the stylistic mannerisms of pagan art had been pruned away. Yet no one can say by whose creative vision or by what bold stroke of initiative the pruning was done. The anonymous artists of the Byzantine empire seem to have been directed by remote control and by an unseen will, or to have worked by a process of visual telepathy. In such a situation, all the historian of art can do is to divide the most important productions of the period into categories and to select from each category what seems to him most worthy of mention.

Among ivories, for example, one could select a diptych from the Ravenna museum, showing an enthroned, beardless Christ surrounded by panels depicting, at the side, four of His miracles, above, two flying angels bearing a cross, and

The Harbaville ivory triptych: Byzantine, late 10th or early 11th c.

below, scenes from the story of Jonah and the Whale. Another, in the Bibliothèque Nationale, coarser and more energetic, is arranged in the same way, though here the Christ is heavily bearded, and the throne more splendid with jewels. Both are of the period of Justinian.

Later ivories - and here one must admit that style does change as the centuries pass - become more refined and more delicate and more formal. A triptych, the 'Harbaville Triptych' in the Louvre, is typical. It comes from Constantinople, yet despite its Byzantine formalism, one feels that it has been almost spoiled by sophistication. The passion of the earlier ivory carvers has evaporated and elegance has taken its place.

51

David playing the harp, in a
Hellenistic setting with allegorical
figures, from the *Paris Psalter:*
Byzantine, mid-10th c.

Paintings on wooden panels and illuminations from manuscripts abound and most of them seem to be of Alexandrian
origin. They begin with the sixth century and provide models
for later painters, so that one has the impression that the most
conservative of all the Byzantine artists were the painters and
illuminators. Yet conservative though they may have been,
the best of the icons and illuminations are immensely impressive
and in a manuscript of the late sixth century, known as the
Rabula Gospels, one is surprised to find a strength of design
and colour that must surely have inspired Rouault in our own
century.

The Iconoclast Edict of 730, in Constantinople, made a
temporary break in the production of illuminated manuscripts,
and for nearly a hundred years - until the middle of the ninth
century - the production of images of divine and holy personages was forbidden and existing images were destroyed in
great quantities; so that in the Eastern portions of the Empire
there is a gap in the production of anything but decorative art,
and especially in the making of icons and illuminated books -
Psalters, Gospels, and Bibles. The Imperial pressure was

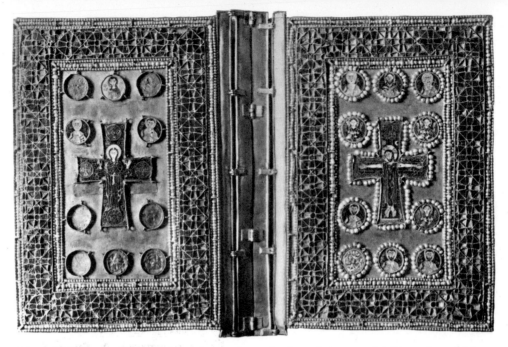

Metal book-cover decorated with pearls and *champlevé* enamel: Byzantine, 10th c.

most effective against the monasteries from which they emana-
ted. And when the edict was relaxed, the manuscripts produced
from the tenth century onwards have a strange air of having
been forced, once more, to rely on classical models and even
of having adapted classical themes to the Old Testament subjects. David playing his harp, in a mid-tenth-century psalter
from Constantinople, is certainly an adaptation of Orpheus,
and the river god lounging at his feet has been re-labelled
'Bethlehem' in a rather desperate attempt to make a Greek
myth fit a theme from Jewish history. In the same psalter, a Byzantine Isaiah finds himself in the unexpected company of
allegories of Night and Day that seem to belong to a Pom-
peian villa.

It was, in fact, only in the works of craft, the book-bindings
decorated with enamels and pearls, or the even more elaborate
reliquaries and portable icons, that the old pre-iconoclastic
style persisted and became even more splendid than ever.

Meanwhile, to glance back at the sixth century and the
ambitious iconographical schemes in mosaic that were contemporary with or a little later than the churches of Ravenna, the

53

Abraham entertaining the angels:
mid-5th-c. mosaic in Sta Maria
Maggiore, Rome

The Virgin and Child, and an angel
of the Apocalypse: 9th-c. mosaics
in Sta Prassede, Rome

most interesting are to be found in Rome. They begin with
the semi-dome in the apse of Santa Pudenziana, where Christ,
with a rhetorical gesture, addresses his assembled Disciples
who gather round Him as though they were Roman Senators.
The effect is so reminiscent of pre-Christian Roman art that
despite its subject, one can hardly connect it with a revolutionary creed.

More important, both to the historian of style and the
student of iconography, are the mosaics of Santa Maria Maggiore
which are divided into two series. The panels high up in the
nave illustrate episodes from the lives of Abraham, Jacob,
Moses and Joshua. Those on the triumphal arch over the
altar are scenes from the Gospels - or rather the Apocryphal
gospels.

As a decorative scheme for a church interior the result is
ineffective, but the competence and skill of the craftsmen
responsible are remarkable. The tesserae are handled with the
same mastery with which Monet or the early Pissarro handled
the divisionist technique. Even the effects of vibrating light
54   and the 'shorthand' suggestions of detail remind one of the

masterpieces of French Impressionism. The date of these mosaics is not known. It is possible but unlikely that they belong to the fourth century, but they are certainly not later than the end of the fifth.

Mosaics of the later of these two dates are to be found at Salonica. Those in Constantinople are almost non-existent and in the interior of Hagia Sophia, the greatest and most impressive church in the Byzantine Empire, the mosaics were started late and were never of the quality that such a context deserved.

The mosaics of the basilica of Parenzo, on the Adriatic coast opposite Ravenna, are heavily but not unintelligently restored, and today the interior is one of the completest and most satisfying examples of a fully decorated church of the sixth or seventh century outside Ravenna. But the most puzzling series of mosaic interiors occurs in Rome in the ninth century, of which the most notable and the most extensive is the ensemble in Santa Prassede.

These strange mosaics have no exact parallel in the whole range of Byzantine interior decoration. They are rigid and stiff, the figures are highly stylized and linear, the faces expressionless, the iconography difficult to read, the symbolism unconventional. And yet the very rigidity of the design increases the sense of awe. On the apsidal arch, for example, is a serious attempt to depict the full flavour of the Apocalyptic vision of St John in the Book of Revelations. The Twenty-Four Elders stand like a regiment on parade in their white togas, offering their crowns. Angels and the symbols of the Four Evangelists float in a sky dotted with clouds. This is as near to pure abstractionism as figurative art can ever manage to get. It is dream-like and impersonal, and it provides an enclosing frame for the semi-dome, which is equally rigid and hieratic but less decorative and, with the exception of San Vitale in Ravenna, makes the most arresting focal point of any of the apsidal churches. The six figures on either side of the colossal standing Christ are spaced with a fastidious eye for the intervals between them and an equally exact sense of their scale relative to the church itself. Below them twelve sheep, symbols of the Disciples, move inwards as solemnly as the martyred saints of Sant' Apollinare Nuovo in Ravenna. These mosaics have been called decadent because of their almost mathematical rigidity. But the dividing line between decadence and hieratic solemnity is not easy to draw. For myself, I find them not so much inhuman and dry as superhuman and aloof.

Tenth-century Italy produced little to excite the historian of Christian art, and one might have supposed that at last the art of mosaics had exhausted its own possibilities, yet the Byzantine phoenix was to rise from its own ashes splendidly on two more occasions, and in widely separated districts, before it disappeared.

In and around Venice, in the late eleventh and throughout the twelfth centuries, the Basilica of St Mark was filled with mosaics as carefully planned from an iconographical point of view as any in Europe and as sumptuous in style and colour as any except San Vitale in Ravenna. On the island of Torcello, the Cathedral's west wall was used for the largest and most detailed Last Judgment to be found anywhere.

In Sicily, at the other end of the peninsula, at Palermo, Monreale, and Cefalù, under the spur of a different patronage,

The Creation: 12th-c. mosaic dome in the atrium of St Mark's, Venice

mosaics equally ambitious, and, in some of their details, more memorable, were completed in the twelfth century under the Norman kings.

The structure of the Basilica of St Mark (it is not the cathedral of Venice but the private chapel of the Doges) was completed soon after 1070 and the decoration of the interior was finished by 1094. Much restoration has interfered with the quality of detail, but the general effect of the whole, despite the deplorable addition of large areas of mosaic done in the sixteenth century, is breathtaking, partly because after the dazzling mother-of-pearl effect of the exterior which hardly strikes one as a large building, one finds oneself, on entering, in a dark, cavernous interior of unexpected immensity, glowing dimly with gold and crowded with imagery. Cippolino marble lines the walls up to the cornice above the arcaded nave. The mosaics lead upwards from the level of the cornice, covering the curves of the walls and the great domes overhead and the pendentives that lead the eye into them.

The general scheme is complex and the plan of the church, with its three cupolas and its cruciform ground plan, is an ideal setting for a complete Byzantine layout. In the domes the Church itself is symbolized in formal, radiating designs with medallions in the centre establishing the three principal subjects - a Christ seated on a rainbow in the Ascension cupola, a throne and Dove in the Pentecost cupola, and a head and shoulders of Christ in the Christ Emmanuel cupola. On the vaults below are the great feasts of the Church, and on the adjacent walls, Christ's life, His miracles, and the Life of the Virgin. In the baptistery are scenes from the life of John the Baptist, and in the narthex outside the west entrance, in the six shallow domes overhead, the story of the Old Testament beginning with the Creation and followed by the stories of Cain and Abel, Noah, the Tower of Babel, Abraham, Joseph and Moses.

These last are the latest of the great Biblical series and were probably completed as late as the mid-twelfth century, but they have the fascination of good strip-cartoons. They are diagrammatic in their clarity and the sequence of the events related, full of readable symbolism (the stages of the creation of the world

Noah's drunken sleep, reproof of his son Ham, and death: 12th-c. mosaic in the atrium of St Mark's, Venice

miraculously sum up the opening chapters of the Book of Genesis) and equally explicit gesture (Joseph's escape from Potiphar's wife has even a hint of Gothic humour in it); one can well imagine the pilgrims, assembled in the narthex, spending instructive hours reading the narratives they had so often heard expounded in sermons.

On the lonely island of Torcello stands the great barn-like Cathedral which was reconstructed in the form we now see early in the eleventh century, though the mosaics were added a century later. Those on the vaulting and the eastern semi-domes are conventional echoes of scheme from San Vitale, but covering the whole expanse of the west wall is a huge Last Judgment that is unique in the whole corpus of Byzantine iconography. Indeed nothing resembling it existed in Christian art until the Romanesque sculptors of France attempted the same theme on the western façades at Bourges and Autun. Only a specialist in iconography could discuss its elaborate content - the Judgment of Souls, the Rewards of the Blessed and the Punishment of Sinners, but even the uninstructed eye grasps immediately the rigid categorization of the five horizontal bands that split the wall into sections, each with its own message and the gradual diminution from the huge images of the archangels and the 'Harrowing of Hell' (the 'Anastasis') at the top to the Punishment of the Sinners in the lower sections. It is a composition that only an artist of exceptional

Detail of the Last Judgment, early 12th-c. mosaic covering the west wall of Torcello Cathedral, near Venice

Interior of Monreale
Cathedral, looking east to
the mosaic of Christ
Pantocrator, late 12th c.

vision could have invented, with the rhythmical, serene group-
ing of the Blessed, the agitated 'Punishment' sections and the
swiftly moving angels of the 'Hetimasia' - the preparation
and guarding of the throne.

Venice, isolated from the mainland and always in close
cultural touch with the East, developed her own type of
glowing and expressive imagery in the eleventh and twelfth
centuries. But at the Southern end of Italy, at precisely the
same moment, the Normans invaded the island of Sicily -
always a meeting-place of mixed races - occupied it and built
up, on the Saracenic culture they found there, a period of
occupation in which Palermo became the brilliant centre of
a new hybrid art, with Greek craftsmen to serve as decorators,
and elements of Northern Gothic architecture to provide the
walls for their decoration.

On the North coast of the island, the apse of the Cathedral
of Cefalù (the earliest of the Norman churches in Sicily)
contains the huge head and shoulders of Christ Pantocrator,
the most daring example of Christian symbolism in Southern
Europe and one which was repeated in two other Sicilian
churches - in the Cappella Palatina in Palermo and in the
Cathedral of Monreale outside the city - so that it establishes

62

Interior of the Cappella
Palatina at Palermo,
looking west, 1132-89

itself as a Sicilian convention, though it was by no means a
Sicilian invention. In Byzantine churches, the Pantocrator was
traditionally placed in the dome overhead where the eye has
to search for it. In Sicily, no dome being available, it occupies
the whole of the half-dome of the apse where it arrests the
eye at once by its position and dwarfs the whole interior by
virtue of its colossal size.

The Pantocrator of Cefalù is the most memorable of the
three great figures. One is confronted with a celestial judge
who is both relentless and benign. He is implacable yet His
hand is raised in blessing. And as though to emphasize the
terrifying aspect of sheer size, the curved walls below are
filled with rows of hieratic standing figures - the Virgin,
Archangels and Apostles - themselves large enough to dwarf
the worshipper and yet themselves dwarfed by the inescapable
image above them. This is no longer symbolism; it is a product
of purely visual imagination in which all the laws governing
architectural scale have been broken for the single purpose of
overwhelming the spectator with a sense of awe.

The Cappella Palatina is a small, jewel-like church. Architecturally it is a confused mixture of a Western basilica with
a Byzantine church added to its eastern end: stylistically it

63

attempts to combine a Saracenic roof with stalactite forms with normally constructed windows and walls. This aesthetic mixture should cause acute discomfort to the sensitive eye. Yet in fact one hardly notices these absurd juxtapositions, for the general effect is that of a richly inlaid casket and the mosaics in the sanctuary (which include a spirited 'Entry into Jerusalem') are among the most effective in Sicily. But more famous, because more ambitious and larger in scale, is the interior of the Cathedral of Monreale.

It is the last of the Sicilian churches, built by the last of the Norman Kings in Sicily, William II. It attempts to combine the virtues of the apse at Cefalù - the same immense Pantocrator above, the same solemn standing figures below, on two levels - with the nave and aisles of the Cappella Palatina. The colour is colder, the design stiffer, the craftsmanship less accomplished than in the two earlier churches. Yet the effect, because of the completeness of the whole interior, cannot fail to be impressive.

Scenes from the Gospels cover the walls of the aisles, the nave walls contain scenes from the Old Testament, on the vaults and the transept walls are the Feasts of the Church. Heads of Saints fill medallions in the borders that run round the soffits of the pointed Gothic arches. And, as in San Vitale, there are two historical panels, in one of which King William II offers a model of the church to the Virgin: in the other, Christ places His hand on the crowned head of the King.

This Sicilian interlude, the result of the irruption of Northern warriors into a Mediterranean island, is a strange but not unimportant tailpiece to the history of Christian mosaics. What is unexpected is that these adventurous sailors should so quickly have absorbed and been absorbed by the civilization they discovered. A few Gothic features in the churches they built make it clear that they were invaders. But their willingness to adopt a medium they had no experience of, and to use artists and craftsmen brought up on traditions so remote from their own, prove that they were colonists of an exceptionally enlightened kind, as well as Christians who had the good sense to adopt the kind of Christian art that had established itself centuries before their arrival.

Catacombs, mosaics and monasteries

WILLIAM NEIL

It may seem surprising that Christianity struck roots so readily in the Gentile world since it remained basically a faith grounded in Jewish thought and history. The answer is to be found in the fact that when Christ was born there were far more Jews outside of Palestine than inside. The dispersion of the Jews which had begun with compulsory exile centuries before had continued for military, economic and commercial reasons until there was hardly a city of any consequence in the Roman Empire which did not have a Jewish community. Although more liberal in outlook than orthodox Jewry, the Jews of the Diaspora were faithful to the beliefs of their fathers and provided an oasis of stability in a changing world.

Many pagans who were attracted neither by the abstractions of Greek philosophy nor by the popular mystery religions of the time, found themselves drawn to the local synagogues by the high moral standards and monotheistic faith that they found there. They were not prepared to become Jewish proselytes, which involved circumcision and full acceptance of Jewish Law. But as fringe adherents of the synagogues, known in the New Testament as God-fearers, these Gentile sympathizers with their respect for the Old Testament formed the bridge between the Palestinian Gospel and the pagan world.

It was to the synagogues of the Empire that the first Christian missionaries went, assisted by the splendid system of imperial roads and the universal peace which Rome provided, and using the common language which was the legacy of Greece. There, when as normally happened, they were rebuffed by their Jewish countrymen, they found the pagan God-fearers ready to listen to what appeared to them to be an even better variety of Judaism. Here was a powerful and

65

The fierce persecutions to which the early Christians were subjected began in AD 64 under Nero (*left*), and lasted until the reign of Diocletian in the 4th c. Thousands were slaughtered by gladiators or thrown to wild animals, as in this mosaic (*right*) from Roman North Africa

coherent faith, rooted in the Old Testament heritage which had initially attracted them but freed from the narrowness of Jewish nationalism and legalism.

This, then, was the foundation on which the Christian missionaries built, developing into a multiplicity of mixed Jewish-Gentile Christian house-churches competing with other faiths throughout the Empire, but growing in numbers until finally Christianity became the established state religion of the Empire itself. It offered a solid body of doctrine, a high standard of morality, a closely knit fellowship. Its doors were open to people of all nations, and within them slaves were the equals of free men. It gave women the status that paganism withheld. Its membership was distinguished for joyous living and wide charity.

Why then was such an admirable and exemplary community subjected to so much persecution? For the record of history, to which the Colosseum at Rome is a lasting memorial, is that violent sporadic attacks upon Christianity by the Roman government dogged the progress of the Church until it finally triumphed. 'The Christians to the lions!', the dramatic cry so familiar from Hollywood spectaculars of life in ancient Rome, pinpoints only one of the ways in which martyrdom was inflicted upon the early Christians.

Tacitus, the Roman historian, gives a graphic account of the first major persecution of Christians by the Emperor Nero in Rome in AD 64. On this occasion they were made the

scapegoats for a mysterious fire which had destroyed more than half the city and which Nero himself was suspected of starting. Christians were covered with the skins of wild beasts and torn to pieces by dogs, they were crucified and burned alive, or used as human torches to light up the grisly scene of their own destruction. It was in all probability in this persecution that the Apostles Peter and Paul were martyred.

But if Nero's madness accounts for this particular persecution it does not explain why under his successors Domitian, Marcus Aurelius, Decius and Diocletian, not only in Rome but throughout the Empire, Christians were for the next two and a half centuries either subject from time to time to major attacks ordered by the government or were liable to find themselves at any time at the mercy of some local mob. Yet they exercised no political power, they were law-abiding hard-working citizens, and the Romans were notably tolerant in allowing people to practise whatever religion they chose provided they behaved themselves.

Part of the reason for the persecutions was that the Christians made no secret of the fact that they regarded the Empire as an evil institution which was doomed to perish as other world empires had done in the past. It was godless, corrupt and ruthless and altogether contrary to the will of God. The emperors were mere men, often bad men, and to give them divine honours as was expected of all citizens was utterly blasphemous. The Christians like the Jews refused to do so. They further made no secret of the fact that they regarded any other form of religion as superstitious, immoral, and inspired by the Devil. They disrupted home life, undermining the authority of the head of the house by converting his wife, his children and his slaves.

Their exclusiveness and failure to mingle with the rest of society, to share in the public entertainments, to participate in statutory pagan religious ceremonies, could only be described as 'hatred of the human race'. Their 'love feast', the name the Christians gave to their common eucharistic meal, must obviously be some kind of sexual orgy, and the 'kiss of peace', the normal Christian salutation, pointed in the same direction. The Church was moreover no longer a collection of gathered congregations under some loose form of leadership, but a highly organized institution subject to its bishops, bound by its own rules, suffused by a devotion and enthusiasm to which no other religion offered a parallel. It was in fact a danger to the stability of the Empire, which must either destroy the Church or be destroyed by it.

So persecution followed persecution in a vain attempt to stamp out this growing menace. How many Christians suffered martyrdom it is difficult to say. What is certain is that every persecution strengthened the faith of those who survived it. The blood of the martyrs was the seed of the Church. Men and women went to their deaths proud to die for Christ, displaying almost unbelievable heroism, confident that beyond the death of the body lay the crown of glory reserved for those who shared the suffering of their Redeemer.

This extract from a letter of a Christian apologist of the second century sheds light both on why the Christians were persecuted and why persecution served only to strengthen the Church. 'For Christians are not distinguished from the rest of mankind by country, or by speech, or by dress. For they do not dwell in cities of their own, or use a different language or practise a peculiar life ... But while they dwell in Greek or barbarian cities according as each man's lot has been cast, and follow the customs of the land in clothing and

food, and other matters of daily life, yet the condition of
citizenship which they exhibit is wonderful, and admittedly
strange. They live in countries of their own, but simply as
sojourners; they share the life of citizens, they endure the
lot of foreigners; every foreign land is to them a fatherland,
and every fatherland a foreign land.

'They marry like the rest of the world, they breed children,
but they do not cast their offspring adrift. They have a common
table, but yet not common. They exist in the flesh, but they
live not after the flesh. They spend their existence upon
earth, but their citizenship is in heaven. They obey the established laws, and in their own lives they surpass the laws.
They love all men and are persecuted by all. They are unknown,
and they are condemned; they are put to death, and they
gain new life. They are poor and make many rich; they lack
everything, and in everything they abound. They are dishon-
oured, and their dishonour becomes their glory; they are
reviled, and are justified. They are abused, and they bless;
they are insulted, and repay insult with honour. They do
good, and are punished as evildoers; and in their punishment
they rejoice as gaining new life therein. The Jews war against 69

God was seen as the supreme artist, the Great Architect using mason's dividers to order His Creation (13th-c. French miniature)

them as aliens, and the Greeks persecute them; and they that hate them can state no ground for their enmity.

'In a word, what the soul is in the body Christians are in the world. The soul is spread through all the members of the body, and Christians through all the cities of the world. The soul dwells in the body, but it is not of the body. Christians dwell in the world, but they are not of the world. The soul, itself invisible, is detained in a body which is visible; so Christians are recognized as being in the world, but their religious life remains invisible ... The soul when it is stinted of food and drink thrives the better; so Christians when they are punished increase daily all the more. So great is the position to which God has appointed them, and which it is not lawful for them to refuse.

'For this is no earthly discovery, as I said, which was delivered into their charge; it is no mortal idea which they regard themselves bound so diligently to guard; it is no stewardship of merely human mysteries with which they have been entrusted. But God Himself in very truth, the almighty and all-creating and invisible God, Himself from heaven planted among men and established in their hearts the Truth and the Word, the holy, incomprehensible Word, sending to men not a servant, as one might imagine, or an angel or ruler, or one of those who administer earthly things ... but the very Artificer and Maker of the universe himself, by whom He made the heavens ... [Do you not see the Christians] flung to the wild beasts, to make them deny their Lord, and yet unconquered? Do you not see that the more of them are punished the more their numbers increase? These things do not look like the achievements of man; they are the power of God; they are the proofs of His presence.'

Such an invincible faith could withstand what we must now regard in the light of Auschwitz and Belsen as the amateurish attempts of the emperors to exterminate it. But the evidence of the power of Christianity to survive and eventually triumph is not confined to written documents like this Epistle to Diognetus, it is to be found on the walls of the catacombs at Rome where the first Christian artists proclaimed their faith on behalf of all who took refuge there in this troubled

In Rome the labyrinthine catacombs, lined with burial niches, became a refuge for the outlawed Christians

time. Christians were constantly being accused by the pagans of being secretive about their religious rites but in time of persecution secrecy was forced upon them and they took their faith underground until the worst of the storm blew over. Often martyrdom pursued them even there.

The Romans cremated their dead; Christians, like Jews, buried them. But according to Roman law interment must take place outside the city walls. Consequently, as visitors to Rome well know, the catacombs, the burying-places of the early Christians, are situated outside the city on the main highways. The soft tufa was easily manipulated and a network of subterranean passages was excavated, with recesses in the walls for the reception of the corpses, and with larger vaults for families, notable martyrs, or bishops. It is reckoned that the total length of passages may have been anything up to seven hundred miles. One small catacomb, with as many as five tiers of burial niches, has been calculated to have held almost six thousand graves. 'Catacomb' is a relatively modern word, deriving from the name of the locality, Catacumba, but the first Christians called their burial-places 'cemeteries', meaning sleeping-places, in accordance with their belief that death was merely a sleep which would end in resurrection.

There was nothing secret about their construction, their entrances, or their use until the killing-times of the third century when their extensive and tortuous passages offered access to convenient meeting-places for the celebration of the sacraments and the preaching of the Gospel, as well as affording personal safety from imperial decrees and malevolent informers. When Christianity became the state religion the catacombs reverted for a while to their normal use as a burial-ground. Pope Damasus in the second half of the fourth century made provision for the veneration of the martyrs who had died there, but when their relics were later removed to the churches in the city the catacombs were largely forgotten. It is only in recent times that a proper study has been made of the contribution they have to make to the history of Christian art.

The earliest wall paintings in the catacombs do not have a specifically Christian character. They might appear on the walls of any Roman dwelling-house, as they do indeed at Pompeii, except that obviously anything offensive or suggestive of pagan cults is omitted. Landscapes, gardens and flowers in which pagan art delighted could serve equally well for Christians as a foretaste of Paradise. But soon it would seem that subjects were chosen which although common enough in classical painting were capable of being understood in a deeper sense by Christian believers. Pictures of the four seasons, for example, which spoke to pagan minds of seed-time and harvest, would suggest to the early Christian beholders death and resurrection, Christ's or their own, as they recalled the words of Jesus and St Paul: 'In truth, in very truth I tell you, a grain of wheat remains a solitary grain unless it falls into the ground and dies; but if it dies it bears a rich harvest' (*John* 12:24). 'The seed you sow does not come to life unless it has first died; and what you sow is not the body that shall be, but a naked grain, perhaps of wheat, or of some other kind; and God clothes it with the body of his choice, each seed with its own particular body' (*I Corinthians* 15 : 36 *ff.*).

So also the paintings of funeral feasts, which would mean no more to the pagans than a representation of the normal

Feast scenes - here in the Catacomb of Calixtus - were reminders of Christ's promises, the feeding of the five thousand and the great supper where 'the poor, the maimed, the halt, and the blind' were fed

commemorative feast in honour of some departed worthy, meant for the Christian the heavenly Messianic banquet, the great supper of *Luke* 14 : 16 *ff*. In the catacomb of St Calixtus the table is actually laid with the eucharistic symbol, the fish. Similarly, pictures of Orpheus, who moved all hearts by his sweet music and had the power to wrest the dead from Hades, would undoubtedly suggest to the Christian the Lord whose sweet words touched men's hearts and who could save their souls from death.

Despite the dubious tradition that St Luke was a painter - the ancient picture of the Virgin, now over the altar in the Borghese chapel in the church of Santa Maria Maggiore but found originally in the catacombs, claims to be 'one of seven painted by Lukas' - it is unlikely that the earliest Christians, who were mostly small shopkeepers, artisans or slaves, included creative artistic skill among their attainments. They were content to copy classical motifs and no doubt the first stage of the decoration of the catacombs was in the hands of the pagan artists who were normally employed in painting the walls of Roman villas. But by the end of the second century original Christian themes begin to appear.

These are mainly scenes from the Old Testament: Moses striking water from the rock, Noah in the Ark, the three men in the fiery furnace, Susanna, Daniel in the lions' den,   73

Abraham sacrificing Isaac, Jonah. New Testament incidents also are represented, such as the healing of the man who was sick of the palsy, the Raising of Lazarus, the Adoration of the Magi, St Peter's denial of his Master. Christ Himself, who had previously been suggested by the symbol of the fish, or depicted as the Good Shepherd, now appears in majesty accompanied by the apostles as Judge of all the world.

It is clear from the frequency with which certain Biblical scenes recur that this art of the catacombs was not art for art's sake, but art for the sake of instruction and inspiration, symbolism which underlined Christian doctrine. Thus the picture of Noah in the Ark shows nothing but a man standing in what is little more than a box, with arms outstretched in prayer. Towards him flies the dove with the olive twig. No variety of zoological specimens, or crested waves, or the other members of Noah's family must distract the attention from the lesson to be taught: as God saved Noah from the Flood so He saves the soul from everlasting death.

Similarly pictures of Abraham's sacrifice of Isaac eliminate all detail that would come between the spectator and the message of Christ's sacrificial Death which it is intended to convey. Abraham and Isaac stand side by side, with hands extended in supplication. The ram and the bundle of faggots alone suggest the context of the original narrative. More significant is the presence to the right and left of the patriarch of the dove with the olive branch, the symbol of the saved soul. The same motif of salvation is conveyed also by the pictures of Daniel in the lions' den, the three men in the fiery furnace and the vindication of Susanna.

One of the commonest themes is that of Moses striking water from the rock in the story of the Exodus. As the Lord had then preserved His people from dying of thirst, so He now saves His people from death by the water of Baptism. In the same way pictures of the miracle of the Feeding of the Multitude turn the thoughts to the Bread of Heaven which nourishes man's immortal soul. And as we should expect the doctrine of the Resurrection to feature prominently in these symbolic paintings, we do indeed find the Raising of Lazarus frequently represented in the catacombs, together

In the Catacomb of Priscilla, Noah's story is reduced to its essential significance: the dove returns to Noah, alone in his box-like Ark

with the Old Testament allegory of Jonah's emergence from the gullet of the whale.

Unlike the later stages of Christian art when Biblical scenes were reproduced on the walls of churches in considerable detail, these frescoes in the catacombs prune the incidental elements in their subjects to a bare minimum. In critical times it is the fundamental doctrines that matter and the age of persecution was indeed one such time. What anxious and harried Christians needed then was, above all, reassurance that death was not the end. This is the underlying theme of all artistic activity in this testing-time of the Church's faith.

No one would describe the art of the catacombs as comparable in excellence with that of the period which followed the establishment of Christianity. It is primitive in expression and execution, much of it has suffered from later restoration and

Isaac, bearing the wood for his own sacrifice, was seen as a 'type' of Christ

the ravages of time. The astonishing thing is that under cramped conditions and working by torch-light, with the speed that frescoes necessitate, these early Christian artists should have achieved so much. With one accord they preach the gospel that Christ has made men free - free from the fear of death and the worst that pagan persecutors can do. So in these subterranean caves of the dead the total impact of their work is the opposite of melancholy reflection on man's mortality. It is rather the joyful proclamation of hope and confidence that man's true home lies beyond the hazards and bitter trials of this present world.

An age of persecution may be one in which men's faith is strengthened but it is not likely to be one in which the arts flourish. The first generation of Christians, living in expectation of the speedy end of the world as they knew it and the return of Christ to found His Kingdom, could still be urged by St Paul to accept the authority of the state as ordained by God. The growing hostility of the state to the Christian community had made their successors regard the Empire as a monster and the emperors as Antichrist. Christians in such circumstances could not be anything but otherworldly, conscious of being strangers in a pagan civilization with which they had nothing in common. If, as is likely, the art of the catacombs made use of pagan motifs mainly for practical or prudential reasons, there was during the same period a deliberate movement within the Church at Alexandria to come to terms with pagan thought instead of condemning it. The two great names in this connection are those of Clement and Origen, spanning between them the century from about AD 150-250. Both were extremely learned and both were impatient with what they considered to be the obscurantism of current Christian thinking. It was their contention that Greek philosophy was in fact a preparation for the Gospel and that for Christians Plato was as important as Moses. Highly influential, they represented a way of thought that was to come into its own when Christianity ceased to be a persecuted sect.

The last great persecution, that of Diocletian (AD 303-305) having failed, it only remained for the Emperor Constantine, who acceded in the following year, to accept the inevitable and proclaim toleration for Christianity throughout the Empire. He himself had become a Christian, as were his successors with the notable exception of Julian the Apostate, and the final step was taken by the Emperor Theodosius who before the end of the century had established the Nicene Creed as the sole faith of the Empire, proscribed all pagan and heretical gatherings, and demolished all heathen temples. The most startling indication of the changed status of the Church was that the Emperor was excommunicated by Ambrose, Bishop of Milan, for taking unnecessarily repressive measures in quelling a riot in Thessalonica and massacring several thousand citizens. He was not readmitted to communion until he had done public penance.

The baptism of Constantine in 337 marked the official acceptance of Christianity throughout the Roman Empire

Thus in the words of Julian the Apostate, who had made an abortive effort to restore paganism, the Galilean had conquered. Christianity which had been in all probability still a minority movement when Constantine published his Edict of Toleration was now the religion of the Empire which had tried in vain to destroy it. Its progress had been fantastic but its ultimate triumph was far from an unmixed blessing for the Church or for the world at large.

It was a far cry from the faith of the martyrs, still farther from the spirit of the Gospels, to the acceptance of a credal formula which now became the hallmark of a Christian. Political chicanery, persecution, cruelty, ostentation and corruption began to be practised in the name of Christ by a Church which at times in its history has behaved as if the Devil were its master and not God. No enemy of Christianity could say worse things about the sins of the Church than have been said throughout the centuries by Christians themselves. Many a time churchmen have wished that history could have been otherwise when they contrast the temper and atmosphere of apostolic days with the Church as it came to be - or as it now is. The worst advertisement for Christianity has always been Christians.

Yet if we believe that there is a divine purpose in history this was the way it had to happen. If Christ had not been in the Church throughout the centuries it must have died time and

77

time again. We have to set against the stains on the Church's scutcheon the battle honours won against ignorance, collective selfishness, inhumanity and superstition. The honours may have been won by individual Christians in opposition to the organized Church, but this is the way the battles have to be fought.

The Church could have remained a minority movement, relying, as it did in the days of the catacomb Christians, on the power of example and the enthusiasm of a persecuted sect. It chose, or God chose for it, the far harder role, which after all is implicit in the Gospel, of being the leaven in society with all the compromises that that involves. If society is to be revitalized, changed and renewed, it cannot be done by standing outside. Christians must take their cue not from the Pharisees, who stood aloof from the life of the community and set themselves up as men of God, not as other men are, but from the fact that they are sinful mortals conscious of their own shortcomings who do their best in an imperfect world to translate their vision of the truth into the humdrum atmosphere of everyday life. This is the corollary of the Incarnation.

When Christianity became the established religion of the Empire the Church could no longer sit in the audience and criticize the actors in the drama of civilization. It was now part of the cast. It consisted of pagans who were Christians only in name, of Christians who were as devoted to their Lord as the first apostles, and of those - probably the majority - who were somewhere in between. With this mixed material it had somehow to maintain and advance the Faith, to remain true to the Palestinian Gospel while translating it into terms that were meaningful to men and women who had become 'Christians' by an imperial edict; to harness all that was best in paganism to the service of Christ and to try to eliminate all that was contrary to His Spirit; to learn to exercise power with Christian responsibility in the knowledge that whatever might be the results they were bound to fall far short of Christian standards. The choices were no longer between black and white but between varying shades of grey.

For Christian artists the task was to maintain the heavenly vision while making use of the forms that pagan civilization provided, seeking all the while to revitalize them. The wealth and technical resources of the Empire were now at their disposal as a result of their new status. Classical art must be baptized into Christianity. Clement of Alexandria had paved the way not only by emphasizing the relevance of Greek philosophy for Christian thought but by reminding the Church of its Master's delight in the beauty of the world for its own sake.

Constantinople - personified on this medal - replaced Rome as the imperial city, and eventually became the centre of Eastern Christianity

'Do not', he said, 'encircle my head with a garland, for in the springtime it is delightful to while away the time on the dewy meads, while soft and many-coloured flowers are in bloom, and like the bees, to enjoy a natural and pure fragrancy'. To enjoy beauty, according to Clement, is to praise God: 'As beauty, so also the flower delights when looked at; and it is meet to glorify the Creator by the enjoyment of the sight of beautiful objects'. Clement was arguing that to see the world through eyes which have been opened by the grace of God is to see that everything in it except sin has in principle been sanctified by the Incarnation.

The historical developments in the Empire brought it about that when this rediscovery was made by Christian artists of the value of cultivating beauty for the enrichment of the mind as well as for the nourishment of the soul, it was not in a Western but in an Eastern setting that the first great upsurge of creativity took place. The Emperor Constantine, having defeated all rival claimants to the imperial throne, decided to found a new capital. He chose the ancient city of Byzantium, on the Bosphorus, which he renamed Constantinople and dedicated to the Blessed Virgin. The Western half of the Empire, centred on Rome, was a little later to be overrun by the Goths, but Constantinople remained the heart of the Eastern Empire for over a thousand years.

Rome had its own artistic tradition, largely borrowed from Greece, but Byzantium, at the crossroads between east and west, was heir also to the ancient cultures of Egypt, Mesopotamia, Persia and Asia Minor. It was a cross-fertilization of Oriental and Graeco-Roman art forms which produced the distinctive style known as Byzantine. If the former Church,

79

Hagia Sophia in Constantinople, now a Mohammedan mosque, may be regarded as the climax of Byzantine art, it is in Ravenna, in Italy, that Christian artists have left the most perfect expression of how pagan art forms could be adapted to convey the new consciousness of architectural and pictorial beauty.

Honorius, son of the Emperor Theodosius who finally abolished pagan religion in the Empire, fearing rightly that Rome would be sacked by the invading Goths, moved the capital of Italy to Ravenna, which then became for more than three centuries a royal residence and the scene of a brilliant artistic development which makes it second only to Rome in importance for the study of early Christian art. Its almost impregnable position in what was formerly marshland, difficult of access from the sea, made this Adriatic city, now a provincial backwater, a suitable haven of refuge for Honorius, who was in any case more interested in rearing poultry than in maintaining power, and for his successors.

But whether in the comparative isolation of Ravenna, where Christian artists flourished in two sustained periods of imperial patronage, or in Rome or Venice or Sicily, under the patronage of various Popes, Doges and Norman kings, the dominant theme of Byzantine art is the Majesty of Christ. In a world where barbarism bade fair to engulf civilization, where incursions of Huns, Vandals or, even worse in the eyes of the Church, of Mohammedan infidels, threatened the very fabric of newly established Christendom, the note that needed to be struck was that of the serenity and order of the heavenly kingdom. Anarchy might prevail on earth but Christians must be recalled to the basic order that ruled the world. In the catacombs the figure of Christ as the Good Shepherd had been a beardless youth, a David or more likely an Orpheus, tending His flock and winning their allegiance. The Good Shepherd in the Galla Placidia mausoleum at Ravenna, even allowing for the difficulty of expressing gentle emotions in mosaic, is already a shepherd who dominates His flock rather than loves them. When we reach the ultimate peak of Byzantine interpretation, Christ sits enthroned as Pantocrator. He is Emperor, Monarch, Ruler, surrounded by His heavenly Court of saints and angels.

II The Good Shepherd:
mid-5th-c. mosaic in the Mausoleum of Galla Placidia, Ravenna *(above)*

III Christ separating the sheep from the goats at the Last Judgment: early
6th-c. mosaic in S. Apollinare Nuovo, Ravenna *(below)*

IV The Ascension, from the *Rabbula Gospels,*
   painted in Northern Mesopotamia in the late 6th c.

A Byzantine Christ Pantocrator, Emperor, and Judge, dominates the 12th-c. cathedral built by Norman conquerors at Cefalù, in Sicily

It is difficult to see how it could have been otherwise. The loving Shepherd was what the Christians of the catacombs needed to steady their nerves. Christ the King was just as much the need of a world that saw before it nothing but chaos and disorder. Both aspects are true to the Gospel. The danger was that the love and grace of God would be forgotten in an age when the fear of God and of His law was constantly being pressed upon the Church. Christ as Emperor implied a spiritual hierarchy, elaborate ritual, and solemn ceremony. This was good enough in its way, but it was not all that Christianity had to say.

The Byzantine mosaicists called into their service all the richness of detail and wealth of colour which the consecration of pagan art forms now put at the disposal of the Church. No one who has seen Ravenna can ever forget the haunting beauty of San Vitale - and many thousands of ordinary soldiers involved in the Italian campaign during the last war found themselves in the odd situation of viewing these wonderful mosaics while perched on planks above the flooded floor. Nor can anyone fail to be grateful that by good fortune the shelling that damaged the walls of Sant'Apollinare in Classe left its mosaics undamaged. But the cold formalism of the Byzantine style, whether in Ravenna or St Mark's in Venice or the Cathedral of Monreale near Palermo, its concentration on the awful majesty of the heavenly Kingdom, forces us to our knees but barely touches our hearts. Christian art had to rediscover how to convey also the love of God and the way to this rediscovery was made possible by monasticism.

The story of the Church in the West after the Emperor Constantine had transferred the imperial capital to Byzantium is overshadowed by the disintegration of temporal authority. The next six centuries, generally known as the Dark Ages, are politically chaotic. Wars and invasions, pillaging and plundering, are hardly a propitious atmosphere for the development of Christendom. Yet somehow or other Christendom emerged. Somehow or other amid all the political upheavals and accompanying misery, the Church succeeded in establishing a workable code of public morality, in abolishing slavery,

82

During the politically chaotic Dark Ages, art and learning were kept
alive by the monasteries; here, in 851, monks of St Martin-des-Champs
in Paris present a great illuminated Bible to King Charles the Bald

in banning gladiatorial shows, in establishing hospitals, and
infusing the spirit of charity into common life.

In the absence of secular control the leadership passed to
the bishops of Rome. Gregory the Great, the sixth-century
Pope who sent St Augustine of Canterbury to evangelize
England, is only the most notable of a long line of occupants
of the Apostolic See who fought successfully to protect
Christendom from threatened extinction at the hands of pagan or Muslim invaders. It was one of his successors, Leo III,
who crowned Charlemagne first Holy Roman Emperor in

St Jerome's Latin version of the Bible (which he is seen dictating to a scribe) was made in the late 4th c., and remained the standard text throughout the Middle Ages

AD 800 and gave for a time at least some stability and cohesion to the Western world.

The Dark Ages were not without their great figures - St Augustine of Hippo in North Africa, whose great conception of Christendom as the City of God rising out of the ruins of the old Empire paved the way for the great age of the Papacy and the Holy Roman Empire, and St Jerome, whose translation of the Bible into Latin, the Vulgate, not only made the scriptures accessible to the West but also gave to Latin Christendom a sense of its own unity as distinct from the Greek-speaking East.

But the true strength of the Church in the Dark Ages lay in the monasteries. They were the real powerhouses of Christianity and the moulders of its culture. When Europe emerged from the Dark Ages it was seen that it was only because the monasteries had preserved the faith, and, however tentatively, sought to express it in concrete artistic forms that the great and lasting memorials of mediaeval Christendom became possible. In art and architecture, in music and drama, in the whole splendid outburst of the Christian spirit in the Middle Ages, the seeds were sown and nurtured by the monastic

84

orders which began as a flight from the world and ended by becoming the world's benefactors.

The monastic life was a by-product of the establishment of the Church as the state religion. Those who feared that the faith would be submerged by the world fled to the deserts of Syria and Egypt. Thousands turned their backs upon civilization and chose to live in solitude, supporting themselves in extreme asceticism by the work of their own hands, finding in the Scriptures and in devotional writing their only interest. Some of them, like St Simeon Stylites, who is said to have lived on top of a pillar for thirty years, were pathological cases. Many of these early hermits for all their devotion

St Augustine of Hippo displays the manuscript of his *City of God*

85

to Christ seem to be poles apart from the Friend of publicans and sinners, and more akin to the obscurantist precursors of the prophets in Old Testament times who shunned the world to save their own souls in the wilderness.

But as it was from such ambivalent beginnings that an Isaiah or an Amos came, so it was from the ranks of these culture-shy anchorites that St Benedict and others like him founded the monastic orders. For good or ill these desert solitaries were the saviours of Christian culture, for without roots in a personal faith no culture can be Christian. Hermits, whether Jewish or Christian, were, for all their narrowness, men for whom God was the supreme reality. If we speak in terms of Christian art, it was such men, themselves culturally 'barbarians', who supplied the dynamic which inspired their contemporaries and successors. For there is something in us which makes us doff our hats to men who give up everything for what they believe to be the truth.

So, in fact, it worked out. As in Old Testament times, the solitary found the need of fellowship. Anchorites began to form communities and in the sixth century St Benedict founded the first Western monastic order of Benedictines, with Monte Cassino as the mother-house. His wise rule, prohibiting extreme asceticism and emphasizing the value of useful work, led to the monastic concentration on education and the arts. Many of the great figures of the Dark Ages were the products of a monastic upbringing - St Augustine, St Jerome, and Pope Gregory the Great, creator of Gregorian plain chant. Literature and art were nurtured by the very movement which had sprung from renunciation of a world which cultivated them.

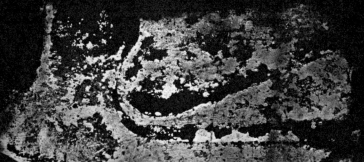

III ROMANESQUE AND GOTHIC

The mediaeval craftsmen

ERIC NEWTON

So far I have told the story of the beginnings of Christian art as though everything worth serious consideration had happened around the shores and in the hinterland of the Eastern Mediterranean, and as though the style evolved by artists, as Christianity spread, had been a constant, slow modification of the traditions left behind by Greece and Rome, a gradual and almost imperceptible series of shifts from classical grace and beauty to spiritual and symbolic expression in which the emphasis on the human soul replaced that on the human body, so that the Good Shepherd of Galla Placidia became, in the end, the awe-inspiring Pantocrator of Cefalù.

But to concentrate on what is roughly known as the Byzantine era is to ignore more than one half of the story. Civilization in Northern Europe was less stable. To the citizens of the gradually decaying Roman Empire it must have seemed that the restless and warlike tribes of the North - Goths, Vandals, Saxons, Danes and Vikings - were 'barbarians'. And in the sense that they had never come under the direct influence of Hellenic cultural traditions, their civilization was unfamilar and the reverse of homogeneous. Also, since they tended to be raiders and pillagers, it was natural that their ventures into Southern Europe should be regarded with fear and mistrust, although the Normans eventually set up a stable government and a glittering court at Palermo in Sicily.

Yet the word 'barbarian' need not imply an absence of skill or craftsmanship or a lack of awareness of what is meant by art. We know well enough that Northern Europe has developed its own styles and has produced its own masterpieces of painting, sculpture and architecture. That development began to take place a century or two later than in the South, but as far as Christianity was concerned, the Gospel continued to spread northwards, carrying with it its inspiration

The Mission of the Apostles: inner tympanum of La Madeleine at Vézelay, early 12th c.

though not in the same artistic forms. From the point of view of subject-matter there never was a definable frontier between North and South. The same themes, the same formulae for Christian imagery appear on both sides of the chain of the Alps, though what I described in the first chapter as the 'shape appropriate to the emotion' was very different.

We are accustomed to regard the art of Southern Europe as serene, orderly and classic in its clarity, while in the romantic North the idiom is tortuous, restless, spiky and what art criticism tends to call 'expressionist'. The difference in skyline between the spires of the Cathedral at Chartres and the domes of Hagia Sophia in Constantinople gives one a key to this dichotomy, and when one examines the detail, the intricacy and angularity of the tympanum of Vézelay or the illuminations of the Book of Kells, and compares them with the serenity and solemnity of the Byzantine ivories and icons, the contrast becomes more acute.

Moreover, 'barbarian' certainly did not imply a resistance to the Christian creed. The monasteries of Ireland and Northumbria in the seventh and eighth centuries produced illuminated books and manuscripts certainly more elaborate than their counterparts within the Byzantine sphere of influence,

89

The Evangelist Luke, from the *St Gall Gospels:* Irish, mid-8th c. and *(right)* the Evangelist Mark, from the *Lindisfarne Gospels:* Northumbrian, *c.* 700

but no less devout. The Book of Kells from Ireland and the Lindisfarne Gospels from Northern England have no parallel South of the Alps.

Both of those remarkable examples of the illuminator's art are admittedly less intelligibly related to the human story contained in the Gospels than those of Italy or Constantinople. The descriptive and narrative elements in the Book of Kells are primitive as compared with the Rabula Gospels of three centuries earlier or the Homilies of Gregory done for the Emperor Basil I (867—886), but they are evidently done by artists passionately dedicated to their task. And their task was certainly that of the Christian propagandist, even though their references to human anatomy and facial expression and their descriptions of gestures or the appearance of drapery, whenever they found it necessary to introduce a human figure, were stiff and diagrammatic.

90   There is surely nothing surprising in the fact that the North

European artists of the eighth century were less successful in the depiction of the visible world than the Mediterranean artists of two centuries earlier, for they were faced with a different and, in many ways, a more difficult problem. The Byzantine artists were attempting to adapt an old, highly sophisticated, realistic style to a new and mystical purpose - a purpose it was never intended to serve. But the North Europeans, who had inherited no stylistic traditions at all, had to start from scratch and invent for themselves a set of formulae that could be used to serve the demands of the new religion. Those demands were the most exacting that any artist could be called upon to meet, but they certainly did not include the need for visual accuracy. A portrait of St Luke in an illuminated Gospel would certainly have to be solemn, mysterious and hieratic, but it would not have been more impressive had it been anatomically accurate or had its draperies more closely resembled those worn by the reader of the book. On the contrary, realism and hieratic solemnity, visual truth and spiritual intensity were and always must be at loggerheads

God admonishing Adam and Eve after the Fall, a panel of the bronze doors cast in 1015 for the Church of St Michael at Hildesheim

Christ in Majesty: tympanum of St Trophîme at Arles, *c.* 1170-80

with each other. The gaunt and stylized images of the enthroned
Christs carved above the doors of St Trophîme at Arles
in Provence or the great basilica at Vézelay in Burgundy owe
their power, their impact on the eye and the mind, precisely
to their daring departures from the visible facts as we know
them. Like the Byzantine icons they are universal and timeless
because they are not portraits. The very distortions by which
we recognize the Romanesque sculpture of France and Germany
in the eleventh and twelfth centuries are the source of their
almost hypnotic symbolism.

Yet it would be absurd to attribute the hypnotic effect,
without which no Christian work of art can make its full
appeal, merely to the presence of distortion. One of the most
difficult puzzles for the critic to solve in any branch of the
arts - in music and poetry as well as in painting, architecture
and sculpture - is to explain the relationship between form
and content and especially that between realism of form and
profundity of content. In poetry we are familiar with the
discovery that to impose a formal rhythm or a pattern on
a sequence of words can alter and intensify the meaning. The
rhythms and the patterns themselves produce an incantatory
effect that goes far beyond the mere meaning of words. That
same incantatory effect, whereby even the doggerel of a
nursery rhyme becomes magical and memorable, applies
equally to the visual arts. And no set of visual rhythms could
be more magical than those of the Romanesque sculptors and
painters who worked in France and produced their best work

in the middle of the twelfth century, or of the craftsmen who later echoed them in Limoges enamel. Whether they would have been capable of abandoning those rhythms in the interests of realism is a question hardly worth answering even if it could be answered. Like the solemn processions of saints and martyrs in Sant'Apollinare Nuovo in Ravenna, these are symbols, not descriptions. They are concerned with spiritual truth and not with material fact. What makes Romanesque - and, later, but to a lesser extent, Gothic art - so potent as an expression of the Christian religion, is the remarkable fact that it succeeded in discovering a set of stylistic conventions that could make the meaning of Christianity clear with a minimum of reference to visible facts, and that if it had not done so its impact would have been immeasurably weakened.

What distinguishes the Romanesque style from the Byzantine is the vast range of the moods it could evoke. Energy and solemnity can find themselves side by side: humour and dignity, fantasy and tenderness, the awe-inspiring and the trivial. The list of masterpieces or near-masterpieces is long, and although, as with the Byzantine artist, most of them are anonymous, an occasional name emerges - as, for instance, that of Gislebertus who carved his name boldly on the great Last Judgment tympanum at Autun.

The Temptation of Christ: capital by Gislebertus at Autun, *c.* 1130

93

Even more important than the distortions of the best Romanesque art, fearless though they may be, are its omissions and its generalizations. For the artist whose chief concern is with a spiritual message must reduce his symbols to a minimum. Nothing inessential must distract the eye. It is a sure sign that the Renaissance has at last arrived when we find that art is beginning to insist on the detail that does not reinforce the central theme - the landscape that was introduced because the beauty of the material world could not be ignored. The Madonna and Child who are seen against the background of an enchanting meadow under a blue sky flecked with clouds may lose their divinity and, with it, their meaning because they too seem to succumb to the enchantments of the material world. No Romanesque illuminator would have permitted himself to yield to such distractions or to allow the reader of his book to be so distracted.

This single-minded will to insist on the essence of the message, however simple or however complex, runs through the whole of Romanesque art. The Christ in Glory from a missal of the Cathedral of Limoges (now in the Bibliothèque Nationale in Paris) is an instance of simplicity in which the swinging draperies are no more than a diagram that either ignores the limbs beneath them, or never allows them to suggest weight or solidity. The purpose of the figure is to indicate awe-inspiring majesty. The mandorla within which the figure is contained, the four symbols of the Evangelists that steady the design, the patterned background with its six rosettes, are there merely to suggest that an effect of jewelled richness will add to the effect of splendour. The elaborate border isolates the whole, as though to separate the divine figure from the world of triviality and humanity. Beyond this, nothing that is not essential has been allowed to intrude. It is a work completely dedicated to the expression of the supernatural.

And yet, when action is needed and narrative is included, the Romanesque artist can produce an effect more dynamic than any other. The urgency and cruelty of the three figures who thrust St Lawrence downwards into his metal grill could hardly be more simply or more clearly expressed. And

94

Christ in Glory, from the *Limoges Sacramentary*: French, *c.* 1100

the helpless nakedness of the saint (no need for an agonized expression on the face) completes the message by the contrast between cruelty above and vulnerability below. The flames thrust themselves upward, like teeth, from below.

When the message is complex and filled with intricate detail, as on the great tympanum at Vézelay with its huge enthroned Christ dominating the whole of the crowded area, or the tympanum over the door at Autun in which nothing is omitted that could add to the meaning of the Last Judgment and nothing is included that could detract from it, the Romanesque sculptor never hesitates. He is in full control of the steady architectural design and never lets it conflict with the strength of the architectural context, yet he is never afraid to add those touches of pathos or dignity that belong to the sinners thrust into hell or the blessed seated in glory.

Throughout the façades of the Romanesque churches of France and on the elaborately carved capitals in their interiors, one finds examples of this creative energy. Within the rigidity of the design the imagination expands freely. Single figures, like the Isaiah of Souillac (1110), solemn statues like the seated Virgin with a patterned and jewelled surface in Saint Denis (1130), animated groups like the Resurrection of the Virgin at Notre Dame de Senlis (1190), startling reliefs like the St Peter on the Portal at Moissac (c. 1135), great carved areas full of decoration and imagery like the façade of the Cathedral of Angoulême produce a cumulative effect that belongs to no other century than the twelfth and no other country than France. This is the most complete expression we have in art of the mediaeval attitude to Christianity.

The same steadiness and rigidity of design combined with the same richness of surface is to be found in the stained glass of the period and in the elaborate craftsmanship in metal and in the enamels whose production centred round Limoges. The east window of the Cathedral at Poitiers (1180) is a wonderful example of its kind, though one has to wait till the development of Gothic imagery and a more flexible use of the medium for the full flowering of stained glass in the thirteenth century.

V Gold cover of the *Codex Aureus of St Emmeram* (detail):
   Carolingian, *c.* 870. Christ, seated in Glory, is surrounded by the four
   Evangelists and scenes of His life

The martyrdom of St Lawrence: 11th-c. wall painting at Berzé-la-Ville

It would be tempting to overcrowd this chapter with illustrations to show the variety of mood, and the steadiness of purpose of these Romanesque carvers. But the temptation must be resisted in this outline of the history of Christian art. If the chief emphasis in the title of this book were on the word 'art' rather than the word 'Christian', the temptation would be lessened, for it must be admitted that, as examples of pure art, later centuries produced masterpieces in far greater numbers and with a far greater sense of both the beauty of the world and the personality of the artist than the twelfth. But

97

Romanesque sculpture: Isaiah, on the portal at Souillac, *c.* 1110 (*left*), Virgin and Child of painted wood, from St Martin-des-Champs in Paris, *c.* 1130 (*centre*), and St Peter, on the portal at Moissac, *c.* 1135 (*right*)

if we are to regard the artist as a man whose main task was to discover visual equivalents for the hieratic, the mystical, and the supernatural elements in Christianity, then the supremacy of the best Romanesque art cannot be denied.

Nor was it limited to Northern Europe. It existed also in Northern Italy. The same single-minded economy of means and the same insistence on 'meaning' as opposed to 'beauty' is to be found in the bronze doors of the Church of San Zeno in Verona and in the figures carved by the Lombard sculptor-architect Benedetto Antelami in the Baptistery at Parma. He dated his great panel of the Deposition in the Cathedral at Parma 1178. The bronze doors of San Zeno are about half a century earlier.

'Romanesque' and 'Gothic', for the historian of architectural styles, are words that have a fairly precise meaning. But if one is tracing the development of pictorial or sculptural style in Christian art, the transition is gradual and the distinction between them anything but precise. And yet the difference between the two, if one compares fully developed examples, is profound.

What strikes one immediately as one searches for examples that will make this difference apparent is that whereas the masterpieces of Romanesque art - and especially of Romanesque sculpture - are detachable from their architectural contexts, and yet still retain their meaning even when we imagine them as separate items in a museum, no such isolation is possible with the main body of fully developed Gothic. It would, in fact, be true to say that whereas the carved tympana at Vézelay and Autun live an austere life of their own, independent of the buildings they adorn, the life of Gothic art is to be discovered only in the building itself. The word 'Vézelay' conjures up an image of a hundred carvings - capitals, statues, reliefs - each one of which asks for a separate scrutiny. The word 'Amiens' suggests a greater unity, crowded certainly with

Benedetto Antelami. *The Deposition,* 1178, in Parma Cathedral

detail, but with detail whose primary function is to add a richness of texture to the whole expanse of the vast construction.

It is of course true that as one goes nearer in order to 'read' each separate detail of the all-over pattern, the details do, in fact, turn out to be readable. A huge iconographical system, carefully and logically thought out, slowly reveals itself to the searching eye, but it is rarely a sequence of sculptural masterpieces; the parts are so completely absorbed into the whole that one could say that examples of Gothic art at its best tend to be either gigantic or minute. Each one of the great Cathedrals of France is like some huge galactic system that contains within itself a thousand stars or planets, each related to its neighbours by virtue of the stresses and strains, the tensions and attractions, that govern the whole. The result is an effect of dynamism that is hardly ever to be found in Romanesque art but which runs like an electric current through the whole of Gothic from the end of the twelfth century until the growing spirit of the Renaissance began to invade it from the South and cut off the supply of energy towards the beginning of the fifteenth. This pervasive Gothic dynamism is sometimes restless and disturbing, often mysterious and visionary but always elusive and magical. Every manifestation of Gothic art seems to have its origin in the all-embracing spirit of Gothic craftsmanship dedicated to a single end - the glorification and intensification of Christianity.

Ultimately, when one comes to explain the origin of Gothic art, one finds it, quite simply, in an architectural - one could almost call it an engineering - discovery. The ribbed vaults radiating outwards from the summits of immensely tall piers made it possible to envisage a building of an entirely new kind in which the strength of the single support from below could be made to spread outwards and upwards into a vast coverage of roof which needed no walls to justify it or hold it in place. Once that had been done (and students of architecture agree to credit the Abbot Suger of St Denis with the discovery and all that it was to imply during the course of the next century) everything that followed was both architecturally inevitable and aesthetically revolutionary. To dispense with the areas of wall that had hitherto seemed essential

100

Detail of the west front of
Angoulême Cathedral, c. 1140

Aerial view of Notre Dame in Paris, showing the structure of a Gothic cathedral with its 'external skeleton' of buttresses, late 12th - early 13th c.

to the very existence of an important building made it possible to allow the window to invade the space where the wall had once been. To fill the window with imagery and colour of the most intense kind followed naturally. And in tracing the development of the art of stained glass in the thirteenth century one discovers the one exception to the rule that Gothic art tends to be either immense or minute. For the window that took the place of the wall could be split up into any convenient size by the patterns of stone tracery that divided the whole glass-filled space into manageable sub-divisions.

It soon appeared that the outward thrust of the vault required a counter-thrust to make the whole structure stable. The solution - not yet discovered when the choir of St Denis was completed in the mid-twelfth century - was the extraordinary device of the flying buttress, the buttress that rocketed upwards into a pinnacle from the outer limits of the ground-plan and leaped across to the point where the outward thrust of the vault was strongest, in an upward-sloping stone bridge. The purpose of this device was originally purely functional,

West front of Reims Cathedral: perfectly developed
Gothic façade, begun in the
mid-13th c. and completed in the 15th c.

but it soon became apparent that the flying buttress itself was an integral part of the dynamic pattern of Gothic architecture, not merely a means of resisting a thrust with a counter-thrust, but an impressive way of making Gothic dynamics apparent to the eye. In Notre Dame in Paris, at Narbonne, at Le Mans, at Rouen, the flying buttresses are, in themselves, a kind of aesthetic adventure. At Beauvais, where the immense height of the choir must have demanded special treatment, the vertical buttresses are doubled and so are the flying arms that leap inward towards the roof and walls. The effect is of a fantastic animal that is forced to wear its skeleton outside its skin and has decided that its own bones must be fashioned as objects of slender beauty.

Gothic art, therefore, as an expression of Christianity, owes much of its stylistic vividness, its vertical rhythms, its spikiness and its slenderness, to the engineering feats of Gothic architects: and if this outline of Christian art were concerned with causes rather than with effects, it would be necessary to examine in far greater detail the structure of the great cathedrals rather than the nature of the works of art that are contained within them or that cling to their outer surfaces.

Needless to say, it is not part of my intention to follow the development of Gothic as a way of building. Architecture was never more truly the mother of the arts than in Northern Europe in the thirteenth century and the decades that preceded and followed it. It is with the complex family to which it gave birth - the sculpture, the stained glass windows, the illuminated books, and to a lesser extent, the wall paintings - that we are concerned.

It is natural to consider the sculptural aspects of Gothic first, for not only are the cathedrals themselves massive examples of sculpture but their outer surfaces seem designed for enrichment by sculptural detail. The central doorway of Bourges Cathedral is a marvellous assemblage of carved surfaces in which row upon row of fretted surfaces are inter-related within the enclosing frame of the gable that contains them. Above the doorway, three niches are recessed to contain sculptured groups. The doorway itself is framed by an arcading that contains seven statues on either side:

The Last Judgment: tympanum of the main west portal of Bourges Cathedral, *c.* 1270-80

from their canopies rise six rows of carved mouldings, within each of which are fitted small statues; the outer moulding contains twenty of these single figures; the next eighteen, and so on, as the radius decreases, until the inner row contains ten. This makes a total of ninety in the curved archivolt alone, and with the fourteen standing figures below (seven of them have disappeared or were perhaps never completed) and the five in the niches above makes a total of 109 in the outer framework alone. To this number must be added the complexity of carving in the crowded Last Judgment on the tympanum over the doors themselves - a grand total of over 200 figures. And when one adds to this the other doors in the same cathedral and then multiplies it by the number of equally if not more ambitious sculptural schemes at Reims, Amiens, Paris, Chartres and half a dozen less famous structures, one begins to be overwhelmed by the sheer exuberance of the Gothic output in France alone during the century and a half when Gothic was at its most confident.

105

Quantity is no test of the aesthetic value of any creative movement, but quantity can at least be a measure not only of religious enthusiasm but also of the ubiquity of craftsmanship which only enthusiasm could provide. Not all the carvings are imaginative masterpieces and some of them are no more than competent, yet in an art that was, after all, largely anonymous and in which the notion of creative genius had not occurred to the minds of either the artist or the public, quantity is a factor of considerable importance. When one looks at the figures in the archivolt at Senlis or at Chartres, at the Resurrection at Rampillon, the quatrefoil reliefs at Auxerre or the lively carvings at Chartres which depict the months in the life of the peasants, one begins to feel that sculpture is not merely a possible outlet for genius, it is a normal means of communication, as conversation might be in another, less inspired, but more sophisticated age.

In Spain, at Santiago de Compostela, the pattern was richer but less disciplined. In Germany, in the statues of Magdeburg and Naumburg, the artist's vision was more dependent on close observation and less on inspiration. In Italy, on the carved relief surfaces at Orvieto Cathedral, we are still in the world of Gothic intensity and complexity but the sculptor is no longer anonymous. We begin to recognize the personal handwriting of men like Lorenzo Maitani, and somehow our very knowledge of the artist's name seems to make art a less effective means of expressing the collective consciousness of an age.

To enter any of the great Gothic cathedrals of France is to move into another world. Outside is a concentration of fretted and carved surfaces that vibrate because they catch every variation in the direction of light. Inside are smooth mathematically calculated vertical rhythms, that bend over and meet overhead to form a soaring avenue. The light is inevitably subdued, as it must be in any roofed enclosure, and the windows that occupy the spaces between the clustered piers were destined for the kind of stained glass whose imagery could certainly be read in the same way and with the same kind of effort that is needed for the reading of the external sculpture. But just as the effect of the sculpture is a function

106

Choir of Beauvais, 1247-72: highest of all Gothic cathedrals, its plan was too ambitious and it was never completed

of its texture, so the effect of the windows is a function of their colour - intensified to an extent that no painting or mosaic can achieve because the light is transmitted and therefore even the deepest tones register on the eye as a glow against the comparative darkness of the surrounding stone. The effect of stained glass both on the eye and on the mind depends on a jewel-like multiplicity of intense colour broken up by small-scale imagery and contained within borders of even smaller-scale decorative patterns, surrounded by the immense, unbroken verticals of the piers that sweep past it, ignoring it as it were, on their upward journey to the point where they begin to curve over into the vault as the stem of a leaf spreads out into the web of the leaf itself. Photography cannot achieve this effect of jewelled colour set among dizzy verticals, but it is certainly the contrast of the two that is responsible for the awe-inspiring effect of the whole; as though coloured fire were smouldering in the midst of moulded icicles.

Gothic sculpture: details of *The Last Judgment* by Lorenzo Maitani, on Orvieto Cathedral, *c.* 1310-30 *(left)* and of *The Betrayal, c.* 1230, in Naumburg Cathedral

The Dormition of the Virgin, 13th-c. stained glass in Chartres Cathedral

The interiors of Chartres and Bourges Cathedrals are, justly, as far as stained glass is concerned, the most famous in Europe. But by being so incessantly quoted and so enthusiastically praised, they have perhaps become more famous, in relation to their lesser competitors, than they deserve. Yet it is true that in the whole field of Christian art there are two major visual experiences which can never be enjoyed except in the physical presence of the works of art themselves. One is the Sacristy and apse of San Vitale in Ravenna, the other the glass of Chartres. The former depends on the construction of the wall, the latter on the placing of the windows. It was not fortuitous that, in the intense sunlight of Southern Europe, the window should have been reduced in size in order to provide the ideal amount of illumination for the mosaic, whereas in the North the window was enlarged to replace the wall and then filled with colour that would tone down

109

English illumination: the Virgin and Child, from the mid-13th c. *Missal of Henry of Chichester*, and the Crucifixion, from the early 14th c. *Arundel Psalter*

the light and, again, produce the calculated ideal of illumination to serve a great enclosure. It would be absurd to compare the two either as means of intense religious expression or of satisfying interior decoration. But in both cases what is impressive is not the concentrated statement of a single creative mind - Giotto, Tintoretto or the unknown painter of the Pietà of Avignon - but the total impact of a building whose architect with his team of artists were working under the stimulus of a Byzantine Emperor or the Abbot of St Denis.

When we move out of the realm of the immense, and direct our attention to the minute - the reliquaries, the chalices, the small ivories and the illuminated manuscripts - the scale changes but the spirit remains the same. Reliquaries tend to reproduce the forms evolved by architects, even though the functional basis of these forms has disappeared. And the illuminated books certainly derive a good deal from the masters of stained glass. What distinguishes the reliquary from the building, the illuminated book from the window, is their intimacy and their privacy. The illuminated book is essentially a personal possession, to be used, held in the hand. It

110

The fall of the rebel angels,
from the
*Très Riches Heures du
Duc de Berry:* by the
Limbourg brothers, 1413-16

is designed neither for the public eye nor for the library. Even the art critic or art historian of today finds it difficult to familiarize himself with the immense corpus of Gothic illumination. To examine each book page by page is a very different kind of task from the study of the imagery of the stained glass masters; yet the essential spirit of Gothic art - its fantasy, its grace and its gaiety as well as its devotion - can be concentrated as surely within the pages of a book as across the spread of a façade or the area of a window.

One of the turning points, social historians tell us, in the history of European civilization is marked by the invention of printing. Certainly it made the spread of knowledge possible but in doing so it reduced the preciousness of the book for its maker and its reader. To the mind of the artist who produced it the idea of mass production had never occurred. What he made was unique and therefore worthy of meticulous care and skill in the making of it. Both in France and England, during the thirteenth century, Gospels, Missals, and Psalters of astonishing beauty made their appearance.

'Beauty' is not a word that one can easily apply to the solidity and seriousness of Romanesque art, but as Gothic replaced it, the illuminations become more fanciful, more delicate, and more human. What the artist had in mind by the end of the thirteenth century was surely a self-conscious attempt to make the page beautiful rather than meaningful - to turn what had once been strength into elegance. A Virgin and Child in the thirteenth-century Missal of Henry of Chichester has a swinging line that expresses the tenderness inherent in the subject. Towards the end of the century, in the Arundel Psalter, a greater refinement, almost mannerist in its delicacy, is to be seen in a Crucifixion page.

Both in England and in France this refinement was bound to lead into prettiness, but with the fourteenth century prettiness was slowly replaced by a kind of decorative realism that was still Gothic in spirit though the awakening preoccupation with the material world was steadily shifting the emphasis of the illuminated book from heaven to earth. The climax of this compromise between the affectionate illustration of life and the mystical vision of the rapidly disappearing Middle Ages is to be found in the Duc de Berry's *Très Riches Heures* of which the enchanting pages were illuminated by Pol de Limbourg, the Duke's valet, and his brothers. This famous book is not only a climax but a turning point. Its Northern counterpart in panel painting is the Wilton Diptych in the National Gallery, which marks the end of an age dedicated to the spiritual and the beginning of what was to develop into the Renaissance. Historians of style have agreed to use the term 'International Gothic' to describe it. Only another step is needed to move into another world - the world in which Italy took over the lead that had begun in the North. It is a world no less reverent and religious, but more attentive to the information supplied by the observant eye - that of Pisanello and Gentile da Fabriano, of Fra Angelico and Benozzo Gozzoli. In order to understand such a world one must cross the Alps and focus one's attention on the cultural centres of Italy, in particular on Florence.

112

VI The Virgin and Child:
   14th-c. stained glass window in the church of St John the Baptist at
   Fladbury, in Worcestershire

The faith that built the cathedrals

WILLIAM NEIL

Building cathedrals is not a common practice in the modern world. It is perhaps something to be said in favour of the twentieth century despite its indifference to religion that it has set about building three in England - Liverpool, Guildford, Coventry - which is more than any other century has undertaken since the craftsmen of the Middle Ages studded not only England but the whole of Northern Europe with masterpieces of Romanesque and Gothic design which leave us as much aghast at the boldness of the enterprise as overwhelmed by the splendour of the execution. Whether the cathedrals and abbeys of the Middle Ages were designed to serve a metropolitan area like Notre Dame in Paris, or a rural diocese like Salisbury, or a religious community like Melrose, the enlightened patronage and piety which built them could only have achieved these miracles in stone as a result of some extraordinary impulse.

We cannot dismiss them as merely the product of an age when labour was cheap and plentiful. Nor can we put it down to a vagary of fashion which might equally well have occurred in the seventeenth or eighteenth century. Cathedrals and abbeys were built in the Middle Ages because it was the one age in history when St Augustine's dream of the City of God on earth seemed likely to come true. It was an age of buoyant faith, when for the first time a united Christendom felt itself moved to build and think and write and sing to the glory of God. There was undeniably poverty and squalor, political insecurity and violence. But there was an underlying certainty, an overruling authority, and a common system of belief. The Catholic Church was the patron of the arts and men felt that there was no higher service than to extend Christ's Kingdom on earth and to devote the utmost energy of mind and body to that cause.

It is too much to say that the pointed arch of the Gothic cathedral replaced the rounded arch of Romanesque as a symbol of men's increasingly upward aspirations. It was, we are told, a practical device to give more window space and reduce the risk of fire to the earlier wooden roof. Nevertheless the soaring columns and spires of the Gothic cathedral do express this characteristically mediaeval heavenward look. God was for them without any doubt 'up there', and man's life on earth was meant to be lived in constant awareness of His Sovereignty.

In the long history of the Papacy before the Reformation, Roman Catholic historians would be the first to admit that many of the Popes were sorry caricatures of the Vicar of Christ on earth. By the same token Protestants would be less than fair if they did not recognize that it was due to the Christian witness of most of the Popes and the real greatness of many of them that the Church was guided through the stormy seas of mediaeval Europe. Temporal power was a necessity and on the whole it was exercised with wisdom and charity. Without a doubt it was the Papacy which created Christendom and held it together.

Hildebrand, who became Pope Gregory VII, was the real artificer of this great Age of Faith. It was his aim to make the Church supreme over the national rivalries of kings and the pretensions of the emperors. His triumph in 1077 at Canossa has become part of the stuff of legend, when the Emperor stood barefoot in the snow doing penance until the Pope would receive him back into the fold. Hildebrand's successors built on these foundations. They carried through reforms within the Church, they evolved a legal system, they battled with popular superstition, they founded the first universities.

This was the age of the great Crusades, which were, like everything else in the history of the Church, the result of a mixture of worthy and unworthy motives. On the credit side there was the legitimate abhorrence of the idea that the Holy Land and the sacred places of pilgrimage should be in the hands of Islam, on the debit side there was the behaviour of the Christian Crusaders. In the two hundred years

114

Henry IV's submission to Pope Gregory at Canossa was a dramatic though temporary victory for the Papacy. Here he begs Abbot Hugh of Cluny and Matilda of Tuscany to intercede for him

from 1095 to 1270 eight Crusades were launched. Most of them turned into appalling travesties of what the word implies. Yet they sparkle with tales of individual heroism and gallantry and despite the fact that the original purpose was largely lost in political struggle and bloody slaughter they were promoted and permeated by the same idealism and religious fervour which built the cathedrals. Christendom felt itself united in a common cause and men were ready to give their lives for Christ and His Church.

It was an age too when saintliness and scholarship walked hand in hand. We may feel that local piety conferred sainthood too readily on founders of churches and monasteries, on worthy abbots or bishops, but, after canonization had been more strictly controlled by the Church, the rightful claims of such men as St Bernard of Clairvaux, St Thomas Aquinas, and above all St Francis of Assisi to be included among the saints would be denied by few. Yet they were only the most outstanding among a host of men of God, whether statesmen or bishops, missionaries or writers, who in this age sought to make the whole fabric of society worthy of its Redeemer.

From the monasteries the monks took with them on their educational enterprises not only the works of the Christian Fathers but the legacy of the best of Latin literature - Virgil, Horace, Ovid, Cicero, Juvenal. Within the monasteries they copied faithfully by hand, in the days before the invention of printing, manuscripts of the psalms and the Gospels, illuminating them skilfully and devotedly, so that they became

115

The Dominican St Thomas Aquinas holds his great work, the *Summa*; St Bernard, less concerned with thought than with action, championed the Cistercian reform and preached the Second Crusade

no longer mere copies of ancient writings but testimonies of a living faith. From such places and from the cathedral schools sprang the first universities, whose teachers saw the spread of knowledge as part of the purpose of God and therefore the business of His Church.

It is easy now to make fun of the mediaeval schoolmen who argued over how many angels could balance on the point of a needle, or what would happen to a mouse which ate the consecrated wafer, but the scholasticism of the Middle Ages was basically a valiant attempt to save Christian truth from irrationality, misguided piety, and popular superstition, and to demonstrate that revelation was compatible with reason. Christianity must be shown to be a logical coherent system, capable of co-existing with the best thought of pagan philosophy.

Peter Abelard's tragic love-affair with Heloise is more familiar in the modern world than his writings or his gifts as a teacher, which drew thousands of students to the young University of Paris to hear him expound his arguments. But the great master of this noble attempt at a synthesis of all human thought was, of course, St Thomas Aquinas. His

Summa Theologica is one of the most influential works in the history of man's attempt to find an explanation of the mystery that surrounds him. Aquinas taught that there are two sources of knowledge, revelation as contained in the Scriptures and interpreted by the Church, and human reason. Neither is adequate without the other. Reason can prove the existence of God; only revelation can tell us what God is like. Hebrew-Christian thought must be married to Greek philosophy. Both come from God because there is only one Truth.

These splendid advocates of the reasonableness of the Faith, Abelard and Aquinas, contributed also to the mediaeval legacy of song. Aquinas, who was responsible for the universal observance of the feast of Corpus Christi, composed several hymns which are well known in all parts of the Church, including 'Thee we adore, O hidden Saviour, Thee', while Abelard's great hymn 'O Quanta Qualia' - 'O what the joy and the glory must be' - is deservedly a universal favourite. But, by the irony that lurks in human affairs, Abelard's theological views were opposed and he was denounced as a heretic by a saintly otherworldly monastic, St Bernard of Clairvaux, who, however, has expressed his own deep faith in hymns that are even better known than those of Aquinas and Abelard: 'Jesus, thou joy of loving hearts', 'Jesus, the very thought of Thee', 'O Jesus, King most wonderful' and 'Light of the anxious heart'.

Perhaps hymns like these can teach us more about the nature of the faith that built the cathedrals than the *Summa Theologica*. At all events they lead us inevitably to the most beloved, and perhaps most Christ-like of the saints who made the concept of Christendom come alive for ordinary men and women, St Francis of Assisi. G. K. Chesterton has said of him: 'Of all the heroes of the great Catholic effort no one has made himself so comprehensible to this Protestant people as that amazing man of the thirteenth century in Umbria.'

This tenderest and sweetest of the saints, son of a prosperous cloth merchant, meant to be a soldier. But like St Paul and St Augustine he was 'apprehended by Christ'. The story is told of how he overcame his natural horror of lepers by recollecting what Jesus had done and embracing one of these poor

117

sufferers, and how he thenceforward devoted himself to their service and that of all sick folk. So also is the story of how he was moved to restore the ruined church of San Damiano in Assisi. He had no money, so with a sublime disregard for business principles he removed a load of cloth from his father's warehouse and sold it in a neighbouring market. From his enthusiastic point of view he was conferring on his father the inestimable privilege of assisting in the rebuilding of a house of God.

His father looked upon it in a different light and took his son to court. He regarded him not only as a thief but as a madman. He saw his fortune and the hopes he had placed in his heir tumbling to the ground. Francis was told by his bishop that no good could come of money dishonestly acquired and he was ordered to restore it to his father. This was the last straw for the zealous Francis. He stood up in court, renounced his rights to his patrimony, his name, and the very clothes he wore. Stripping off everything except a coarse hair shirt on which he roughly chalked a Cross, he went out into the world alone. He was penniless, half-naked, and fatherless. The snow was on the ground. Yet it is recorded that as he went under the frosty trees he burst into song.

San Damiano was rebuilt with his own hands and the help of some like-minded enthusiasts. One morning at Mass the priest read from St Matthew the story of Jesus sending out the twelve disciples to preach the Gospel. It came to Francis that these words were meant for him and in that moment the order of Barefoot Friars was born. He too would go forth with neither gold, nor silver, nor wallet, nor shoes, nor staff and with but one cloak to his back. He would recall men to righteousness and to God.

As he preached, disciples joined him. His power was extraordinary. Whenever it was known that he was on his way the whole life of a community would come to a standstill. Bells were rung, merchants left their desks, tradesmen their work, women and children ran to meet him and strove to touch the hem of his tunic and kiss the footprints which he left on the ground. Many legends are told of his preaching; he did not confine himself to men and women, but addressed

St Francis preaches to the birds near his convent: 13th-c. sketch by Matthew Paris

As a young man St Francis
founded the mendicant friars,
with their twin vows of Holy
Poverty and Holy Obedience;
his love of all things led to
a new celebration in art of the
minutiae of God's Creation.
This portrait was painted
during his lifetime in St
Benedict's sacred cave
at Subiaco

the flowers and trees, the birds and animals. For St Francis,
they were all the children of God. The wind, the sky and
the streams were his brothers and so even was death his kind
and gentle sister. His great hymn in which all Creation joins
in the praise of God takes us very close to the heart of this
great saint.

Masses of people were moved by his words and by the
example of his life: enemies were reconciled; vows were
taken; lives were dedicated to God under the power of this
little man's fervour. Soon his followers were so many that
he had to establish settlements all over the country, which
became centres of charitable and missionary activities. The
sisterhood of the Poor Clares was founded under his inspiration and the Franciscan Order grew in his lifetime to over
five thousand. As was to be expected, not all of them lived
up to the ideals of their founder.

Before his death he received the stigmata, the wounds of
Christ in his own body, and he died singing a psalm. Two
years after his death he was canonized, but Christendom had
already conferred on him the title to sainthood by common

The Friars were teachers and itinerant preachers, using example and oratory (as in this 13th-c. English miniature) to combat heresy and stimulate faith

consent. He was the most joyous of saints and always rebuked any of his friars who looked gloomy or melancholy. His followers were to be 'minstrels of God', scattered about the world to sing the gospel truths. 'At times,' said Thomas of Celano, 'I have seen him with my own eyes draw a stick across his arm in the guise of one playing the viol and sing in French praises of the Lord'. He treated all men as his brothers, whatever their rank or character, and his whole career was a passionate attempt to put into practice himself and to get others to follow the life set out in the Sermon on the Mount.

Alongside the Franciscans grew up the order of Dominicans, founded by St Dominic in Spain. Both traversed Christendom, working among the poor, tending the sick, preaching and teaching. No doubt there were petty jealousies between the settled parish priests, the older monastic orders and these new mendicant friars. But the Friars sent the lifeblood of the Faith coursing through Europe, inspiring, uplifting, reviving. Like the Salvation Army in more recent times, they carried the simple Gospel to people whom the schoolmen and learned doctors of the Church could never reach.

If the two seminal works of the Dark Ages may be said to be St Jerome's *Vulgate* and St Augustine's *City of God*, the correspondingly significant literary milestones in the Middle Ages are St Thomas Aquinas' *Summa Theologica* and the *Divine*

120

Dante stands between his beloved Florence and the cosmos he described - Hell, Purgatory, and Paradise. *The Divine Comedy*, he wrote, was undertaken 'not for speculation, but for practical results'

Comedy of Dante Alighieri. This was not only the greatest of his works, and indeed one of the greatest literary masterpieces of all time, it also embodied the mediaeval mind. In it he describes how in a vision he is taken through Hell, Purgatory and Paradise. But it is in effect an allegory of man's aspirations, from the morass of human existence, through purification of all that separates him from God, to the Beatific Vision of the Heavenly Throne.

It is indeed a veritable cathedral itself, a monument to mediaeval faith, expressing that sense of the reality of the supernatural world and man's need to find his true home there. Our duties on earth and our destiny in heaven, these are matters beyond question or dispute. Love is the key to life, and the soul's pilgrimage through this world is meant to end in perfect union with the Love which is God. Dante draws into his vision the richness of his knowledge of the classics and the Christian philosophy of the schoolmen, but he makes all of this come to life for ordinary men by the intensity of his own religious feeling.

This humanizing of the Faith, if we may call it so, evidenced in the *Divine Comedy*, is a reflection of the Middle Ages as a whole. Even if we imagine the Romanesque churches and cathedrals not as the rather severe Christian fortresses which they now appear but, as they were originally, brightly

121

decorated, with almost Oriental variety of colour, they still express the Byzantine sense of the remoteness, aloofness and majesty of the Divine. In the Gothic style there is not only the movement of the human spirit upwards to God, but outwards towards all created things.

The comic element in Gothic sculpture, the oddities of the human shape, the delight in carvings of little animals, are part of the rediscovery that God not only reigns in glory but loves His creatures. It is over-simplifying the picture to say that the Risen Christ of Byzantine art was replaced by the Crucified Sufferer of the Middle Ages. There had been suffering enough in all conscience in the earlier centuries. It was no new discovery of the sombre texture of life which turned men's thoughts from the Majesty of Christ the King to the Crown of Thorns upon the Head of the Crucified.

Contemplation of Christ's Passion may well have become at times morbid, both in art and in private devotion, but concentration on the Cross is basically a recognition of the Love of God which was not content to reign in majesty but came down among men to suffer and die for them. So together with the new concern for men as sinners for whom Christ died, and for all God's creatures, so perfectly embodied in the life and work of St Francis, there came into the forefront of popular devotion the Crib, the Rosary, the Virgin Mother, the Blessed Sacrament. None of this was new but it acquired a new significance.

The Church of the Middle Ages in its liturgy and in its buildings managed to preserve the balance between the adoration of the Godhead and devotion to the human Jesus. The Crucified reigned as Judge above the rood screen. Trinity Sunday matched Corpus Christi. And the cathedrals remain, like the *Summa Theologica* and the *Divine Comedy*, as mirrors of a faith which was big enough to comprehend the whole of life. Their soaring arches and pointing spires still have the power to lead our thoughts upwards to the Sovereignty and Authority of God, their sculpture and stained glass remind us that the world and its concerns, its saints and sinners, its achievements and its follies, are gathered together under the symbol of His Love.

The triumph of physical form

ERIC NEWTON

Much has been written about the Italian Renaissance for it marked one of the most conclusive turning points in the history of European civilization, yet the very word 'point' gives a mistaken impression. There was no specific moment at which one could say that it had begun. Still less could it be said that its meaning and its influence have even today come to an end. All one can be sure of is that the change from mediaeval to modern ways of thinking was gradual but decisive and that, as it developed, it brought with it the profoundest kind of revolution. At the beginning of the fourteenth century one could detect the first signs of it: by the middle of the fifteenth the whole pattern of human thought and behaviour had taken on a new flavour and, in particular, literature, architecture, painting and sculpture had developed not merely a new set of outward appearances but also new inner meanings.

From the art historian's point of view the word 'Renaissance' can be taken literally. Something that had once existed and had been taken for granted - the Hellenic view of life in which man was the measure of all things, and the gods had been fashioned, with the addition of certain intensifications and idealizations, in man's image - had been virtually destroyed by the advent of Christianity, and, at last, phoenix-like, had begun to stir again into a new life.

That it should have been regarded as a rebirth was inevitable. It was equally inevitable that the new life should have been thought of not merely as a replacement of the old, mediaeval pattern but also as a destruction of it. Historians of art, who themselves took part in it, men like Giorgio Vasari, assumed without fear of contradiction that Giotto was the forerunner, in the art of painting, of a new and a better era and that those who came after him, up to the death of his friend Michelangelo, were all contributing to a new kind of tradition which had developed, with ever increasing splendour, over a period of three and a half centuries. To Vasari, in fact, it could not occur that the moment in which he completed his great work on the lives of artists in the mid-sixteenth century was not the moment of ultimate climax and that Raphael and Michelangelo were not the greatest artists of all time. The word 'genius', which had hardly been a meaningful word up to his day, could be used of Michelangelo without any sense of its being an extravagant or exaggerated term of praise.

Vasari thought of 'art' in a rather specialized sense, and from the Renaissance point of view he was right. If a 'work of art' is to be thought of as the complete expression of his own personal experience by a man of genius who is also a superb craftsman, a master of his chosen medium, then no artist has ever surpassed Michelangelo, and few of his successors have equalled him in imaginative power. Titian, Velazquez and Rembrandt could certainly claim to possess 'genius' in the same sense in which Vasari applied the word to Michelangelo. But, for the purpose of a history of Christian art, the word, if it is to be used at all, must be used in rather a different sense.

What had happened, as the Italian Renaissance steadily built up the traditions that divided it from the mediaeval world, was a new faith in the importance of the individual. It was no longer the relationship of man with God - or, to be more precise, with man's concept of the Trinity - but the expression of each separate artist's delight in the world he lived in that counted in any estimate of his 'genius'. True, the world he lived in included his experience of divinity, but certainly not to the exclusion of his new-found faith in physical and material beauty. Once more, as in pre-Christian Greece, God was conceived as made in man's image - a symbol not of the Supernatural but of the idealized 'natural'. In addition, for 'Renaissance man' the human being was no longer thought of in isolation (though Michelangelo himself was an exception to this rule) but as part of 'Nature', an environment of whose beauty he became increasingly conscious until, to

125

some extent, the art of landscape became, for the painter, as enthralling and as full of emotional overtones as the art of figure painting. And, as always happens when man is engaged on exploring new fields of discovery, he brings a new kind of intellectual curiosity to bear on his researches. Leonardo, the supreme type of 'Renaissance man', was positively consumed by the kind of intellectual curiosity that nearly prevented him from being an artist at all and certainly interfered with his efforts to be a Christian artist.

One other notable characteristic of the Italian Renaissance must be mentioned before referring to its attitude to Christianity. The rebirth of Hellenic thought naturally led to a rebirth of paganism and especially of pagan attitudes to mythology which differed considerably from pagan attitudes to religion. When Botticelli painted 'The Birth of Venus' for the villa of his Medici patron, he was announcing his faith in something that no Romanesque artist of the twelfth century could have taken seriously. It was not, of course, that Botticelli believed in the existence of a goddess whose special concern was with human love and physical beauty, but that he was convinced that love and beauty were in no way opposed to the basic tenets of Christianity, and that therefore, unless his patron specifically required it, he was under no obligation to refer, in his art, to a specifically Christian theme. Almost every writer on Botticelli has noted that his Venus and the three Graces in his equally famous 'Primavera' have the same wistful innocence, the same aloof gaze, as his Madonnas, but that whereas they were manifestly unashamed of their nakedness and proudly conscious of their physical perfection, his Madonnas were unconscious of possessing bodies at all.

Botticelli was not, of course, the first post-mediaeval artist to attempt this fusion between the body and the soul. But he was one of the first to discover that the unveiling of the body need not interfere with or diminish the significance of the soul. The circle of patrons among whom he moved was a circle of poets and philosophers as well as of ecclesiastics. For that reason he was able to tackle themes belonging to pagan mythology as easily as Christian themes and to feel

126

Giotto. *The Lamentation, c.* 1306, fresco in the Arena Chapel at Padua

that he was not involved in any basic contradiction between the two.

It follows that the most noticeable change in the appearance of the visual arts brought about by the Renaissance is the arrival of this new faith in material beauty and the attempt to link it with spiritual truth. The attempt was bound, in the end, to fail. I have already pointed out in my introductory chapter that Rubens's enthusiasm for physical and material beauty makes one doubt his capacity to express spiritual truth even when it was his central theme and even though his patron was the Christian Church. But that point, when the

Giotto. Detail of *The Betrayal*, *c.* 1306, in the Arena Chapel at Padua

competition between material and spiritual experience was developing into a decisive victory for the former, did not arrive till the beginning of the seventeenth century.

Vasari, looking back at the first hint of the new spirit in art, and deciding that Giotto was the great initiator of it, could hardly think of it as a 'competition'. For him, if he analyzed it at all, it must have seemed a fusion of two forces, neither of which could produce the necessary impact without support from the other. For us, knowing as we do well enough, that Giotto took the first step in a chain of development that continued at least until the death of Rembrandt, his arrival contained within itself the seeds of destruction. The re-birth that we can so easily and so hopefully notice in his frescoes in the Arena Chapel in Padua was the first scrap of evidence that the Romanesque and early Gothic artists had

VII SIMONE MARTINI
Christ returning to His Parents, 1342

Giotto. Detail of *Joachim and the Shepherds*, in the Arena Chapel at Padua

worked in a style that he himself was making obsolete and that what they had done could never be done again.

What one notices at once in the world that Giotto created in his frescoes is, first, that it has solidity and weight and, secondly, that it is concerned with essentially human situations. His account of the Annunciation, for example, is a description of a Florentine girl visited by an angel bearing a message that she can hardly understand. His characters are involved in a human drama from which the mystical or supernatural overtones have almost disappeared. That marvellous panel of the mourning over the dead Christ laid reverently at the foot of the Cross seems to be a summing up - perhaps the most fully charged with pathos ever painted - of the grief of a mother lamenting the death of her son. And the equally moving description of the Betrayal and the kiss of Judas is

129

certainly a profound essay in tragedy but on a human scale; it is a description of human ambitions wrecked by human treason. The painting of Joachim, bowed with shame before the wondering shepherds, is equally dramatic, with a Shakespearian understanding of the gestures and emotions that can take place at a climax in a human story.

In order to produce this new kind of impact, Giotto had to approach his purely artistic problem with an equipment that no previous artist had possessed. He had to observe as well as to imagine - to note purely physical appearances. For the first time since the end of the Hellenic era, a painter insisted that the world he lived in was made of solid objects, and that the men and women in it were themselves solid, that their feet pressed on the ground they stood on, that they expressed their own moments of shame, triumph or defeat in gestures that were appropriate not to the mediaeval concepts of a timeless Heaven or an earth that obeyed its commands but to the life of his own day. However deeply Giotto may have felt the divinity of Christ, he was primarily a fourteenth-century Florentine, the first artist to be quite certain that whatever message he had to convey could only be conveyed in terms of the life around him.

What makes him revolutionary and original is the fact that he had few predecessors on whose work he could build. For the sculptor, engaged on translating Christian themes into marble, there were plenty of available pagan examples at hand, and, a century before Giotto, Nicola Pisano had picked up hints from existing Roman sarcophagi and used them for Christian purposes, so that magnificently composed though they are and carved with faultless skill, his women have the air of Roman matrons and his men of Roman statesmen. By the time his son, Giovanni Pisano, was old enough to carry on the work his father had begun, Gothic influences had begun to find their way across the Alps and Giovanni's versions of his father's themes developed a more nervous, gracious, less consciously dignified mood. Yet in neither Nicola nor Giovanni can one detect the beginnings of the Renaissance.

But Giotto's frescoes in Padua derive only from his own understanding of human behaviour: and his realization of the

Nicola Pisano. *The Adoration of the Magi*, one of the panels of the hexagonal marble pulpit in the Baptistery at Pisa, 1260

drama of the New Testament was based on his own humanity. It was from the moment when, early in the fourteenth century, he completed the great series of narrative paintings in Padua, that the artists of the Renaissance began to discover and solve a new set of problems in art. In doing so they immeasurably enlarged the scope of what painting and sculpture could achieve: but also, in doing so, they unwittingly narrowed the range of what the mediaeval artists had expressed.

The story of the arts of the Italian Renaissance has been so often told, and so much is known about the forging of each separate link, each step in the long upward climb from Giotto to Michelangelo, and after him, from Titian to Velazquez and Rembrandt, that it would surely be a waste of the reader's time and a contradiction of the central purpose of this book, to go over the ground again in detail. If I have suggested

131

that each link in the chain brings art - by which I mean, of course, the representational arts - nearer to the visible world and further away from the world of the unseen expressed in the only way available to the artist, by means of symbols, all that this chapter need do is to pick out landmarks in the long journey from the Arena Chapel in Padua to the Sistine Chapel in Rome (completed in 1508), and then continue the journey through Titian in the sixteenth, and Rubens and Rembrandt in the seventeenth century, noting, as we examine each one, how the mood changes and how each change of mood brings with it a change in the artist's approach to his Christian theme.

To do that, however superficially, compels us to view the whole sequence in a way of which Vasari would certainly not have approved. His *Lives of the Artists* is an essay in progress. For us the sequence, though it is certainly concerned with problems solved - and often solved triumphantly - is evidence of change rather than progress. For the problems were not those of how to interpret Christianity but of how to come to grips with the world of phenomena. What interested the followers of Giotto, first in Italy, then, later, throughout the whole of Europe, were such problems as how to express concepts like space, the impact of light, the examination of volume and structure (especially the structure of the human body), movement, the harmonization of colour and, from the purely technical point of view, the hitherto unexplored possibilities of the handling of the medium itself.

All this is evidence of the concern of the artist with *visualizing* rather than with *vision*. To state the situation in its simplest terms, the mediaeval artist depended largely on his mind's eye, the Renaissance artist on his physical eye, and though the two were not, of course, mutually contradictory, and in all the visual arts of painting and sculpture, a fusion of both is essential if art is not to degenerate into mere decoration, yet the balance between the two, towards the middle of the fifteenth century, was beginning to be upset and the old interpretations of spirituality in terms of symbolism were being replaced by descriptions based on observation and carried out with an ever-increasing fund of technical skill.

Fra Angelico. *The Annunciation*, upper section of a painted tabernacle, *c.* 1425-35

In this book, I am concerned less with the progress of art than with its relationship to Christianity, and as art increases its concern with the nature of the visible world a dangerous moment may arrive, and, in fact, *did* arrive, when the inner meaning of the Christian religion was obscured by all kinds of interests that have no bearing on religion itself. At that dangerous moment the usual standards of judgment must change. What, to the art critic, must be regarded as the very climax of artistic achievement, will not necessarily be also the climax of religious expression. It is true that at every period there have been artists who, by the very intensity of their own inner vision, have circumvented the danger - and it is they who must emerge as the heroes of this book - but it was always in spite of and not because of their undoubted grasp of the world of phenomena. We shall find, for example, as we follow

133

Fra Angelico. Detail of *The Deposition, c.* 1440, fresco in S. Marco at Florence

the chronological sequence, that Velazquez was not even conscious of the danger, while Rembrandt could avoid it with ease: that Tintoretto found no difficulty in tackling the profounder levels of Christianity while his contemporary, Veronese, rarely made the attempt.

Giotto's death was followed by a period of nearly a century during which hardly anything that Vasari would have described as 'progress' occurred. There were plenty of artists who imitated his innovations without understanding them, but it was not until the beginning of the fifteenth century that the Renaissance began to build on the foundations Giotto had laid. Two painters of considerable importance mark the early years of the century. Both were Florentines. Fra Angelico, a

Dominican monk, could be said to mark the end of the mediaeval world, for his whole life was dedicated to the expound-
ing of Christian themes, and even though his technical equipment as a painter was based on that of Giotto, he approached
his theme in a mood of ascetic devotion. His pupil, Benozzo
Gozzoli, learned how to solve the fresco painter's problems
from his master but the problem of spirituality he could not
solve. The procession of the Three Magi on their journey to
adore the Christ Child in the chapel of the Riccardi Palace in
Florence is no more than a hunting party headed by members
of the Medici family. His frescoes of the life of St Augustine
at San Gimignano tell us much about everyday life in fifteenth-
century Florence but little about the inner life of a saint.

Fra Angelico's contemporary, Masaccio, was an undoubted
genius, though his death at the age of twenty-eight came too
early for him to have reached full maturity. But his series of
frescoes in Santa Maria del Carmine in Florence prove that
it was he who took the first inevitable step towards Renaissance
realism and dedicated his short career to vivid descriptions
of the life that passed before his eyes. It was the dignity of

Benozzo Gozzoli. Detail of *The Procession of the Magi*, fresco begun in 1459,
in the Chapel of the Medici Palace in Florence

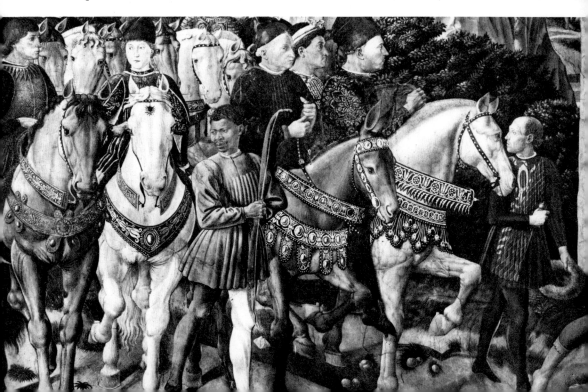

man rather than the divinity of Christ that obsessed him. It was he, more than any other artist of his time, who focussed the eyes of his successors on what was to be the supreme achievement of Renaissance art - an art dedicated to the beauty of the world and the nobility of man.

There is something in the series of frescoes he painted in the Brancacci Chapel of the Carmine church in Florence that convinces us of his unceasing attempt to depict the world as he saw it - so much so, in fact, that he begins to look to us like a genre painter, a man more interested in the momentary happening than in its timeless significance. To a far greater extent than Giotto he is a recorder of events. The naked figures of Adam and Eve expelled from the Garden of Eden are not symbols of shame and repentance but records of two personages fleeing from punishment: the girl with her infant in her arms who stretches out her disengaged hand to receive money from Peter is a study in momentary gesture seen with the eye of a Dutch genre painter of two centuries later.

Masaccio was, in this respect, ahead of his time. The pursuit of the momentary was not what chiefly engaged the attention of his successors in fifteenth-century Italy. For them, the painter's task was not merely to observe and record but to understand and idealize the world of phenomena. In Florence they followed each other in rapid succession, contributing cumulatively, during the space of less than a century, more than at any similar period in the history of art, until what I have called 'the dangerous moment' - when description ousted symbolism - arrived.

It did not arrive till the middle of the sixteenth century, and even then a few exceptional artists - men whose deeply religious faith enabled them to circumvent it - managed to resist the temptations that eventually translated Renaissance sensitivity into worldliness. Meanwhile, out of the long sequence of fifteenth-century Florentines and central Italians who paved the way to the climax of Leonardo, Michelangelo and Raphael, one can select certain innovators. Piero della Francesca, in his series of frescoes in Arezzo on the theme of the Golden Legend - the story of the cross on which Christ was to be crucified and of its subsequent history - painted with such

Masaccio. *The Expulsion,*
c. 1425-28, fresco in the
Brancacci Chapel of
Sta Maria del Carmine,
Florence

:o della Francesca.
  Resurrection, c. 1460,
:co in Borgo San Sepolcro

Pollaiuolo. *The Martyrdom of
St Sebastian, c.* 1475

fastidious understatement (Berenson has called him 'the non-eloquent painter') that his very reticence amounts to reverence. The brothers Pollaiuolo studied the human body in action with such intense seriousness that they set a new standard in the artist's understanding of the human body. Their researches brought the danger-point nearer. Their impressive altarpiece in the National Gallery of the Martyrdom of St Sebastian never fails to give the impression that, fascinated though they were by the noble gestures involved in the practice of archery, they were incapable of realizing the meaning of martyrdom. Botticelli, as already noted, only just succeeded, by the delicacy of his enchanting linear arabesque, in distinguishing between pagan and Christian meanings. Blind until his final mystic phase to the central grandeur of the Christian faith he substituted for it a delicate, attenuated poetry that was equally

139

appropriate for his Madonnas and his pagan goddesses. His contemporary, Ghirlandaio, a competent master of prose, tackled religious themes but robbed them of both mysticism and poetry.

It is at this point - the last decade of the fifteenth century - that the High Renaissance arrives, and with it three men whose genius was able to accept and use the discoveries of their forerunners and yet avoid the dangers those discoveries brought in their train. Leonardo, Michelangelo and Raphael inherited everything that the questing Renaissance mind and the searching Renaissance technical skill had prepared for them, and yet they succeeded in presenting the Christian case - the fusion of physical beauty with spiritual tensions - with a completeness never achieved before.

Leonardo's achievement is almost inexplicable for he possessed the curiosity of a natural scientist and the logic of a mathematician, both of which should have acted as brakes on his imagination as a portrayer of the Christian theme, yet, in his 'Last Supper' and the two versions of the 'Virgin of the Rocks' (one in the Louvre, one in the National Gallery, London) he proved himself capable of interpreting the mystical implications of the Christian tragedy and of the Christian mystery. Michelangelo's lifetime as both sculptor and painter raises even more unanswerable questions. How could an artist whose knowledge of human anatomy was so complete that every gesture he invented for his figures seemed both human and inevitable, manage also to suggest that each gesture, with all its muscular tensions and relaxations, was a product of the restless, aspiring human soul? And how, having achieved this remarkable harmony between the flesh and the spirit, could he go further and, in the Sistine Chapel ceiling, imagine those astonishing images of God creating the world, dividing light from darkness, creating the first man, himself a miracle of physical beauty and mortal submission to the will of his omnipotent Creator? Admittedly, unlike any of the founders of Renaissance painting, Michelangelo seems to have been indifferent to the beauties of nature. He allowed his Adam to awaken to life on this planet not in a Paradise that had been fashioned to receive him but on a featureless slab of rock.

Almost every previous artist of the Italian Renaissance was acutely aware that nature was as worthy of his attention as man, and hence would have been a potential landscape painter had he been born two centuries later. But such was Michelangelo's obsession with the significance and splendour of the human body that his figures need no context. They are utterly self-sufficient. They do not need to be related to each other, and in their isolated grandeur they pay homage to the omnipotent Deity who created them. Where Giotto and Masaccio adopted the yardstick of humanity and hence failed a little in spirituality, Michelangelo's human beings seem to express the essence of the divine and his image of God the Creator is so compelling that, despite His physical strength, the complete realization of His material presence, He is still a symbol of the supernatural and therefore he, alone, can be compared with the Romanesque sculptors as an interpreter of divinity. He alone, among Renaissance humanists, finds it possible to rise above humanism without denying it. The danger point, the competition between

Botticelli. Detail of *Mystic Nativity*, 1500

Leonardo da Vinci.
The Virgin of the Roc...
(London version), 148...

Michelangelo. Detail of *God separating the Earth from the Sea*, on the Sistine ceiling

physique and faith which every other artist had to circumvent was, for him, the source of his power. In his earliest major sculpture, the Pietà of St Peter's (done at the age of twenty-three), one sees him struggling against the temptation of his own skill and knowledge, perilously near to the disaster of virtuosity. In his last, the Rondanini Pietà, virtuosity has been abandoned as though he were casting away his shackles. The wraith-like figures are pure symbols. They are oddly related to some of the most expressive figures on the twelfth-century tympanum of Autun. To be able to say that may be one's ultimate homage to Michelangelo. But it is also a tribute to Gislebertus and, consequently, to Romanesque sculpture in general.

Raphael presents a different problem. As one traces his progress (for once one is forced to adopt the Vasarian view) one sees him emerging from the suave purity of his master Perugino, gathering speed and power, emulating the Michelangelesque terribilità, but diluting it because his instinct for the graceful always conquered his desire for the meaningful, and his acute sense of classic beauty always got the upper hand over his sense of spiritual tensions. Where Michelangelo, in his old age, went back to mediaeval awe, Raphael succumbed, at the end of his short life, to the temptation of rhetoric, but one could say, sadly, that his last picture, 'The Transfiguration'

Michelangelo.
Pietà, c. 1500,
in St Peter's, Rome

Michelangelo. *The Rondanini P*
unfinshed at Michelange
death in 1

in the Vatican, represented his complete failure as a statement about Christianity. It was also something even more destructive. Its self-conscious rhetoric was one of the fatal influences that made it difficult for many of his successors to paint Christian pictures at all.

It is at this crisis in the history of religious art that a parenthesis becomes necessary. It must start with a reminder that up to a date late in the eighteenth century, the artist was almost invariably a servant - a man dedicated, perhaps to a cause, but the cause was primarily that of his master, or rather his patron.

The history of patronage is one facet of the history of civilization, for the patron is a person or an organization with sufficient power, and usually with sufficient wealth, to employ the artist as a propagandist and, hence, to dictate terms to him as regards subject-matter. As long as power and wealth were largely in the hands of the State religion, as they were

144

PIETÀ DI MICHEL ANGELO BVONAROTA

in pre-Christian Greece, or pre-Hellenic Egypt, the artist's subject-matter was largely dictated by the priest who required it for the temple, or the priest-king (in Egypt) who required it for purposes centering round the tomb. Later, the Roman Emperors, more closely concerned with political ambition, required the artist to turn his attention not to gods but to conquests. As Christianity developed a civilization centred on the monastery, requiring symbolic propaganda for the Church, the subject-matter became once more religious and art was, perforce, a sacred art which had the Church as its patron. And as long as this patronage was unchallenged (that is to say from the fifth century, throughout the Middle Ages and during the early decades of the Renaissance) the work produced by the artist, in architecture, sculpture, painting and the most elaborate and demanding of the applied arts, was essentially sacred. It was also the best. The Church had, as it were, a monopoly of craftsmanship as well as of faith.

But the new spirit engendered by the Renaissance and the new belief in the importance of the individual and the power of the intellect, and the consequent growth of secular organizations, was bound, in the end, to lessen the hold of the Church over the average mind. By the middle of the fifteenth century the Church, though its role as a patron continued, no longer had a monopoly. Italy, split up as it was (and to a great extent still is) into city states, each of whose rulers wished to assert himself both as a political and a cultural force, soon began to develop a secular as well as a religious patronage. In Florence the Medici, in Milan the Sforzas, in Mantua the Gonzagas, in Rome the Vatican as a political party governing the Papal States, in Venice the aristocratic élite that ruled the city, all developed a tradition of patronage that, in the end, introduced a new flavour into art - or, to be more precise, a set of new flavours each of which reflected the spirit of the new secular patron. In Florence, the intellectual and philosophical interests of the Medici and their circle exercised a recognizable influence on Florentine art. In the palace at Mantua, Mantegna produced a series of frescoes that reflect the dignified daily life of the Gonzagas. In the Schifanoia palace in Ferrara there are rooms which record the life of Borso d'Este's

146

Raphael. *The Ansidei Madonna, c.* 1505-7 (*left*), and *The Transfiguration,* begun in 1517 but completed only after Raphael's death

court, the love of sport and outdoor occupations. In Venice the great family palaces and the even greater wall spaces of the Ducal Palace forced the Venetian painters to embark on ambitious schemes celebrating not the city's piety but its pride. Even in the famous papal apartments in the Vatican one of Raphael's most successful frescoes paid homage to Apollo and the Muses, with the poets of antiquity gathered together on Mount Parnassus.

This outburst of secular patronage or the commissioning of secular subjects did not, of course, interfere with the ecclesiastical patronage that continued to run parallel with it, but it gave the artist a new set of interests and preoccupations. The gap between Earth and Heaven which had begun to narrow with Giotto narrowed still further as the demands of governments, princes and merchants increased. So that, by the beginning of the sixteenth century, and especially in Venice, 147

Earth and Heaven approached each other more nearly and the distinction between sacred and secular art became less sharp whether the priest or the prince acted as patron.

In many of the great mural paintings in the Venetian Ducal Palace one has the curious impression that the Doge and the Deity meet on equal terms. And in that most Venetian of institutions, the Scuole, organizations dedicated to a saint but managed by the lay members, the religious and secular elements are so closely fused together that one can hardly decide whether the artist has tackled a spiritual or a material theme. Carpaccio's great series of paintings, once in the Scuola dedicated to St Ursula, seem to be descriptions of elegant social occasions and when, at the climax of the series he is obliged to present us with a 'St Ursula in Glory' accompanied by her crowd of martyred virgins, he fails to rise to the occasion at the very point where a Romanesque or Gothic artist would have reached the point of highest intensity.

Titian's pagan mythologies invariably strike one as more eloquent and convincing than his Annunciations or his Assumptions, heroic though the latter may be. Veronese is always happier when he is celebrating the pomp of Venetian life than when he tries for the nobility or the tragedy of the Christian story. And he, of all artists, most confuses the two, so that a marriage at Cana or a feast in the house of Levi become state banquets that have lost all their symbolic meaning.

Only Tintoretto, in the Venetian sixteenth century, can rise to the demands made on his creative imagination by Christian themes. In the Scuola of San Rocco, to which he was appointed as official artist, his greatest works are not concerned with the life of the saint but with the deeper meaning of the story of the Gospels and with miraculous healings. His Crucifixion, full though it is of closely observed human action, is one of the most profoundly moving of all Crucifixions. His 'Last Supper' in the Church of San Giorgio makes Leonardo's more famous version look like a brilliant essay in composition. His 'Temptation of Christ' penetrates to the heart of the problem of the struggle between good and evil.

Tintoretto's San Rocco series is the most striking proof we have that what I have called the 'danger point' in the

Vittore Carpaccio. *St Ursula in Glory*

development of Renaissance art can be avoided by the artist
who is more conscious of the meaning of Christianity than of
the beauty of the visual world. It hardly needs saying that only
a man with unusual depth of feeling could have achieved this
almost impossible feat. For Tintoretto was certainly not un-
aware of human physical perfection. The four famous allegories
of Venice he painted for the Ducal Palace are among the most
radiant tributes to physical beauty ever painted; they contain
no trace of a Christian message. They are as expressive of
pagan optimism as the San Rocco Crucifixion is of Christian
tragedy. What the Ducal Palace required from Tintoretto -

149

Titian. Detail of *The Assumption of the Virgin,* 1516-18, in Sta Maria dei Frari, Venice

what, indeed, it required from almost all the artists it employed - was a combination of Hellenic pagan mythology and civic pride, and the great public rooms in the building are filled with masterpieces of precisely that kind. Titian and Veronese were as capable as Tintoretto of producing them. But Tintoretto alone could find the means to paint the deepest spiritual levels of Christian dogma and narrative. And when he was required to do so during his twenty years of work in the Scuola of San Rocco, he painted his most memorable though not his most opulent pictures. No other artist in the whole of the Venetian sixteenth century was capable of rising to such an occasion. Tintoretto had, in fact, two styles as well as two levels of subject-matter. His Ducal Palace style was part of the opulent Venetian tradition: his San Rocco style was entirely his own - dark, often forbidding, always in search of the eternal conflict between good and evil, and always (it is here that Tintoretto is unique) finding the meaning behind the appearance.

150

Tintoretto. *The Last Supper, c.* 1590-9
in S. Giorgio Maggiore, Veni

It must be realized that Renaissance attributes of mind,
and, hence, Renaissance ways of interpreting Christian themes
in art, were beginning to spread across Europe where their
impact was very considerable. In Germany, for example,
Dürer, Grünewald and, to a lesser extent, Altdorfer, responded
to Italian influences, and though their response was remarkably
un-Italian, it would certainly not have happened but for the
Renaissance. In Spain - after a sojourn in Venice and Rome
- El Greco produced a series of paintings that threw an
entirely new light on the possibilities of Christian symbolism
and iconography. These, too, would never have been envisaged but for his Italian training. In the Netherlands a group
of artists, of whom Jan van Eyck, Rogier van der Weyden
and Memling were the most important, made their contribution to religious painting. In France another group, centred
on Avignon, produced Christian paintings, one of which,
the 'Pietà' by an unknown artist, is, by any standards, one of
the undoubted masterpieces of religious art in any period.

It was painted about the year 1460 - roughly at the same
moment when Gozzoli was completing his Riccardi chapel
frescoes in Florence. Yet there is no trace in it of Florentine

152   Tintoretto. Detail of *The Crucifixion,* 1565, in the Scuola di S. Rocco, Venice

influence. Representing the International style the Avignon 'Pietà' is oddly timeless and would be difficult to place as the product of any local school or district of Europe.

In that the background is an expanse of plain gold, it is archaistic, for the use of gold to represent symbolic space had become obsolete a century earlier. The mood of the picture is one of austere tragedy. The silhouettes of the three mourning figures, St John, the Virgin Mary and the Magdalen, rise like mountains above the low horizon. The pale, angular figure of the dead Christ below them is unforgettable. The kneeling priest at the side is an irruption from the material world - a reminder that a mortal human being can be allowed to share the timeless grief occasioned by Christ's death. The three mourners do not see him, yet his presence among them, stated

Avignon School. *Pietà*, *c*. 1460, formerly in the Charterhouse of Villeneuve-lès-Avignon. The identities of artist and donor (kneeling on the left) are unknown

Hubert and Jan van Eyck.
The Adoration of the Lamb,
central panel of the
Ghent Altarpiece, 1432

in the most realistic terms, marks the contrast between divinity and humanity. Yet the contrast, even the contradiction, is given a stylistic unity by the metallic, map-like line that runs through the whole. Such a picture, a summing up, as it were, of the meaning of the Christian story, could only have been envisaged by an artist in a moment of strange inspiration. The fact that we do not even know his name seems to add to its power.

No such moment of sensitive inspiration occurred in Renaissance Germany, for neither Dürer nor Grünewald, both of whom were greater artists, if greatness is to be judged by confident grasp of the pictorial problem to be solved, were capable of such subtle symbolism.

As a painter Dürer can hardly be said to have made a serious contribution to Christian imagery. Intelligent and intellectually curious about what was happening in Italy, he travelled south to meet his contemporaries, in particular

Late Gothic German woodcarving:
The Assumption of the Virgin by Tilman
Riemenschneider, from the Creglingen
Altarpiece *(left,)* and *The Dormition of
of the Virgin,* centrepiece of Veit
Stoss's altarpiece in Cracow

Dürer. *The Four Horsemen,* woodcut from the *Apocalypse* series of 1498

Giovanni Bellini in Venice, but though his paintings make
it clear that his vision was broadened by his Italian contacts,
he was incapable of absorbing the lyricism or the poetry of
Bellini. But as a draughtsman he developed a German vitality
that turns the best of his engravings and woodcuts into the
noblest works of art that Germany produced. His masterpiece
in the field of religious art was the great series of illustrations
156   to the Book of Revelations. In these passionate woodcuts the

Grünewald. Detail of *The Entombment*, from the Isenheim Altarpiece, *c.* 1509-15

medium itself seems to have released in him a vein of apocalyptic splendour that has no parallel in European book illustration. The plate of the Four Horsemen plunging forwards
across the bodies of their victims is the best - certainly the
most memorable - of a series of plates that catch the full
flavour of the exuberant imagery of the text. The Book of
Revelations had always attracted the Gothic artists of an earlier
epoch (the series of tapestries from Angers is an outstanding
example) but no Renaissance artist had dared to tackle its
complexities so fearlessly.

But Dürer, even at his most fearless moments, never succeeded in introducing anything to compare, in intensity and
variety, with the great polyptych by Grünewald, now at Colmar.
Here, at last, is a cumulative effort on the largest possible
scale, that could never have been envisaged by any Italian. The
Colmar Crucifixion is unique in the history of religious painting. It strains the possibilities of the tragic, the static, the
mystical and the macabre to a point never reached before or
since in Christian art. Perhaps it is the one great series of
paintings that dwells, almost hysterically, on horror and yet
never loses the spirit of reverence for suffering without which
Christian imagery would be repellent - that tackles the expression of triumphant ecstasy and yet never falls into sentiment
or undue sweetness - that attempts the gruesome without slip-
ping into bathos. No other artist has approached so nearly to
excess on a religious theme without falling into the traps that
often await the use of the excessive. In Grünewald's case the

157

danger of seduction by concentrating on the grace of the human figure and the beauty of its worldly environment, which occurred so frequently in Italy, was overcome by a temperament that never felt the temptation of such seductions.

The altar-piece at Colmar is an elaborate structure made of hinged panels that open up to reveal further panels. The outer pair, when closed, combine to show the famous Crucifixion in which no aspect of spiritual tragedy or physical suffering has been avoided. The torn, lacerated body is described in detail that verges on the repulsive and yet evokes compassion rather than horror. The monstrous crown of thorns, the writhing fingers, the agonized feet, the cross itself bent downwards by the weight of the body, somehow succeed in making their effect as timeless symbols and not as records of an event. A refusal to use the device of symmetry in a theme that seems to demand symmetry, the use of agonized diagonals (the thrown back bodies, the thrust out arms, the entangled fingers, the pointing hand of St John the Baptist) and the sinister black of the sky all insist that we are not concerned with an event that could happen on earth.

The outer panels fold back to reveal two more, equally charged with an unworldly mood. In the left an Annunciation, unlike any other Annunciation, a feverish miracle; on the right, a Resurrection rapturous with explosive light and equally feverish. Between the two a central panel in which symbolism is worked out with such intensity that subject-matter itself seems to disappear. One can only guess that Grünewald has attempted a pictorial Incarnation - the central point of Christian dogma. Two further panels representing St Anthony and St Paul surrounded by hideous vegetation, impossible mountain ranges and diseased monsters, complete the whole of this unearthly feat of the imagination. Tragedy, rapture and the world of Satan himself on the three levels of the altar-piece show Grünewald's immense emotional range.

Even in this brief account of Christian art the Colmar altar-piece needs examining in some detail for here is an artist with the full technical equipment of the Renaissance, a contemporary of Raphael, who could combine the mysticism of sth mediaeval world, including its sheer ugliness, with the realime

Grünewald. *The Resurrection*, wing c
the Isenheim Altarpiece, *c.* 1509-1

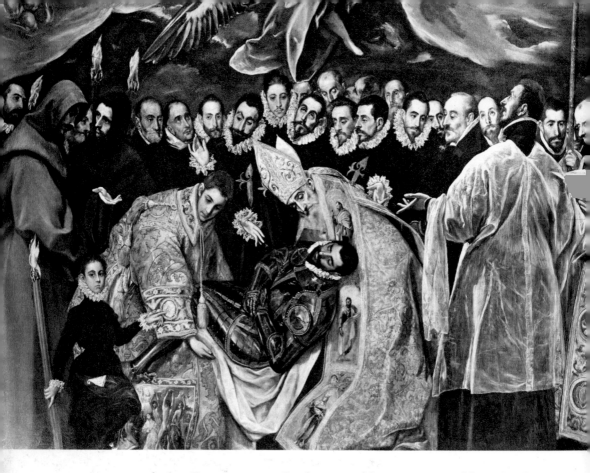

of the Renaissance. Such an achievement could only have happened in the romantic North of Europe, and only in Germany where excess and intensity were essential features of the national temperament.

The study of Mannerism must begin with an artist who is an exception to my over-all view of 'Mannerist' art. But El Greco's career is exceptional enough from many points of view. He was born in Crete in 1545 and therefore subjected in his youth to Byzantine influences. He moved to Italy where, first in Venice, then in Rome, he absorbed some of the sensuous materialism of the Venetians and then some of the intelligent virility of Michelangelo. With this strange set of contradictory experiences in his mind he mysteriously moved to Spain where he spent the rest of his life developing one of the most personal and the most eloquent of styles in the history of European art.

Greco. Detail of *The Burial of Count Orgaz, c.* 1586 (*left*) and *The Resurrection, c.* 1597-1604

There is a general agreement that El Greco, especially in the later phases of his career, was not only one of the greatest but also one of the most daringly original of all painters. But what, for the purposes of an account of the history of Christian art, is of ultimate importance is that his originality enabled him to discover a new way of relating art itself to the Christian religion. To state the case for El Greco briefly, he discovered a new set of rhythms - the rhythm of flames - and a new kind of world - a world that was weightless. Clouds, bodies, draperies, trees, rocks all seem caught up in these unearthly flickering rhythms. Where Grünewald's world is hard, cruel and merciless, El Greco's is ghostly, radiant, soaring. No one has ever possessed a more convincing command of the energy of upward movement. His pictures - not only of the Assumption or the Resurrection which demand, by the very nature of their subjects, an upward thrust, but even the Baptism or the Adoration of the Shepherds - tend to be vertical and the forms in them drift upwards and accumulate in their upper halves.

Such an artist could hardly fail to be a master of the unworldly; his skies are full of clouds that stream upwards, bearing not only angels but bodies with them. And such an artist could equally not fail to find a language for the interpretation of the heavenly. His great picture of the burial of Count Orgaz depicts the descent from heaven of St Stephen and St Augustine who miraculously lift the body into a crowded heaven that is itself a miraculous organization of flame-like forms. The very clouds, for all their cold harmonies of colour, are on fire, and the draperies are caught up in the same rhythm.

No wonder, with this strange imaginative equipment, that El Greco managed to seize on a new aspect of Christian art. No other artist has ever invented such convincing formal symbols of the world of the spirit. El Greco's temperament drove him into rebellion against the spirit of the Renaissance. For two hundred years art had been striving to understand the problems of structure, volume, space and solidity. And here, suddenly, was a genius who could deny the weight and solidity of the world without robbing it of its reality.

Christian humanism

WILLIAM NEIL

The two centuries between roughly 1300 and 1500 were a period of disintegration and rebirth. On the one hand there was the breakdown of the mediaeval order, of the Papacy, of the Holy Roman Empire, of the concept of Christendom; on the other, there was the stirring of new life, the discovery of nationalism, the spirit of scientific enquiry, the growth of criticism of authority, the revival of classical learning, the new emphasis on man and his interests, in short the Renaissance. It was out of this conflict between the old and the new, and the crosscurrents set up by the ferment of religious and secular thought that Christian art reached its apogee in the field of painting.

First, let us look at the collapse of what appeared at one time to be the monolithic structure of Christendom, when the Church under its great Popes provided the framework which called forth the highest endeavours and aspirations of the human spirit in all its manifestations. It was not for long that the power of the Church, as evidenced by Hildebrand's triumph over the Emperor at Canossa, remained unchallenged. Rivalry between secular rulers who resented the domination of the Popes, and Popes who used their spiritual authority for secular ends, ended by vitiating both the Papacy and the Empire.

It is understandable that a vast ecclesiastical organization needed money and that the voluntary contributions of the faithful were pitifully inadequate to cope with the administrative costs of running Christendom. Temporal and political power were vital, as were the revenues from Papal estates. But while the Pope as a Father in God could command the allegiance of high and low, emperor and serf, the Pope as a secular potentate and a landlord put himself in competition with princely ambitions and lost the sympathy of the people.

163

When it became difficult to tell the difference between the Vicar of Christ on earth and a manipulator of politics or a business tycoon, the glory had departed from the Papacy.

The Holy Roman Empire, under weak rulers, was becoming less significant in Europe than the rising power of national states, such as France and England. When a king of France felt strong enough to organize the kidnapping of a Pope without thunderbolts being cast down from heaven or even military reprisals being taken, and when he did so with the support of the French bishops, obviously the authority of the See of St Peter had reached its nadir. A few years later a French Pope had been installed at Avignon, under the control of the King of France, a 'Babylonian Captivity' which was to last for seventy years.

The Pope was now virtually a tool in the hands of the French. The Holy Roman Emperor was little more than nominal head of a collection of petty German states, each under its own ruler. With the growing sense of nationhood, where Englishmen felt themselves to be English, and Frenchmen, French, the cohesion which had made Christendom a supra-national organism had disappeared. For an English king, or a German prince, the authority of the Church was still paramount, but the Pope was now an 'Italian' or a 'Frenchman', a 'foreigner' as well as the Head of the Church, and therefore resented.

The situation became grotesque when by the end of the fourteenth century there were two Popes, one in Avignon and one in Rome, each claiming to be the Vicar of Christ, each vilifying the other, and each demanding financial tribute. The natural rivalry between the two rising powers in Western Europe, England and France, made it inevitable that so long as the Papacy was in French hands at Avignon, Englishmen would not feel themselves inhibited from giving tongue to their criticism of a Church which was governed from enemy territory. Chaucer's scathing indictment of the traffic in religion practised by unworthy representatives of the Church is matched by Langland's *Piers Plowman*. Both are not merely nationalistic protests against a 'foreign' organism, but rightful indignation at a degenerate presentation of the Faith. Both

Wycliffe's late 14th-c. translation made the Bible available to a growing middle class, able to read but ignorant of Latin; it weakened the Church's absolute authority in Scriptural matters, and incidentally fostered national feelings against Rome

Chaucer and Langland recognize the piety and honesty of true servants of Christ.

A more trenchant critic was John Wycliffe, Master of Balliol towards the end of the fourteenth century. He trounced the hierarchy for its exorbitant demands in papal taxation, claiming that the Church's wealth had become its greatest curse. But he went much further. The head of the Church in any nation, he said, should be the king and not the Pope. A priest is no different from an ordinary man and certainly has no power to change the sacramental bread and wine into the Body and Blood of Christ. The true Church consists of all true Christians and depends on neither Pope nor bishops. It derives its sole authority from the Bible.

This radical call, not for reform of the Church but for its replacement by something different, attracted little support, and Wycliffe became the founder of the sectarian Lollards, who were more interested in political anarchy than in a religious revival. The Bohemian Hussites, who were protesting as much against German domination as against the abuses of the Church, were directly inspired by Wycliffe. His translation of the Bible into the vernacular was his greatest legacy, but the climate of opinion which he engendered was not one in which art of any kind would find much encouragement.

165

Faced with heresy and rebellion, and the added complication of a third Pope, a last attempt was made to set the Church in order at the Council of Constance in 1414. It was agreed on all hands that the Church must have one head and not three, that there was clamant need for reform and that false doctrines must be suppressed. In the event, after four years of deliberation only the question of the Papacy was settled. No reforms worth speaking of were carried out and the method of suppressing false doctrine was to burn at the stake the leader of the Bohemian revolt, John Hus. A further Council held at Basle ended with equally derisory results. The Church was obviously by 1460 unfit either to set its affairs to rights or to retain the respect and allegiance of its own members.

Yet to offset this depressing and tragic story, the two centuries which saw the progressive crumbling of the structure of Christendom saw a flowering of mystical religion. Popular devotion directed to the Name of Jesus, to the Mother of God and to the Blessed Sacrament, working powerfully on the imagination and the emotions, maintained a real and living faith which ecclesiastical expediency could not corrode. But beyond this was the outstanding witness of saintly men and women throughout Christendom.

Unlike their predecessors St Francis, St Dominic and St Bernard, they did not dominate their times, found new movements, change the trend of events or receive popular acclaim. Their spiritual insights have rather been handed down in their writings, or have influenced small groups of like minded men and women to cultivate the contemplation of the Divine, in prayer and vision, as the highest activity of the soul. Such a one was St Thomas à Kempis, author of the incomparable *Imitation of Christ*, who spent most of his life within the walls of a monastery, but put all Christendom in his debt. From Germany came the autobiography of the Blessed Henry Suso, from England Mother Julian of Norwich's *Revelations of Divine Love*. Other mystics played a larger part in human affairs, like St Joan of Arc, or her Italian counterpart St Catherine of Siena, who tried in vain to solve the Papal tangle.

It was undoubtedly the intense popularity of the devotional movement and the influential if limited impact of these mystics

The seal of the Council of Basle, which met fruitlessly in 1431

and their followers that enabled the Church to survive its own follies and to turn to good account the winds of change which were sweeping through Europe. This was a source of power which was able to resist the pagan elements of the Renaissance or rather to transpose them into a Christian setting.

There were many facets of the Renaissance, many factors which combined to produce this remarkable change of outlook which turned mediaeval Europe into modern Europe and constituted nothing short of the rebirth which the word implies. It was something much wider than merely the revival of classical learning or the rediscovery of the riches of pagan literature and civilization. It was an intellectual revolution which affected art, letters, philosophy, science and religion. It comprised the effects of new discoveries and inventions, such as Copernican astronomy, voyages of exploration, the printing press and gunpowder. Trade and commerce expanded with new methods and new markets. The mediaeval guilds with their restrictive practices gave place to individual initiative.

It would be wrong to think of the Renaissance as a complete break with the past. The world was still the same world, and the people who inhabited it did not suddenly feel that they had passed from the Middle Ages to modern times. It was a period of transition and fluidity, which meant that the generation living around 1300 had a different view of life from the generation of, say, 1500. But it would be very difficult to put a finger on any year within these two dates and say that this was when the change took place.

The year 1453 is often regarded as the vital date in the transition from the old to the new Europe. This was the year in which the Turks took Constantinople, the capital of the Eastern Empire, founded by Constantine, the first Christian emperor, and still at that time the centre of Greek culture despite the fact that like its Western counterpart the Eastern Empire was by then a shadow of its former greatness. Greek scholars fled westward into Europe and so stimulated the revival of classical learning which played so important a part in the Renaissance. In fact, however, the end of the Byzantine Empire had been obvious for a long time and the

Petrarch, though one of the greatest of Italian poets, valued classical writing far higher than any achievements in the vernacular

scholars had largely departed to find less turbulent academic havens in the West long before the city actually fell.

Nevertheless 1453 is a convenient date to pinpoint what was in effect one of the major features of the transition from the old mediaeval outlook to that of the modern world, the rediscovery of classical art and literature, and with it the spirit of critical enquiry which is characteristically Greek. As we have seen, the Middle Ages had never lost touch completely with Latin literature. The monasteries above all had preserved the study of the great Latin authors, Virgil, Horace, Terence and the rest, and both in their libraries and in their educational activities scholarly monks kept Latin letters alive.

The study of Greek authors, on the other hand, had not survived in any comparable measure, despite the fact that the Greek language had persisted in parts of the South of Italy as the common tongue and the University of Salerno was noted for its Greek scholarship. It was due above all to Petrarch and Boccaccio that long before 1453 Greek scholars had been encouraged to settle in Italy and that the significant contribution of Greek civilization was made available to the Western world. Petrarch was so convinced of the glory of classical learning that he dismissed his immortal Italian sonnets as unimportant and extolled his dreary Latin effusions as masterpieces. He is said to have venerated the manuscript of Homer which he was unable to read as if it had been the relic of a saint.

Instead therefore of encouraging other young Italian poets and writers to become their pupils Petrarch and Boccaccio were largely instrumental in ensuring that for almost a century creative and original Italian literature was stillborn. Imitation of classical authors, both Latin and Greek, became the height of civilized writing. Textual criticism, compilation of grammars, encyclopaedias, commentaries and dictionaries engaged the attention of the ablest minds. But by the end of the fifteenth century the whole range of classical literature had been absorbed into the blood stream of Italian writers so that when native poetry came into its own again at the beginning of the sixteenth century it touched new heights of beauty and emotion. Ariosto, whose *Orlando Furioso* ranks in

VIII PIERO DELLA FRANCESCA
The Finding of the True Cross, c. 1452, fresco in S. Francesco at Arezzo

literature with the artistic masterpieces of the Renaissance, displays all the power of Petrarch with the added enrichment of the fruits of the classical revival.

A rather different development took place in the plastic arts. Cimabue made his mark before the revival of interest in Greek and Latin civilization set in. Giovanni Pisano, who influenced Giotto, was inspired to some extent by the study of classical marbles. But in the period when writers were pursuing the arid path of classical imitation and modelling themselves upon the styles of ancient authors, no such wealth of specimens of classical art emerged to divert the Italian painters and sculptors seriously from the natural development of their own genius. They too absorbed the spirit of the Graeco-Roman civilization, mainly through literature, but without going through the antiquarian cult which stultified progress between Petrarch and Ariosto. Like Ariosto, however, the perfection of Titian, Donatello, Raphael, and Michelangelo expresses the deepest insights of the intellectual reawakening.

With the publication in 1516 of Ariosto's *Orlando Furioso,* original Italian literature was fully established

What then was the contribution that the classical spirit had to make which came as a revelation to the Italy of the Middle Ages? It was briefly the rediscovery of the value of this world as compared with the world to come. It was the realization of the worth and dignity of man and all his interests, of the beauty of the human body, of the need for the free exercise of the human mind in critical appraisal of ideas and institutions. In classical literature men found the record of a highly cultured civilization which asked searching questions about the meaning of life and found answers which did not necessarily accord with Christian teaching. There was an atmosphere of freedom in the field of intellectual enquiry in the ancient world which was invigorating and stimulating to men who had been brought up to regard all the major issues as having been settled once and for all by the Church.

Latent in all this was of course the danger that the mediaeval cry of 'Glory to God in the Highest!' would be replaced by the modern cry of 'Glory to Man in the Highest'. But to begin with there was no sense that the new learning was hostile to the Church or destructive of Christianity. Clement of Alexandria and St Thomas Aquinas afforded good precedents for combining the best of Hellenism with Hebraic thought, for reconciling reason with revelation. Christian Platonism seemed to be a feasible compromise. If it should turn out that pagan morality infiltrated into society as well as pagan philosophy this was not apparent at the time.

Indeed the Popes were among the most notable supporters of the new movement and their patronage of art and letters was enthusiastic and enlightened. Pope Nicholas V founded the Vatican Library and furnished it with manuscripts culled by his agents from monasteries all over Europe and salvaged from the destruction of Constantinople. He gathered around him a veritable bevy of artists and scholars, including Fra Angelico, and encouraged them to paint, design and write. Sixtus IV was the builder of the Sistine Chapel; Julius II commissioned Michelangelo to paint its ceiling and Raphael to decorate the papal state apartments (Stanze). So the heads of the Church sponsored and directed art and learning in happy alliance with theology.

It seemed indeed as if the new humanism could flourish in an atmosphere of wealth and sophistication in complete harmony with Catholic orthodoxy. But there were inevitable and real tensions which were hard to overcome. There was a difference between the kind of humanism which the Renaissance encouraged and the respect for human reason which Aquinas taught, or the delight in human foibles which the craftsmen of the mediaeval cathedrals exhibited, or the love for human kind which St Francis so movingly displayed. The old Catholic humanism was a concern for man, as a child of God. His interests and activities were all seen as part of the divine economy. He was still basically a soul to be saved, imprisoned in an evil world, finding release and fulfilment only in the life to come.

It needed men of the calibre of Aquinas and St Francis to keep the balance and perspective right. In the normal devout mediaeval Catholic there was a strong puritanical streak which deplored the arts as frivolity, unless they served some high religious purpose, looked on sex as something unclean and entertainment as unworthy of a Christian's vocation. The less devout, of course, behaved as the common

170

The Popes themselves were great patrons: Sixtus IV commissioned masters of the
15th c. to paint the walls of his chapel in the Vatican, and the decoration was
completed for Julius II and Paul III by Michelangelo's ceiling and Judgment wall

On the ceiling of the Sistine Chapel - frescoed between 1508 and 1512 - Michelangelo's God, floating in swirling space, separates light from darkness on the first day of the Creation

run of mankind has always behaved except that they recognized that what they were doing was wrong.

But the new humanist would have none of this. The world was there to be enjoyed, the human body was both a thing of beauty and an instrument of pleasure, asceticism had no place in this brave new world and if the Church taught, or seemed to teach, anything different he preferred to be a pagan. Yet the number of those who on genuinely intellectual grounds turned their backs on the Church was at the time probably no greater than the number of those who found that they could reconcile the new humanism with their Christian faith. The majority, despite the large measure of ignorance and superstition in their make-up, had no thoughts of any other system of belief than the faith they had been brought up in, neither classical paganism nor Wycliffe's heresy.

This was the climate in which the great Italian painters of the Renaissance lived and worked. They were heirs to the classical heritage, pagan symbolism and mythology could be incorporated into their work, but they were still members of the Catholic Church, surrounded still by all the evidence of an ancient and powerful Faith, and conscious of the genuine mystical and devotional piety which was centred in congre-

gational worship.

Michelangelo made the human body capable of expressing the most profound spiritual truths: God stretches out His hand to the newly created Adam, waking him to life

If we ask whether a particular artist who painted a Madonna was in fact idealizing his charming model, or whether another painter was more interested in the details of the landscape than the Crucifixion which it frames, the answer is not always easy. Most people would agree, however, that if we were to look for one painting which conveys even to the uninstructed eye the perfect balance between the new humanism and the old Faith it is Michelangelo's 'Creation of Adam' on the ceiling of the Sistine Chapel. Here is something which is unique in that it combines perfect artistry with profound theology. The mystery which shrouds the transcendent Creator is suggested by the mantle which enfolds Him and the angelic figures who surround Him. This is no aloof Being, remote and inaccessible, but one who comes close to man communicating power and blessing. And man, the created, acknowledges his Creator, and reaches towards Him for he is made in His image, the crown of creation. He does not touch Him for God is essentially unknowable, but Michelangelo's Adam is as surely God's son as His creature. This great painting says all that there is to be said. The life of man finds its fulfilment in this kind of relationship to God.

There is a world of difference between Michelangelo's 'Creation of Adam' and Grünewald's 'Crucifixion of Christ', 173

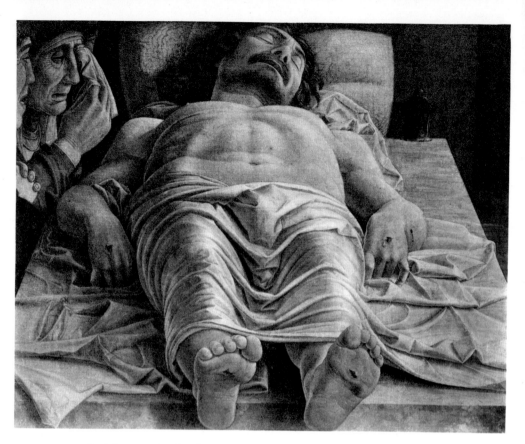

In Mantegna's *Dead Christ*, Renaissance discoveries in perspective and anatomy are fused with an almost Gothic intensity of emotion

yet Grünewald like Dürer stood in the mainstream of the Catholic tradition and the Catholic faith. But they were products of the German version of the Renaissance which although it derived from Italy expressed itself in a distinctive way. Germany has always had close ties with Italy and this was never more true than in the fifteenth century. German merchants had factories in Italy, German students went there to study law and medicine, and the wandering scholars passed backwards and forwards from one side of the Alps to the other. It was therefore inevitable that the revival of learning which had taken Italy by storm quickly made its impact farther North.

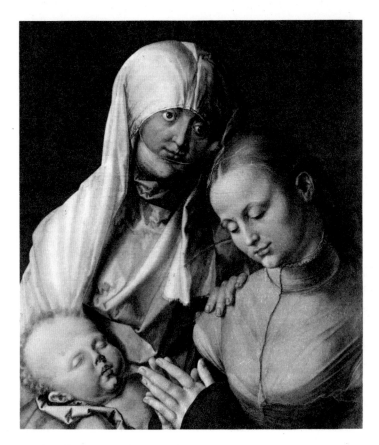

Dürer continued the Northern tradition of realism, painting the Virgin and Child with St Anne in 1519 as a German mother, child, and grandmother

The ground had been well prepared by the high standard of German education. The schools of such communities as the Brethren of the Common Life, which existed for the promotion of religion and learning, were the feeding grounds for the new universities - Prague, Vienna, Heidelberg and many more - which benefactors or civic authorities were busily creating. When the Renaissance came to Germany it flourished first in the wealthy imperial cities, where poets and artists formed circles for the study and cultivation of the new ideas. Holbein was a member of the group at Augsburg, Dürer belonged to the Nuremburg group.

Their Italian contemporaries had turned from painting scenes from the Old Testament or from the lives of the saints

Popular devotion to the Virgin was intense, and her shrines - such as that of the miraculous *Schöne Maria* of Regensburg - attracted crowds of fervent and at times hysterical pilgrims

to subjects from classical mythology. In Germany, however, the Renaissance painters tended to turn more to subjects from everyday life. They began by painting the Madonna as a comely German mother, with the accompanying angels depicted as frolicsome children, and ended by concentrating on scenes from the life they saw around them in the streets, in the countryside, in the farmyard. Since humanism extolled the value of the here and now, commonplace things were as much worth painting as heavenly themes.

The patronage of literature and art which was exercised by Popes and cardinals was in Germany in the hands of the Emperor, some of the princes, but more notably the wealthy merchants. Despite the squalor of the towns and the uncouth personal habits of the patrons, it was they who commissioned

X LEONARDO DA VINCI
Head of an angel, from *The Virgin of The Rocks* (London version), 1483

architects to build great churches and splendid public buildings, and filled their houses with rich tapestries, handsomely carved furniture and excellent paintings.

Religious life was extremely strong. The land was filled with churches and monasteries, the festivals of the Church were observed with enthusiasm, pilgrimages were highly popular and devotion to the Blessed Virgin was intense. Family religion of a simple kind was widely practised, and although there is a long story of unrest among the German peasants who included wealthy clerics as well as oppressive landlords among their enemies, together with some elements who shared the views of Wycliffe and Hus, it would be true to say that the effect of the Renaissance in Germany was to stimulate and encourage the piety for which Germany was already famous.

Within fifty years from the end of this period of disintegration and rebirth, that is by 1550, Rome had been sacked, the Pope had become once again a pawn in the hands of a foreign power, and Christendom was divided into two hostile camps, Roman Catholic and Protestant. Viewed from any angle today the Reformation was a tragedy and a disaster. In the following chapter we shall have to ask why it happened and what were its effects. Meanwhile we have to ask if it could have been avoided. Could the spirit of Christian humanism which animated the great Renaissance painters, so that they were able to combine the new outlook with the old faith, have saved Christendom from schism and prevented the bitterness and bloodshed which followed the Reformation?

Savonarola's fanatical puritanism, together with his attacks on the Pope and nobility, led to his execution as a heretic in 1498

Two of the last great Catholic Christians of the Middle Ages tried without success to reconcile the new humanism with the old religion - Savonarola and Erasmus. Savonarola (1452-1498) was the Prior of San Marco in Florence. He defied the power of the Medici ruling house, and by the sheer passion of his convictions became the uncrowned head of the republic. His preaching awakened the nobility and the merchants, the old and the young, to the need for a rededication of the whole life of the community to God. Artists and scholars who felt that the new learning could flourish best under the banner of the Church became his disciples.

177

Erasmus tried to sting the Church into Reformation from within, but his writings fostered the schism he dreaded

But the movement turned into a triumph of Puritanism over culture. The poor were fed but licence was replaced by asceticism. Religion flourished at the expense of art. In a ceremonial 'burning of the vanities' artistic treasures were consigned to the flames. Extremism of this sort would have dug its own grave but Savonarola's trial and execution brought his short-lived experiment to an end. He had very properly denounced Alexander VI, the worst of the Popes, as unfit to hold office and he had to pay dearly for it.

Erasmus of Rotterdam (1466 - 1536) had a far wider influence and far sounder methods. He was immensely learned and as a good humanist ranked Socrates and Cicero with the Christian saints. He believed that the unity of the Church must be preserved at all costs and could not contemplate war in the name of religion. But religion and morals badly needed reform and he relied on a combination of raillery and enlightenment to achieve it. In his 'Praise of Folly' he pokes fun at the arid scholasticism of the theologians, the vices and pretensions of Popes and clergy, the superstitions of popular religion.

He produced an edition of the New Testament in Greek, with a Latin translation which showed up the inaccuracies of the Vulgate. This with his editing of the early Christian Fathers was designed to show the practical simplicity of the Christian Faith, based on the life and teaching of Jesus, which he maintained had been submerged in the ceremonial and dogmas of the Church. His writings were condemned as heretical after his death but he steadfastly refused to support the Protestants although he lived through the Reformation.

This peripatetic man of letters, whose prim features in Holbein's portraits suggest, it has been said, descent from a long line of maiden aunts, lacked the courage and robustness which form part of the essential make-up of the reformer, but he also genuinely believed that to disrupt the fabric of the Church would bring about the collapse of civilization. He put his faith in the spread of the Renaissance spirit of enlightenment to bring about reform and given time this might well have happened. As on other occasions, however, history did not wait for the scholar.

V

V MANNERISM AND BAROQUE

Theatrical art and Protestant realism

ERIC NEWTON

Aside from a great creation through rebellion, the climax of the Renaissance left the artistic soil of Europe exhausted. In Italy, it proved impossible to follow Michelangelo without parodying his nobility or to imitate Raphael without coarsening his perfection. In seventeenth-century Venice Tintoretto was the last artist to interpret rather than to illustrate Christian themes. In Spain, El Greco proved inimitable; in the North of Europe the intensity of Grünewald turned out to be the last emotional explosion of its kind. During the last three-quarters of the sixteenth century there was no lack of artistic production but it was characterized by a curious and restless insincerity which art historians have agreed to call 'Mannerism'.

It is a phase unlike any that had preceded it. Much has been written about it since; in the early years of our own century, the word 'Mannerism' became an essential addition to the art historian's vocabulary. Yet it has never been sat-isfactorily defined. Nor is it necessary for me to attempt a definition here, for whatever aspect of it one focuses on - its affectations, its preciousness, its exaggerations, its tortuous treatment of subject-matter or its even more tortuous stylistic experiments - it becomes apparent that it suffers from an imbalance that makes it an impossible vehicle for Christian art. It produced a host of skilful artists the best of whom were capable of astonishing *tours de force* but few of them have a place in this book for few of them could avoid the fantasy, the artificiality or even the virtuosity that contradict the deeper levels of experience without which Christian art is meaningless.

Mannerist art is, in fact, an art full of eccentric and charming characteristics, but it has no inner message unless one can call extreme sensitivity to previous art a message. Like the play that is remarkable because it is 'good theatre', it compels

180

one to admire its technical competence and its virtuosity. But such plays, however stimulating and effective, can never be memorable because in them virtuosity becomes an end in itself. And at the moment when virtuosity takes the place of content or message, religion ceases to be a suitable or even a possible theme for the artist.

Consequently, for the writer on Christian art, the age of Mannerism is a barren one. Not that religious paintings and statues were not produced in the latter half of the sixteenth century, or that churches dedicated to worship were not being built in that period. Such works come inevitably into being in answer to the will of the patron rather than the inner urges of the artist: and as long as Christian ritual centering round the Mass itself continued to be practised, the provision of ecclesiastical imagery and ecclesiastical architecture had to continue.

What is missing from Mannerist religious art is the passionate conviction of both patron and artist that Christianity is a cause to be served by art and not an excuse to be eagerly grasped by the artist for the display of his own skill or the advertising of his own vein of imaginative fantasy. That passionate conviction, which is the keynote of all great Christian art, was not to reappear without the arrival of a new stimulus. And that new stimulus, though it gave birth to a new style - the style we have agreed to call Baroque - must ultimately be traced to causes that concern the writer on ecclesiastical history rather than the historian of style itself. For style, as we now begin to realize, is not something that an artist invents as a means of liberating himself from the tyranny of old traditions. It is the inevitable outward expression of what lies beneath those traditions. And at those moments of crisis when a new style is born, however much the art historian may be tempted to analyze and describe its characteristics, he is bound, in the end, to confess that analysis and description are less illuminating than an enquiry into the fundamental causes that have brought about the change, and, indeed, have made it inevitable.

I have chosen Rubens and Rembrandt as types of two extremes of the stylistic divergence Dr Neil and I discuss in our dialogue. But they are by no means isolated examples. And, oddly enough, when one comes to examine the art of Rembrandt's contemporaries in seventeenth-century Holland, one finds that almost all of them are so concerned with material existence and the trivial happenings of everyday life that they are incapable of interpreting the deeper levels of the New Testament and therefore rarely make the attempt. The Baroque artists of Italy, on the other hand, even though religious themes formed the major part of their work, were equally hampered because the rhetorical style to which they were committed too easily degenerated into a set of visual clichés that obscured the very meaning of Christianity.

It follows that only exceptional genius could manage to evade these two pitfalls. Without genius, Protestantism could achieve little but prosaic materialism while Catholicism had little to offer but a set of formulae for religious ecstasy. On the one hand we are restricted to the furniture of the kitchen or the virginals and wine-glasses of the front parlour; on the other, we find rolling clouds, melodramatic gestures, theatrical transports and the whole apparatus of emotional overstatement invented by the Baroque artists in order to replace sincerity by effectiveness.

Despite this double danger, genius did occur during the seventeenth century and some, at least, of the artists who possessed it managed triumphantly to turn it into a means of solving the problem of religious art.

What the Dutch school produced during those vital years of the seventeenth century between the emergence of Frans Hals as a portrait painter in the century's early years and the death of Hobbema at its end, was almost in the nature of a crowded parenthesis in the story of European art. The number of competent Dutch painters who flourished during the middle years of the century was immense. One could describe them all as united by a deep affection for the everyday life of the country, its quiet and seemly domesticity, its wide landscapes, its over-arching skies, its shipping, its cattle, its flowers. It was the outcome of a national temperament dedicated to materialism and a group of artists whose natural means of expression was prose and who therefore were incapable of attempting

Rubens. *The Great Last Judgment*, before 1618

anything that involved the miraculous or the mystical and consequently were incapable of interpreting any but the superficial aspects of Christianity.

Rembrandt, as has been stated, was the great exception to this generalization. He was not only a giant among his contemporaries but he stood apart from them. He was timeless in his humanity even though he was typically Dutch in the sobriety of his style. But because he, like his contemporaries, belongs to this great parenthesis, it will be more convenient to describe his religious paintings later, for they do not belong to the mainstream that had its origins in Italy as early as the fourteenth century and continued to expand and develop across the map of Europe, radiating to Germany, to Spain and, what must concern us now, to the Catholic Netherlands centering on Antwerp and Brussels.

If Holland produced the isolated parenthesis that we now think of as the Dutch school, the Flemish painters carried on the rhythmic grace of Italy, not always understanding it, but almost always paying homage to it until the moment arrived when Rubens uprooted himself from his native Antwerp, visited Mantua, explored the great artistic centres of Bologna, Rome and Venice, discovered the glow of Titian and the virility of Michelangelo and by a metamorphosis that seems almost miraculous, forged out of his discoveries his Baroque style.

One could describe Rubens's style as a fusion of energy and opulence, and his equipment for giving it full expression as a facility in the art of rhythmic composition and in the handling of paint that no other artist has ever possessed to the same degree. The vast mass of work on every kind of theme (with the exception of still-life which he despised as unworthy of his enormous creative energy) includes portraits, mythologies, allegories, historical scenes and religious paintings, all marked with the same heroic opulence. It follows that his religious pictures are impressive and rhetorical rather than profound or spiritual and that the emotional difference between pagan and Christian attitudes to life is hardly noticeable except where tragedy - and usually the tragedy of physical suffering as seen in his Crucifixions - is imposed

Rubens.
The Assumption of the Virgin, 1620

upon him by his subject-matter. The 'Great Last Judgment'
in Munich hardly differs, at first glance, from an ambitious
composition of nymphs and satyrs. The 'Virgin of the Assumption' is a Junoesque vision of his first wife. The disciples of
Christ are athletes, Herculean rather than reverent in their
gestures and actions.

Yet at his best - in the great Antwerp 'Deposition' for
example - he can use the sweeping diagonal rhythms which
he himself invented and the Baroque grandeur which binds
all details into a single pictorial unit for emotional purposes
that no pre-Baroque painter could have achieved.

185

That pictorial unity, in which the eye can never detach a part without detracting from the whole, is the keynote of the Baroque style. When Rubens uses it, as in the great diagonal avalanche that ties together the nine figures in the Antwerp 'Deposition', so that even the dead body of the Christ seems to have no separate existence but is a mere painter's device for emphasizing the central theme of 'descent', he is applying an extreme form of the principle of visual unity to the art of painting. But even so he was applying that principle *only* to the art of painting whereas throughout Italy, guided by the passionate enthusiasm of the Jesuit Counter-Reformation, the same principle was changing the whole spirit of ecclesiastical architecture. As one gazes in bewilderment at the interior of the Jesuit Church, Il Gesù, in Rome, it is impossible to decide where architecture stops and sculpture begins, and as one's eyes at last come to examine Gaulli's painted vision - 'The Adoration of the Holy Name of Jesus' - on the ceiling, it is still impossible to think of that wildly complex vision that rises into a dazzling burst of light in a remote sky as though it were what we normally think of as a 'painting'. It is a visual climax, an inseparable part of a single ecstatic whole which is built up from floor to ceiling. It reminds one, perhaps, of a symphony whose main 'themes' are so closely interlocked that the themes themselves are lost in a complex development of modulations. It becomes comparatively unimportant to know what architect conceived the whole, what sculptor carved the angels that soar upward to support the painted vision or what painter executed the vision itself. Only in the art of grand opera are so many contributions fused together to achieve the final single effect.

It follows that the single names of outstanding geniuses are not the vital factors in the story of seventeenth-century art. Giotto's name is almost all that we remember when we think of the Arena Chapel in Padua, and it is Michelangelo who comes to mind when we remember the Sistine Chapel, and the Scuola of San Rocco is a framework for Tintoretto's interpretations of miraculous events. But Gaulli, in Il Gesù, is the name of an artist who supplied a necessary ingredient in a larger whole. It is the whole church that interprets the event,

186

Rubens. *The Deposition,* central picture of an altarpiece painted for Antwerp Cathedral between 1611 and 1614

Bernini. Monument of Pope
Alexander VII, 1671-78,
in St Peter's, Rome

and the event itself is an indivisible context: the total spirit,
translated into visual terms, of Jesuit militant enthusiasm.

Yet single names do emerge. Rubens is too great an artist
to be ignored, or to be thought of as merely supplying important ingredients to a banquet. So is the sculptor Bernini. The
Vision of St Theresa in the Church of Santa Maria della
Vittoria in Rome is something more than a sculptor's climax
to an architect's design. It may be closely integrated with
the architectural whole, but in our memory we detach it and
it still retains its power as a concentrated study in ecstasy.
His great papal tombs in St Peter's in Rome and the massive
baldacchino he designed for the high altar are immensely
impressive, but the acknowledged genius of Bernini was overshadowed by the even more immense and impressive interior.

188

Gaulli ('Baciccia'). *The Adoration of the Holy Name of Je.*
ceiling of Il Gesù in Rome, 1668-

The pomp and rhetoric of Baroque painting and sculpture in seventeenth-century Italy produced plenty of minor masters, and there were plenty of rich ecclesiastical patrons to urge them on. The names of such artists are known and their skill in producing a theatrical version of the Christian point of view is undeniable. Yet somehow what their work suggests is rather the sumptuous glitter of ecclesiastical vestments and the fumes of incense than the story of the Gospels or the doctrine of Christ. It is the hypnotic power of ritual, not the story of the Bible that primarily concerns the artists and the patrons of the Baroque style in 'Catholic' Europe.

When we turn to Protestant Europe, vestments and incense and theatrical hypnotism are left behind. The artists' patrons are no longer Popes and Cardinals but citizens and merchants for whom not the church but the domestic interior is the focal point for enrichment. Consequently, as has already been pointed out, the unremarkable but affectionately observed details of everyday life, especially in Holland, are what occupy the artist's attention. Christianity, in Holland, may have been no less real to the burghers of Amsterdam than it was to the citizens of Rome, but it was concerned with conduct - one might almost say with 'goodness' - rather than with faith or ritual. Conduct and goodness are not inspiring themes for the artist. It would be almost impossible to argue that the peaceful domesticities of Dutch genre painting, still less the gentle landscapes and the charming still-lifes of fruit and flowers that the little masters of seventeenth-century Holland produced in such abundance had, or could have, any religious significance. In such a situation only an artist of exceptionally profound humanity (I am not here concerned with painterly competence, though admittedly without it human profundity becomes inarticulate) could possibly make Christianity his main theme. And in the whole corpus of Dutch seventeenth-century painting only Rembrandt made a serious attempt to do so, and in doing so did something that had not been done since Giotto painted the life of Christ in Padua. Both artists looked steadily at the world around them, discovered that it was inhabited by people like themselves, but used them as actors in a drama that Christianity alone could have provided for

Rembrandt. *The Adoration of the Shepherds*, 1646

them. Both artists are Shakespearian in their understanding of human appearance and human behaviour coupled with a realization that behind that understanding there must be a depth of feeling that includes divinity, mystery, the unfathomable workings of the supernatural. Giotto was the first painter to possess this almost inexplicable gift, Rembrandt the last.

In Rembrandt's case what makes his achievement even more inexplicable than that of Giotto was that in a school of painters who had specialized in the art of genre - the depiction of scenes from everyday life purged of every hint of the strange or the mystical - he too could approach Biblical themes in precisely the same spirit, as though, for him, Biblical characters were indistinguishable in appearance and gesture from his own Dutch contemporaries, and yet the idea that these are, in fact, genre paintings never occurs to us. The Nativity in the National Gallery takes place in a Dutch barn, the mother and child are surrounded by Dutch peasants. There is no 191 overt reference, as there would have been in a painting by Rubens, to the incarnation of the Son of God, yet there is no mistaking that a miracle, a decisive moment in the Christian story, has occurred. We can only wonder how in this, or in any of Rembrandt's religious pictures, genre has become mystery without any of the usual symbols of mystery. The Descent from the Cross is not, as with Rubens, an essay in diagonals but a description of a grief-stricken crowd doing what has to be physically done. The Miracle at Emmaus has a solemn intimacy that involves the Disciples at the table in reverent wonder, yet they behave less theatrically than Caravaggio's peasants. The Holy Family is a study of a carpenter, his peasant wife and their little son but it is the word 'holy' rather than (as with Rubens) 'family' that is the keynote.

Such paintings can only have been painted by a man who had spent a lifetime of solitary reading and brooding over the Bible and to whom vestments and incense and the sacrament of the Mass had little meaning. For Rembrandt it was the fact not the symbol that counted; the fact was too pregnant with its own meaning to require the addition of rhetoric or splendour.

It is for this very reason perhaps - this almost inexplicable fusion of genre with mystery - that Rembrandt's religious paintings are so unlike those of any other great painter. But it is for a different reason that when we turn to Rembrandt's drawings of Biblical themes we are confronted with a question that needs answering though it is difficult to answer.

Rembrandt like Leonardo was a draughtsman by habit. For him, the act of drawing was not, as it had been with so many of his predecessors, especially his Italian predecessors, a means of preparation for the larger task of painting an altarpiece or of coming to grips with its details. Rembrandt's drawings are independent works of art in their own right, done in the heat of an excited moment of observation or under the sudden inspiration of an emotional idea. For a man so easily stirred into creative activity either by his acute observation or his equally acute understanding of a situation, whether secular or religious, drawing was the ideal, the most rapid

192

Rembrandt. *The Deposition, c.* 1637-

Caravaggio. *The Supper at Emmaus, c.* 1598

method of communication. What one notices first in Rembrandt's pen-drawings to which he gave weight or an added effect of the impact of light by washes of diluted ink, is the furious tempo of them, as though he had done them in a frenzy of controlled impatience lest the original stimulus should evaporate before the statement had been made. Nothing inessential is included in those extraordinary statements, obviously made not for a patron's pleasure but for his own satisfaction and the determination to let no experience pass unrecorded. No drawings have ever been so densely packed with meaning despite the impetuousness and urgency of the hand that held the pen and brush. It is as though the artist had been granted a power to use shorthand instead of the usual laborious syntax of description.

Among the thousands of drawings that resulted from this kind of intimate draughtsmanship are a surprising number of

194

Rembrandt. Detail of *The Pilgrims of Emmaus*, 1648

Biblical illustrations of such directness and immediacy that
one can guess at once how habitually Rembrandt's imagination
brooded on the Bible and its inner meanings. Some, like the
Raising of the Cross or the Entombment, are rapid jottings.
Others like the Annunciation are experiments in the dramatic
relationship of two figures whose reality in terms of dress
and historical setting has hardly seemed to need stating. Some
- Esau selling his birthright for example - are poignant
studies of a situation in which everything depends on a kind
of miraculous passion behind the swift scribble. There is
a nocturne of the Good Samaritan arriving at the Inn in which
outline has almost disappeared and light bears the full
burden, and a 'Christ Walking on the Waves' in which one
would almost guess that Rembrandt was attempting to prove
that even with a match-stick dipped in ink he would still
retain his expressiveness.   195

Rembrandt. *The Good Samaritan arriving at the Inn, c.* 1648

The question we are impelled to ask in the presence of all his religious drawings is a simple one - what, in a country where religious painting was not in demand and the patronage of religious art had almost disappeared, and in a generation where almost every other painter in Holland was concentrating his attention on the material side of life, prompted him to make them? And we can only answer by suggesting that had he not done so, his deepest need would have been unfulfilled. In his fearless realism he did everything that his contemporaries were doing and outpainted them all, yet even so he combined this realism with religious intensity to tackle the problems of translating spiritual values into visual forms. In doing so he proved that he was not Dutch but international, not an artist of the seventeenth century but a timeless one.

Meanwhile, in seventeenth-century Spain, religious painting of a rather different kind was making uneasy attempts to assert itself. Spanish painting had never succeeded in building

197

Rembrandt. *The Raising of the Cross, c.* 1627-28

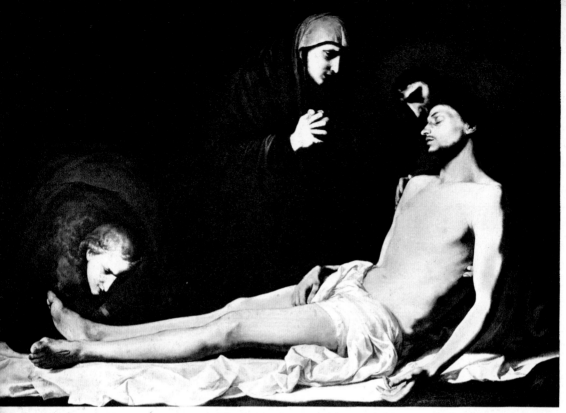

The Lamentation over the Dead Christ, by Ribera, *c*. 1645 (*above*), and *The Death of St Bonaventure*, one of a series painted by Zurbarán in 1629 for the Franciscan church in Seville (*right*)

up a consistent tradition. Neither the splendour of Italian Baroque nor the profound humanity of Dutch art had succeeded in establishing itself in Spain. El Greco's flame-like mysticism had produced some of the most impressive Christian art in Europe but it was too personal to leave behind it a 'school' of religious painting. After his death the greatest of all Spanish painters, Velazquez, found himself, for most of his working life, too closely associated with court circles to apply his genius to religious themes, and in any case, in the earlier years of his career, the few religious works he achieved were done with a Caravaggesque realism that is the exact opposite of Rembrandt's. Where Rembrandt imposed Christian meanings on to a genre formula, Velazquez turned Christian subjects into genre with such imperturbable common sense that little beyond their titles has any connection with Christianity. His contemporaries Ribera and Zurbarán were

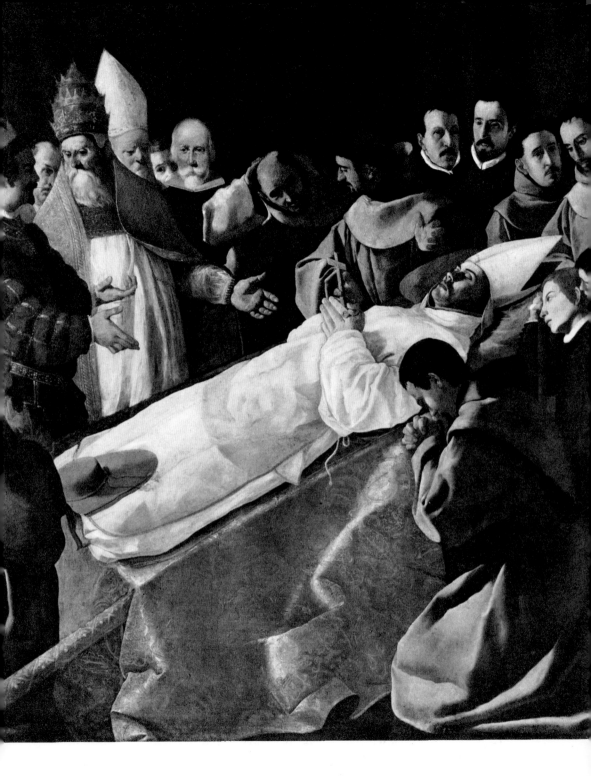

more capable, at their best, of penetrating below the surface of the material world, and his successor Murillo painted altar-pieces based on Italian masters. But where they succeeded in doing exactly what they set out to do with a panache that is, at least, charged with vigour and splendour, Murillo's vision is diluted with a sweetness and a sentiment that robs Christianity of its stern nobility.

In fact, if one asks who, in seventeenth-century Spain, after the death of El Greco, managed to create painting or sculpture of sufficient religious significance to merit inclusion in this brief account, one would be forced to exclude every painter with the exception of a handful of pictures by Zurbarán done in an exceptional moment of inspiration. I have chosen his 'Death of St Bonaventura' (in the Louvre) to represent him. Behind the hard Spanish realism is a gravity and solemnity that is rare in any part of seventeenth-century Europe. One is reminded a little of the lower half of Greco's 'Burial of Count Orgaz'. But one has only to compare the two works to realize that the hieratic grandeur that El Greco derived, ultimately, from Byzantine art has at last lost its magic. Zurbarán's picture is certainly prose of a high order, but it is none the less prose.

The Reformation conflict

ERIC NEWTON AND WILLIAM NEIL

This book has the double task of describing the crucial phases of the Christian story and the growth of the artistic forms which portray that story. The result is inevitably a dialogue in which the religious development has the dominant voice. Artistic forms respond to changes in the spiritual climate, to powerful intellectual and doctrinal movements within the Church. The Reformation and the Catholic response represent one of those crucial moments in history when the active conflict of ideas has produced sharp divergences of styles. And in the seventeenth century 'spirit' and 'style' became so closely interwoven that we have chosen to represent this complex process as a dialogue of two voices where question and answer can seek out different aspects of the truth.

ERIC NEWTON. My first, and indeed my fundamental question, would be to ask Neil to explain the ultimate causes for the Reformation and the evidently passionate reply to it by the authors of the Counter-Reformation. Only on his account of this opposition between two apparently opposing forces can one try to explain the opposition in style between, say, Rembrandt on the one hand and Rubens or Bernini on the other.

WILLIAM NEIL. According to a Protestant anecdote one of the Popes after the Reformation died and knocked on the gates of heaven. St Peter called to him to come in, saying that surely the Pope had the keys. The reply was: 'Yes, but Luther has changed the lock'. A Catholic anecdote records the observation of a candidate for university entrance to the effect that Luther was obsessed by two ideas: Justification by Faith and Invincible Concupiscence. The attitudes reflected in these rather mild and donnish jests merely hint at a history of over four centuries of bitter distrust, violence, persecution and bigotry

The ship of the Church foundering: 16th-c. Protestant woodcut from Germany

with which the two great divisions of the Christian Church in Western Europe have opposed each other, each maintaining and believing in the rightness of its cause and the error and sinfulness of its opponent.

The harm that this schism has done to the cause of Christianity is incalculable and, in the light of the new spirit of reconciliation sparked off by Pope John XXIII, whereby both sides as never before are ready to look again at the issues that divide them and seek to find ways of overcoming their differences, it may seem like reopening old wounds to turn back to the beginning of the sixteenth century and revive memories that were better left to moulder in the past. Any reasonable Catholic or Protestant today would at once want to say that the Church of Luther's day badly needed reforming and that the malpractices against which not only Luther, but untold other devout Catholics at the same time protested, have long since vanished. The Catholic Church in the twentieth century under enlightened leadership, and with a readiness to come to grips with the problems of the day as evidenced by the summoning of the Vatican Council, commands an authority and a respect among non-Catholics which it has not enjoyed for four hundred years.

Cheap jibes about the 'Italian mission' and cries of 'No Popery' are less prominent among responsible Protestants these days than a frank acknowledgment of their own vulnerability. The fragmentation of Christendom, competitive denominationalism, freak sects, an emasculated gospel and individualism run riot seem a heavy price to pay for whatever advantages the Reformation may be claimed to have brought in its train. Over against this stands the Catholic Church with its continuity, its tradition, its internationalism, its architectural and artistic legacy, its rich devotional life and above all its preservation of the *mysterium tremendum* in its faith and liturgy.

Why then, it may justly be asked, do not Protestants who are conscious of all this make their submission to the Holy See, admit their error and return to the fold? Many have indeed done so. But many more hold back because what has been done cannot easily be undone. Catholics and Protestants alike, we are all what history and environment have made us. Italians, Spaniards and Irishmen (unless they are Ulstermen) are born into the Catholic ethos as surely as Dutchmen, North Germans, Englishmen and Scotsmen are children of the Reformation. We cannot unwrite history or lightly bypass what it has made us. What has happened in the last four centuries may take another four centuries to put right. The goal is a reunited Christendom, towards which ecclesiastical and theological leaders on both sides are already working. There is far more which is held in common than that which divides, and there are bigger barriers between sections of Protestantism than between the major non-Roman communions and Rome.

All of which is by way of a preface to saying that to examine the causes of the Reformation from the viewpoint of the twentieth century is to recognize at once that many of them no longer have any relevance. In the light of the present day, the violence of feeling and mutual hostility are barely understandable. Doubtless the modern Catholic rigorist would argue that no issue could be great enough to justify schism, just as his opposite number on the Protestant side would claim that nothing short of a Protestant breakaway could have induced the Catholic Church to set its house in order. Ultra-Protestants would of course maintain that the Scarlet Woman is as great a travesty of Christianity today as she was in Luther's time, just as ultra-Catholics would refute any suggestion that there is room for compromise on such matters as the Index, the celibacy of the priesthood, or birth control, which many Protestants feel to be greater obstacles to reunion than the infallibility of the Pope.

It is idle to speculate what would have happened if the policy of Erasmus had been followed rather than that of Luther and Calvin, and any judgment is bound to be biased by the tradition in which each of us has been brought up and the national ethos we have inherited. What is important is that in stirring up the muddy waters of the Reformation conflict again we should recognize the failure of both sides at that time and ever since to witness to the wholeness of Christian truth. However Catholic and Protestant art would develop in the period that followed the Reformation it could

203

Cranach drew Luther
in 1520, the year
in which he burned
the papal bull
at Wittenberg

not but suffer from the same impoverishment that has affected the theology and devotional life of a divided Christendom. No painter or sculptor could ever again exercise his skill without being conscious that he did so as a Catholic or as a Protestant. He may have felt that he had a monopoly of religious truth on his side but he could not have the same serene assurance of the unassailability of the faith delivered to the saints as the cathedral builders of the Middle Ages or the Renaissance painters. Luther had made that impossible.

The story of this German miner's son is strange and tragic. He began as a brilliant student of the University of Erfurt, with a love of music and the classics, intending to become a lawyer. Then because of personal religious difficulties he entered a monastery in his early twenties, to see if the mediaeval programme of discipline, asceticism and devotion could bring him inward peace. He found the answer, however, not in the intense mortification of the flesh which he forced upon himself but in a spiritual experience which convinced him that the basic truth of Christianity is God's love which accepts us as we are.

It was while he was a teacher of theology in Wittenberg that he first clashed with the established faith. Pope Leo X needed money to build St Peter's in Rome and one certain way of getting it was to sell Indulgences. Whatever the Church might say about the true character of Indulgences the ordinary man believed it was a means of buying himself out of the eternal consequences of the sins he had committed. When an itinerant pardon-seller came to Wittenberg Luther issued an open challenge to debate the validity of the practice. To his astonishment he became at once a public figure. People clamoured to get their hands on copies of his protest; sales of Indulgences dropped dramatically. Luther was summoned to Rome but was protected and prevented from going to certain death by Frederick of Saxony.

This was in 1517, the date generally given as the start of the Reformation. From then on for the next three years Luther poured out a flood of pamphlets criticizing the Church and its doctrine, maintaining the priesthood of all believers, questioning the authority of the Pope over the German churches, disputing the validity of all but the two scriptural sacraments, denying Transubstantiation and recommending married clergy. It is not surprising that in 1520 he was excommunicated or that he burned the papal bull. When he defended himself before the Emperor at Worms he set up the Bible as his sole authority and maintained the right of private judgment against any Pope or General Council of the Church.

The increased sale of indulgences, promoted by Pope Leo X, further inflamed German feelings against the Church

At this point Luther was the hero of Germany. He spoke for all who, like Erasmus, had called for reform of mediaeval practice and a return to primitive Christianity; he voiced the protest of decent citizens against the corruption of the Curia and the scandalous behaviour of so many of the clergy; he struck a responsive chord in all who resented the stranglehold of a foreign hierarchy. The question of schism had not yet arisen and although many felt that he was too radical they could not but see in him the only hope of restoring a sick Church to health. Dürer admired him so much that he painted him as St John, the beloved disciple of Jesus.

Within a few years much if not most of that support had gone. The German peasantry, encouraged by Luther's defiance of ecclesiastical authority and his stand for the rights of the individual, revolted against the system of serfdom which condemned them to poverty and misery. Rebellion against the state was, however, anathema to Luther who denounced the rising and urged the princes to destroy the peasants without mercy. This appalling attitude lost him not only the backing of the masses but of moderate opinion as well. What had begun as a religious awakening ended largely in political expediency. German princes who, like Henry VIII, cast a covetous eye on the wealth of the Church in their territories found Lutheranism a better paying proposition than Catholicism. About half of the German states broke away from Rome, largely in the North, while the South remained Catholic. By 1555 the principle had been established that the religion of the ruler should determine the religion of his territory. Lutherans or Catholics who found themselves in the wrong camp could either conform or quit.

Luther was of course not the only reformer. There were parallel movements in Switzerland and France, but the man

205

At the time of this portrait, about 1550, Calvin had made Geneva into a Puritan City of God

who ranks with Luther as the most influential of the founding fathers of the Reformation is John Calvin. Beside the volcanic and violent German this cold-blooded French intellectual who turned the imperial city of Geneva into a citadel of Protestant rectitude can hardly be called a sympathetic figure even by his friends. He embodied all the strength and weakness of Puritanism and his impact on the religious history of Europe was formidable. His 'Institutes of the Christian Religion', published in 1536 when he was still in his twenties, was the first comprehensive statement of the Protestant case and became the textbook of all subsequent Calvinism.

His position, like that of Luther, was basically an appeal to the authority of the Bible. Where the practice of Catholicism in his view conflicted with the Scriptures it was in error and must be purged. His aim was to make Geneva a theocracy. It became, however, more like Jerusalem under the High Priests than the early Christian communities which he claimed to reproduce. Democracy in Church and State, a highly educated citizenry, strict surveillance of public and private morality, avoidance of frivolity, compulsory attendance at divine worship - these were his plans for the model community and these were the ideas that his disciples carried with them to England, Scotland and Holland.

Calvin held a doctrine of Predestination which was pushed much farther by his successors than he himself probably ever intended. It had however great consequences for the activities and outlook of those who accepted the Calvinist position. Men who believed they had been chosen for salvation by the grace of God felt supremely confident that He was on their side. Neither threats nor persuasion could move them. They took their stand on what they believed to be the faith of the primitive Church, the pure gospel unadulterated by the mediaeval superstition of Rome. Their moral principles were unshakable. Christ had made them free and that freedom had been given to them to build an educated, prosperous, wholesome community to the glory of God. Not by a flight from the world into a monastery, not by mystical contemplation of the world beyond, not by extravagant devotion to the Madonna and the saints, but by a simple faith in Christ

206

centred in the home rather than in elaborate buildings, by plain living and high thinking, and above all by hard work - this was the proper life for men who stood under the judgment of God and this was the way to bring His Kingdom upon earth. No one could deny that this was a noble, if one-sided faith, or that it has produced remarkable results wherever it has been practised.

This was the form which Protestantism assumed in Holland, which, like Scotland, became a Protestant country as much through rebellion against its foreign rulers as by religious conviction. This was therefore the atmosphere into which Rembrandt was born and which had undoubtedly an effect upon Dutch painting in general. Rembrandt himself is said to have been an Anabaptist. The name covers a variety of radical Protestant opinions which before Rembrandt's time had crystallized into a type of religious fanaticism which was little different from total anarchy. It is possible that his membership of the sect was nominal and in any case the Anabaptists in Holland were in his day normal law-abiding citizens.

It would of course be quite wrong to say that the Reformation was the work of Luther, Calvin or any other individual reformers. One has the impression of a horrible inevitability about the whole disastrous business. The Reformation was part of the Renaissance. Apart altogether from the corruption of Popes and clerics, the superstitious practices of the late mediaeval church, the dead hand of scholastic theology, all of which could have been reformed without schism, and have in fact vanished from the Catholic Church, it is difficult not to feel that the new consciousness of nationalism, resentment against the power of an Italian-controlled Church being used for political ends, the growth of individualism, and the rediscovery of the values of this world and human affairs, made the passing of the old order a certainty and reform without revolution highly unlikely.

Political considerations, such as the balance of power in Europe, the old rivalry between the Pope and the Emperor, and the ambitions of territorial rulers, as well as economic considerations, such as the rise of the middle class and the greed of the nobility, had as much to do with the Reformation

207

In yꝛm anſehen iſt er auffgehaßen vnd die wolcken haßen ynn
hinwegt genommen vō yten ougen. Diſer Jeſus der von euch
yn hiͤmmel auffgenommen iſt / wirde alſo wyder kommꝛ wie
yꝛ ynn geſehen haße zu hiͤmund ſharen. Act.1. Seyn reych hat
keyn ende Luce.1. Wer do mir dient der wird mir nach volgat
vn wu ich bin do wirt meyn diener ouch ſeyn Joḣ.12.

Es iſt egriffen die Beſtia vñ mit yr ð falſch pꝛophet der durch
ſie zeychen than hat do mit er voꝛfurdt hat/ die ſo ſeyn zeychē
von yme genommen /vnd ſein bilde angeßet ſeynt verſenckt yn
die teuſſe des ſewirs vnd ſchweffels vnd ſeynd getodt mit dem
ſchwerdt des da do reydt vſſin weyſſen pfande/ das auß ſeynē
mauel gehet. Apocal:19. Danne wirde offenbar werden der
ſchalckhafftige dem wirde der her Jeſus toeten mit dem atem
ſeyns mundes vnd wirde yn ſturgen durch die gloꝛi ſeyner zu
kunſft.2. ad Teſſa.2.

Much Reformation art was propaganda, bitter on both sides: Cranach's woodcut series contrasts the demands and fate of the Pope with those of Christ

as the recovery of Biblical Christianity. Undoubtedly there
was a vast amount of genuine religious conviction, and there
was no monopoly of it on the part of any section of Christendom. Motives were as mixed then as they have always been,
and neither Catholics nor Protestants can in the present day
look back with any great pride on their historical record at
that time.

It has sometimes been argued that national temperament,
geographical conditions, climate and so on determined whether
Catholicism or Protestantism should become the religious
ethos of any particular area; that, for example, the sunshine
of Italy is more conducive to the colourful imagery and emotional richness of Catholicism, while the sombre climate of
Northern Europe encourages the more austere practices of
Protestantism. That this is a fallacy is evidenced by the juxta-
position of Protestant Holland and Catholic Belgium, by
Catholic Ireland and Protestant Scotland, and the contrast
between the progressive industrialized North of Italy and the
lethargic agricultural South, both equally acknowledging the
authority of the Holy See. In any history of Christian art
we are bound to look for religious reasons to explain the
obvious dichotomy between the continuation in Catholic
208   countries after the Reformation of the same concentration

XII EL GRECO
The Agony in the Garden (detail), *c.* 1590

Indulgences remitting years in Purgatory were sold in churches or, as here, out of doors: the papal authorization hangs from a pole on the right

on the soaring themes of the mediaeval faith, and the Protestant emphasis on the more pedestrian realities of the world in which man must work out his salvation.

ERIC NEWTON. You suggest, then, that the Reformation was a logical extension of the Renaissance, with its emphasis on this world - the material world - and that its art therefore concentrated on the factual or narrative elements in the Bible. That would certainly seem to explain the restraint, the lack of exuberance and rhetoric in Protestant art. But would it explain the need for what I have called the 'counter-attack' developed by the Counter-Reformation? It seems to me that one would hardly expect a deepening interest in human affairs - the kind of humanity that one finds in Rembrandt's religious paintings - to stir the Catholic party to such an outburst of rhetorical protest. It is certainly true, as you suggest, that 'The Madonna, Saints and Visions' went 'out' and even that Heaven became, in the minds of Protestant artists, less important as a home than earth. But would that alone account for the intensity of the quarrel? Would it justify the notion that the Reformation involved heresy or that Roman Catholicism contained within itself a contradiction of the true spirit of Christianity? I may be exaggerating the gulf between the two factions in   209 putting the question in this form, but the difference in spirit between Dutch humanity and the Roman or Spanish reply to it seems to need explaining in terms of something rather more deep-seated than a simple opposition between factual statement and visionary rhetoric. Surely one senses a feeling of positive hostility rather than a mere difference of emphasis between the two parties?

WILLIAM NEIL. I think basically it was a difference of emphasis, or if you like, two approaches to Christian truth which are complementary and not mutually exclusive. Both are part of the wholeness of the Faith that the Reformation destroyed. If the Catholic Church at the Reformation had been true to the faith that built the cathedrals or to the faith of Michelangelo there would have been no need for Protestantism. The integrity of Christian art of this calibre shows up the religious witness of both sides of the Reformation conflict as partial and incomplete. In any reunion of Christendom the Protestant emphasis must find a place within the wholeness of a truly Catholic Church.

But of course it is perfectly true to say that the way things developed in Europe in the sixteenth and seventeenth centuries was far more than a matter of differing emphases. Catholics and Protestants were literally at each other's throats. Since the Catholics were in the stronger position their record is blacker, but when the Protestants had the opportunity there was little to choose between them. It is a dismal story of wars of religion, persecution, torture and judicial murder between two antagonists who were avowedly Christian. The only person who can derive any comfort from the record is the atheist.

Perhaps the root of the whole matter is to be found in the circumstances in which the mediaeval Church had developed. When Christianity was proclaimed the religion of the Roman Empire, acceptance of the teaching of the Church became the distinguishing mark between the pagan and the believer, not personal commitment to Christ. In the Middle Ages when the Church was surrounded by barbarians and threatened by Mohammedans, religious orthodoxy became even more important as the factor which held the Church together and kept heathendom at bay. Protestants, who were after all products of the same background, took over the same attitude. Uniformity was paramount whether the state be Catholic or Reformed. No one could be trusted who did not subscribe to the established Church. Religious toleration was eventually dearly won but at this stage it was neither practised nor even understood.

Wycliffe and Hus had therefore been branded as heretics as was Luther. When it became obvious to Rome that the movement he had started was a much more serious threat to the Church than anything that had happened before, an attempt was made at a reconciliation with the Lutherans. After this failed the only course that seemed open was persecution. The Inquisition which had been perfected in Spain was to be the instrument which would extirpate heresy in Catholic countries. But persecution has always meant sowing dragons' teeth. If this had been the only Catholic reply to Protestantism it would merely have strengthened opposition. It is to St Ignatius Loyola and the Jesuits that we must turn to find the origin of the new spirit that suffused the Catholic Church after the Reformation, that gave it vitality and vigour, won back much that it had lost, and provided the dynamic for the Catholic reply to Protestantism in religion, literature and art.

Germany, with its traditional hostility to Rome, was the natural setting for the Protestant revolt. By the same token Spain, with its intense loyalty to the Catholic Church, strengthened by its long struggle against the Mohammedan Moors, was the obvious springboard for the Counter-Reformation. But it needed a man with the religious fire of a Luther to spark it off. Such a man was Loyola and there was not a little in common between these two great Christians whom events forced into opposite camps. Unlike Luther, Loyola was a grandee and a soldier. As a result of a wound he was lamed for life and a distinguished military career was ruled out. Instead he had an experience of conversion similar to Luther's and emerged as a man afire with zeal to fight for God and the Holy Catholic Church.

211

The final session of the Council of Trent, 1564

Ignatius was a Spanish mystic, a visionary and an ecstatic, but he had also a soldier's training. He combined both in his compilation of the 'Spiritual Exercises', a manual of discipline in the devotional life to prepare men for the militant propagation of the Faith. He gathered around him a band of followers whom he had inspired with his own vision and received permission from the Pope to found the Society of Jesus. This was in 1540. Loyola's aim was nothing less than the regeneration of Christendom, by recalling lax Catholics to the Faith, by cleansing Europe of the heresy of Protestantism and thus saving countless souls from eternal damnation.

Shortly after the foundation of the Jesuit Order, the Church at the Council of Trent laid down the policy for the Counter-Reformation. Lutheran doctrines were condemned, a new Catechism embodying the Catholic position was drawn up, and the Index was instituted specifying the books that the laity were not allowed to read. From then until the end of the seventeenth century there is the pitiful history of the

212

St Ignatius Loyola (opposite, by Rubens founded the Society of Jesus revitalize Catholicism; his Jesu still serve as missionaries and teache

religious wars. Fanaticism on both sides was as common as genuine conviction. Political ambitions and exploitation of religion for political ends were more common than either. When toleration was at last adopted as the only possible solution, Europe was exhausted, the division of Christendom into Catholics and Protestants was accepted, and religious uniformity was farther away than ever.

The inspiration of the Catholic side came undoubtedly from the Jesuits. Loyola's concern was to secure a reformed priesthood and an educated laity. From both he demanded implicit and unquestioning obedience to the Church. The faith, enthusiasm and sacrificial spirit of the Jesuits transformed Catholicism. Devotion, tenacity and hope replaced corruption, defeatism and despondency. The Catholics, like the Protestants, naturally overstressed those features of Christian practice which their opponents rejected. At the Council of Trent the traditions of the Church had been declared to have the same authority as the Bible. But since the Protestants rejected everything that could not be justified from the Bible it was inevitable that Catholicism should lay more stress on those elements of doctrine and liturgy which had grown up over the centuries since Biblical times.

The glory of the Church with its pomp and pageantry, the centrality of the Mass, the cult of the saints and devotion to the Virgin were the Catholic reply to Protestant sermons and Bible reading. Adoration, contemplation and ecstasy, angels and archangels, the Divine Light of the Godhead match the sober evangelical family prayers of the Calvinist. Whether the Jesuits created Baroque architecture or whether they simply found it a congenial medium is an open question. There is no doubt that they made the most of it. They too, like the Reformers, were children of the Renaissance. But the Reformers, especially Calvin, looked on the world as the place where men practised their obedience to a sovereign God, busying themselves with the ordering, improving and development of society, harnessing the resources of Nature, concentrating on the practical side of human affairs.

The Jesuits, on the other hand, looked on the world not so much as something to be re-shaped and reorganized, or

214

Rococo exuberance: a detail of the ceiling of the Scuola dei Carmini in Venice, painted between 1740 and 1743 by Giambattista Tiepolo

on men and women as needing to be moulded into a prescribed pattern. They preferred to take the world as it was, and men and women as they were, and point upwards to God as the end and fulfilment of all human activity. If men liked pageantry and display, let them be used in the worship of God. If they wanted plays, let them have drama with a religious message. Let Christian artists delight the eye with the extravagance of their creations, bright colours, rich draperies, riotous ornamentation. All of this can lead men's thoughts to

God if the themes of the paintings and sculptures are con-
sonant with the teaching of the Church. A Rococo church
may look like a theatre or a ballroom, but why should it
not, if altar, crucifix and statuary make men aware of the
presence of God?

The object of the Counter-Reformation had been to recover Christendom as it had existed in the Middle Ages.
Obviously it was not successful and the Jesuits have been
often held responsible, in that they tried to make religion too
easy. Casuistry and abuse of the confessional tended to
make almost any kind of conduct permissible for a Christian
so long as he attended Mass and subscribed to orthodox
theology. But the Jesuits were dealing not with small groups
of committed Christians but with the intractible mass of
humanity who inherited their religion by race or birth. They
did their best, approaching their task from a different angle
from that of the Protestants, to make the nations of Europe
Christian nations.

In the end both sides failed, partly because of their divided
and partial witness, partly because of the deplorable spectacle
they had provided of Christian slaughtering Christian to
the glory of God, but mostly because the humanist revolt
of the Renaissance had unleashed forces with which neither
Rome nor Geneva could cope. Protestant austerity and Catholic
exuberance were both expressions of a common faith in God
which in the following century was violently attacked and
ultimately rejected by a large section of what had once been
Christendom. Man and not God had become the measure of
all things and in the light of that supreme heresy the conflict
between Catholic and Protestant was at once irrelevant.

ERIC NEWTON. That clearly sums up the situation. It is, as you
say, not a simple one. Even though the contrasts between the
opposing forces can be stated in deceptively simple terms, no
single statement can contain the whole truth. It is true that Luther
and St Ignatius Loyola were basically different in temperament
and that the Reformation and the Counter-Reformation, though
each was passionately sincere in its adherence to Christianity,
were equally passionately hostile to each other since conflicting

216

Baroque splendour: Rubens's *Adoration
of the Magi*, painted about 1624

sincerities can hardly fail to engender hostility. It is equally true that Northern and Southern Europe could be thought of as temperamentally incompatible since they are products of a different environment. It could be maintained that the basis of the struggle was between adherence to the Bible on the one hand and adherence to the Papal authority on the other. And this, again, could be simplified into a conflict between faith and works, or even between emotion and reason.

But none of these simplifications explains the central argument of this chapter, namely that in the seventeenth century there developed a cleavage between two kinds of Christian art which was an inevitable reflection in visual terms of a corresponding cleavage within the Christian world itself. Contrasting labels like 'Protestant' and 'Catholic', 'austerity' and 'exuberance', 'pedestrian realities' and 'soaring themes', are convenient for the purpose of dividing the visual arts of the seventeenth century into two stylistic groups. And as soon as one begins to think in terms of style the heat and anger of religious conflict disappear and the art historian takes a dispassionate view of an art-historical situation that is certainly interesting but hardly distressing. An 'Adoration of the Magi' by Rubens may have a glittering splendour, an 'Adoration of the Shepherds' by Rembrandt a quiet intimacy, but apart from the fact that Rubens was manifestly attracted by splendour and Rembrandt by intimacy and therefore Rubens found kings more congenial than shepherds, no art historian would be tempted to regard the two paintings as symptoms of a religious conflict or even to think of them as specimens of 'good' and 'bad' in religious art.

It may be true that, to some temperaments, splendour will seem less appropriate than intimacy as an approach to the interpretation of a Christian theme, but the contrast between the two is certainly not a contrast between religious loyalties. Rather is it a contrast between two attitudes to life itself. Rubens's exuberance can as easily find an outlet in an historical or mythological painting as in a Deposition. And Rembrandt's human understanding can express itself as powerfully in a picture of Dutch citizens as in a Nativity.

218

VI EIGHTEENTH CENTURY

Allegory and decoration

ERIC NEWTON

For the historian of Christian, or even of seriously considered religious art, the eighteenth is the least rewarding of all centuries. It is not that Christian art ceased to be produced. In Italy, above all, the patronage of the Church kept the Baroque tradition alive, but it remained alive merely in that sense that even the best artists could do little more than continue to turn out statues and altar-pieces based on the grandeur and enthusiasm of the seventeenth century, but emotionally diluted and often tainted with triviality that verged occasionally on the swaggering or frivolous.

Any representative anthology of seventeenth-century masterpieces would inevitably include a considerable proportion of Christian pictures, not because the Church (and particularly the leaders of the Counter-Reformation) demanded them, but for the much more compelling reason that they were expressions of a more serious and sincere range of emotion than anything that the following century had to offer. However theatrical the great Baroque altar-pieces and ceiling paintings might be, they were impressive because they had a meaning that could not be ignored and they translated into visual terms an ecstasy that was none the less genuine because it was prone to overstatement.

But what Christian art would be included by the anthologist of eighteenth-century art? With the possible exception of the Rococo art of South Germany - an intense but essentially theatrical art which is a development of the Baroque - eighteenth-century religious art might have competence, charm or dignity, but is neither profound in its religious feeling, nor representative of the essentially secular spirit of its age. What has already been said about the tortured fantasy of Mannerism in the mid-sixteenth century is equally true of the Rococo style of the mid-eighteenth. It is powerless to express the deeper levels of Christian faith or the human levels of the Christian story.

'Century' can be an insidiously tempting word. It leads the art historian as well as the social historian to indulge in generalizations which can never be more than half-truths. The phrase 'The Age of Reason' has crystallized as an explanation of what the century stood for. And certainly reason seemed to the intellectuals of the century an admirable weapon for solving the kind of problems that were beginning to disturb society. We tend to regard Voltaire as the type of thinker who temperamentally mistrusted intuition or mysticism, and who hopefully looked to the scientist to explain the destiny of man with the aid of a measuring rod and principles of logic.

But reason was not the only keynote to the pattern of the century. It could equally truly be called the Age of Taste, the Age of Elegance or the Age of Make-Believe. And according to whichever of those half-truths one chooses to adopt, the resultant anthology will alter its pattern. It was his fastidious taste that enabled Watteau to be so moving in his Fêtes Galantes and his almost heartrending comments on aristocracy at play: it was the perfection of elegance that made Rococo architecture so refined and, at the same time, so lacking in depth, and it was the essential frivolity underlying so much of the life of the Court that turned Boucher and Fragonard into masters of decorative comedy.

All these ingredients dominated the early and middle years of the century, and despite the immense variety of its achievement, gave it all a distinctive flavour, which included and accounted for the sensuousness of Boucher, the cynical and sometimes vitriolic satire of Hogarth, the tender sentiment in the genre painting of Chardin. The variety includes the musical and theatrical effectiveness of a church interior like that devised by the architects of the Abbey of Melk on the Danube, the artifice which so many portrait painters, at the mercy of their patrons' inherent vanities, expended on the depiction of their bewigged sitters, the devotion with which the view-painters of Italy, Canaletto, Guardi, Bellotto and Panini described the appearances of the cities they lived in, and finally the outburst of brilliant and stylish pageantry

221

The Benedictine abbey church of Melk, in what is now Czechoslovakia, designed in the early 18th c. by Jakob Prandtauer, a local architect

which Tiepolo invented to replace the visionary ceilings in Rome of a century earlier.

If we insist on including in the eighteenth-century section of our anthology of Christian art a group of examples that will prove that there were still artists who attempted to translate into visual terms the religious levels of feeling which it must be the main purpose of this book to stress, we must search among the enormous mass of paintings - mostly frescoes - produced by Tiepolo during his immensely active life.

He was born in 1696, and, developing precociously, began to paint in the middle of the second decade of the century and his active career continued for over fifty years. He died in 1770. He was immensely popular, and since he was in demand by courtly patrons all over Europe from Sweden to

Spain, his works are to be found not only in and around his native Venice but in Würzburg and in Madrid.

It was natural that whereas in Italy his patrons tended to be men of the Church and his themes specifically Christian, in Würzburg, in the immense spread of the ceiling of the Residenz, and at Madrid, in the Throne Room of the Royal Palace, the theme was necessarily secular and his nearest approach to religious feeling was by way of allegorical treatment of the Christian virtues.

What distinguishes Tiepolo from his contemporaries is the fact that he could, with no apparent effort, cover immense areas and handle large groups of figures with a skill in composition that almost amounts to genius. The great room in

Giambattista Tiepolo. *The Last Supper*, c. 1745

the Palazzo Labia in Venice is a masterpiece of space filling, airy but never empty. The ceilings over the staircase and the Kaisersaal in the Würzburg Residenz are even larger, yet they are organized with an easy swagger as though no pictorial task were beyond his powers. But what strikes one as one looks at each of his major works is that very swagger which makes him the ideal painter for a palace and a rather less than satisfactory one for a church. At Madrid he is joyfully exuberant; in his altar-pieces - the Adoration of the Magi (in Munich), The Agony in the Garden (Hamburg), The Last Supper (Paris) or the Assumption (Udine) - one can almost guess that he has made valiant efforts to suppress the exuberance and the pageantry that came naturally to him, but his efforts have been in vain; they have a stylish splendour but behind it a Rococo triviality that robs them of much of their religious meaning.

Tiepolo was born too late to give his talents to an intensely religious art. The century in which he lived and the kind of demands it made on him could not be resisted. The Spanish Royal Family and the Princely Court of Würzburg demanded the extreme of swaggering elegance. Tiepolo provided them with it. To tone that swagger down into dignified pageantry and to raise that elegance to the level of grandeur was beyond his powers and ran counter to his inclinations.

In Spain the one great painter of the century who attempted to satisfy his ecclesiastical patrons was Goya, whose frescoes in the Church of Sant'Antonio de la Florida were an equally unsuccessful attempt to provide what the Catholic Church required.

Goya's failure can be attributed to a cause that was the exact opposite of Tiepolo's. Goya belonged to the end of the century. Romanticism was beginning to assert itself in 1798 when Goya was at work in the Church of Sant'Antonio, but what made Goya incapable of tackling Christian themes with conviction was his temperamental realism. The man who was so passionately obsessed with the cruelties and ugliness of the life around him was forced to put all his creative power into painting what he and his contemporaries saw and suffered, in particular the executions of 3 May, or into

XIII REMBRANDT
The Holy Family (detail), 1640

The stylish elegance of Tiepolo's *Adoration of the Magi,* painted *c.* 1745,
contrasts with the directness of Goya's *The Taking of Christ* (1798), where
the contorted faces of the onlookers are those of his contemporaries

making drawings and etchings of the horrors of war. Where
Tiepolo had not been serious enough, Goya was too easily
moved by the immediacy of his own experience. Not the
sufferings or even the triumphs of Jesus concerned him, but
those of his own friends and countrymen.

Yet Goya's almost exact contemporary, William Blake, who was born ten years later than Goya and died a year earlier, managed to prove that, given the temperament of a visionary and a mystic, an artist - it happens rarely, and perhaps Blake was one of the most spectacular examples that ever lived of a man born out of his period - can defy the spirit of the age in which he lived. Whatever label we may choose to attach to the eighteenth century, whether we think of it as The Age of Reason, of logic, of triviality or frivolity, or of Rococo decoration, none of those labels can be applied to Blake. So independent was he of all the pressures both of his contemporary world and of the world of the immediate past that one even wonders whether he could be reasonably described as Christian. And yet no artist who ever lived could more fully qualify as religious in thought, in emotion or in the kind of awestruck visual imagination that spurred him on throughout his life.

It would be absurd to exclude Blake's drawings, watercolours and engravings from this book on the grounds that because he was a visionary philosopher and because his philosophy and his visions were essentially products of his own inner life and experience, he was not a genuine Christian. Orthodox he certainly was not, and one can hardly imagine how the Inquisition, the Vatican or even the conventional theologian would have reacted to his prophetic books or to such aspects of his art as could be described as Christian - and there was a great deal of it. But I feel convinced that if Christianity derives its central meaning from a way of living, a habitual frame of mind that can be truly described as visionary, and not from the kind of faith that can be stated in terms of dogma, or expressed in terms of ritual, then Blake has as much claim to inclusion in a history of Christian art as any artist since the beginning of the fifteenth century.

For the art historian, in so far as he is concerned with an analysis of the roots of style, Blake offers a simple problem. His appearance was unheralded, his detachment from the spirit of his century complete, his scorn of the worldliness and materialism of his contemporaries vitriolic, his refusal to use the world of visible phenomena as his starting point

Blake. *The Ancient of Days* (Manchester version), printed for *Europe* before 1795

for a work of art unshakeable. It followed that his style - stylistic formulae would be a more precise phrase - was almost entirely based on such examples of the work of most other artists that he did not reject as worthless. If one searches in his work for symptoms of derivation one finds that the formula was based on what he knew of Michelangelo, Raphael and the examples of Gothic that he had been set to copy as

227

Blake. *God creating Adam*, 1795; in Blake's view man is not raised to life, but bound to the finite by an evil Creator, the antithesis of Christ

a young apprentice to an engraver. These he absorbed so completely that, as has often been noted, they became the straw from which all his bricks were made. His 'style', once we know that he was an expert engraver and an accomplished draughtsman, is easy to explain. Inevitably it reflected the neo-classicism of his age - the smooth, empty curvature of Flaxman in particular.

But the uses to which he put that style cannot be explained in the language of the art historian. Other artists have had their moments of inspiration based on a natural habit of visionary insight, but for Blake those moments filled the whole of his life, supplying him, as a writer, with unforgettable phrases and as an artist with equally unpredictable images.

Blake. '*Then the Lord answered Job out of the Whirlwind*', detail of an engraved page from *The Book of Job*, 1820-26

Blake's world was based on the heavens as firmly as Hogarth's was based on the streets and drawing rooms of London. Consequently his engravings and drawings are as timeless as Hogarth's are dateable, and being timeless, they are symbolic. They are, of course, in common with all deeply religious works of art, illustrations, but illustrations that are almost independent of the text they illustrate in creating their own symbolic world. 'The Ancient of Days', in which the Almighty leans over the abyss, separating light from darkness with a pair of supernatural compasses, sums up the early chapters of the Book of Genesis; the engravings that accompany the Book of Job are as awe-inspiring as the breathtaking prose itself. The more urgently Blake felt the demands made on him, the more his visionary imagination rose to meet them. The Morning Stars sing together, God speaks to Job out of the whirlwind, Satan strikes Job with boils, God reveals Behemoth and Leviathan to Job as confidently as Hogarth tells his audience about Beer Street and Gin Lane.

Milton, Shakespeare and Dante as well as the Bible provide Blake with the kind of images that spur him on to the creation

229

of imagery that no other artist would have attempted, and most of the images are compressed into sheets of paper of the size that could slip easily into a typewriter. The Creation of Adam may be less sublime, in Burke's sense of the word, than Michelangelo's, but it surpasses it as a translation into visual terms of the act of divine creation. Milton's *Paradise Lost* inspired Blake to a drawing of the Temptation of Eve more rhythmically evocative than Milton's own verse. His final series of drawings linked with Dante's *Divine Comedy* are magical equivalents of a poet's dream.

Even the illustrations to Blake's own poetical and prophetic books have the same timeless splendour, and although the text they illuminate is that of a man who evolved his own personal mythology and his own religious faith, the art that the books give rise to is so completely religious in spirit and so impregnated with what Blake had responded to in the Old Testament that one must either accept Blake as one of the profoundest of all Christian artists in his effortless acceptance of the supernatural, or else reject him as a visionary too personal to identify himself with tradition. The reader of this book must decide for himself whether to accept or reject. For my own part I find Blake so utterly compelling whenever he stands, burin in hand, by the side of the Almighty in the half-created firmament or accompanies Adam and Eve in their journey from the Creation to the Fall or follows Dante and Virgil through the labyrinth of the Inferno or Dante and Beatrice through the visionary bliss of the Paradiso, that I accept him. At the age of seven he had seen a tree full of angels, 'their bright wings bespangling the boughs like stars'. His parents punished him for this precocious venture into what they would have called fantasy but which he was convinced was fact.

He died in 1827. The year - even the century - of his death is unimportant. He could have lived in the thirteenth century and felt at home, or in the sixteenth and rebelled against it. In the eighteenth he was hardly noticed. The reader may be interested to remember that 1827 was the year in which Holman Hunt was born.

The age of reason

WILLIAM NEIL

Sir Leslie Stephen in his *History of English Thought in the Eighteenth Century* makes this comment: 'The Protestant writers against Rome were forging the weapons which were soon to be used against themselves'. He meant by this that once the right of private judgment had been established in matters of religion, the Bible, which the Reformers had exalted to the position of supreme authority formerly occupied by the Pope, was bound to be exposed to the same spirit of critical appraisal as the leaders of the Protestant revolt had applied to the Catholic Church. But the Reformers were, like everyone else in their day, children of the Renaissance, and it is rather to this complex and many-sided urge towards greater intellectual freedom that we must attribute the climate of opinion which characterized the eighteenth century.

The Renaissance had brought liberation, but as so often happens, the new sense of freedom went to men's heads. They had cast off the shackles of an outworn dogmatism which restricted rational enquiry in science, philosophy and religion, and this was clearly desirable and right. But when human reason came to be deified, when religious authority of any kind was rejected, when the lessons of history and the legacy of tradition were scoffed at, when 'enthusiasm' was frowned on and moderation became the chief virtue, the prospects for a vital Christian faith which would inspire poets and painters were indeed bleak. The blight was worst at first in Protestant countries, but Catholic Europe fared little better and in the end suffered most. The eighteenth century with its arid controversy between Orthodoxy and Deism, even when countered by the simple evangelical fervour of German Pietism and English Methodism, and with the looming cloud of secularism which characterized the French Revolution, was wholly unpropitious as a breeding ground for masterpieces of Christian art.

231

In Protestant Europe the ostensible issue was the credibility of the Bible but the real question was about the existence of God. The power of the Establishment was strong enough at first to disguise the radical nature of the attack but by the end of the century it had become clear that what was at stake was the validity of any kind of religious interpretation of the universe. Reason began by questioning supernatural revelation and ended by asking if there was in fact anything supernatural to reveal.

It was inevitable that the Bible should have become the storm-centre of the controversy. In pre-Reformation Europe the Bible had found its proper place within the life of the Church as the title-deeds of the Faith, the record of its origins and the key to its subsequent development. If it had been a loss that it was not readily accessible to the laity, it had been a gain that every Tom, Dick or Harry did not consider himself fully equipped to become an authoritative interpreter and expositor. The leading Reformers, such as Luther and Calvin, had on the whole an enlightened view of the fallibility of the Biblical writers and while they insisted that the Bible and not the Pope must be regarded as the supreme arbiter in matters of religion, they did not fall into the trap which their mediocre successors were unable to avoid. The seventeenth-century divines invested the Bible with an authority at least as oppressive and inescapable as the Catholic Church had ever claimed. In their hands it became the infallible *vade mecum* to all knowledge of God, man and the universe.

Such a ridiculous and untenable claim was bound to be challenged. In the new spirit of free enquiry which the Renaissance had encouraged, thinking men refused to shut their eyes to the obvious gaps and inconsistencies in the Biblical documents, to the dubious behaviour of Hebrew kings, prophets and patriarchs, and to the improbability of many of the miraculous incidents recorded in the Old and New Testaments. If all this was claimed to reveal the truth about God both reason and common sense were bound to reject it. The battle had already begun in seventeenth-century Europe when philosophers like Bacon, Descartes, Hobbes and Spinoza had in one way or another drawn attention to the conflict between what orthodoxy claimed and what reasonable men might be expected to believe.

But it was England that became the storm-centre of controversy between Christianity and Deism in the first half of the eighteenth century. The opponents were not so far removed from each other as at first sight appeared. The Deists were prepared to recognize the existence of a Supreme Being, or as Addison called Him, a 'great Original', while they called in question the eccentric behaviour of the Jehovah of the Old Testament; whereas Orthodoxy claimed that the Scriptures must be accepted in their entirety as the Word of God - in the famous words of Chillingworth, 'The Bible, I say, the Bible only, is the religion of Protestants'. But both sides rejected the claims of Rome, despised the Middle Ages as barbaric and superstitious, and recognized reason as the basic criterion in matters of religion. What was in dispute was whether in addition to the natural religion which was common to all thinking men, there was also a supernatural revelation of divine truth revealed in the Scriptures.

Thus John Locke, the philosopher, as an orthodox Anglican, was at pains in his book, significantly entitled *The Reasonableness of Christianity*, to show that reason was not opposed to revelation and that Christianity could be 'proved' to be 'true'. On the other hand John Toland on the Deist side, arguing from the same premise, proceeded to excise from the New Testament anything which seemed to him absurd or incomprehensible. He chose as the title of his book *Christianity Not Mysterious*, an idea which would have made any pre-Reformation painter turn in his grave. The battle raged in books, treatises and pamphlets over the credibility of Old Testament stories and New Testament miracles, including the Resurrection of Jesus, with Orthodoxy tending more and more to take refuge in the argument that much in the Bible is meant to be treated as allegorical.

The Deist controversy in England died down about the middle of the century. This was partly because the Church had on its side men of the calibre of Berkeley, Butler, Addison, Pope and Swift, indeed in Stephen's words, 'all that was intellectually venerable in England', who were prepared to go

233

so far with the Deists in their desire for a 'reasonable' faith, while showing by superior arguments that in such a faith the Biblical revelation had a proper place. The Deists were men of limited ability and the creed they advocated was a barren and colourless substitute even for Protestant orthodoxy. But they had done enough to shake the foundation of Reformation theology, which was the indisputable authority of the Scriptures. They had raised doubts and questions in men's minds which were reinforced by heavier artillery in the second half of the century.

In the next phase of the conflict between traditional Christianity and the spirit of the times the intellectual giants were not on the side of the angels. Orthodoxy could not muster guns effective enough to silence the fire of a Hume, a Gibbon or a Voltaire. It was now no longer a matter of relatively polite exchanges or peripheral issues on which both sides agreed to differ, but a frontal attack on the validity of any belief in a personal God. In place of such superstition David Hume saw 'blind nature, impregnated by a great vivifying principle, and pouring forth from her lap, without discernment or parental care, her maimed and abortive children'. He flayed both Christians and Deists by arguing that the world, far from exhibiting evidence of design or a Designer, suggests more obviously the crude attempt 'of some infant Deity who afterwards abandoned it, ashamed of his lame performance'.

Edward Gibbon in *The Decline and Fall of the Roman Empire* with tongue in cheek paid lip-service to orthodoxy, but with such exquisite irony that no one could mistake his radical scepticism as he traced the supposedly supernatural origin of the Christian Church. A more effective weapon than irony as far as popular opinion was concerned was the blunt raillery of Tom Paine, whose *Age of Reason* began to appear just before the end of the century.

'Whence', he asked, 'could arise the solitary and strange conceit that the Almighty, who had millions of worlds equally dependent on his perfections, should quit the universe and come to die in our world because they say one man and one woman had eaten an apple?' Of the Old Testament he says:

'When we read the obscure stories, the cruel and barbarous executions, the unrelenting vindictiveness with which more than half the Bible is filled, it would be more consistent that we called it the work of a demon than the word of God'. Turning to the New Testament, he claims that nowhere has he ever found 'so many and such glaring absurdities, contradictions and falsehoods'.

Moderate churchmen doubtless took comfort from such counterblasts as that of William Paley, who likened the universe to a watch constructed by a divine Watchmaker, or of Bishop Watson, who was moved to write *An Apology for the Bible,* but neither of these attempts to restate the faith in contemporary terms was likely to inspire men to build cathedrals. Meantime the influence of English rationalism had spread across the Channel into Catholic France, and in the hands of Voltaire Deism became a half-way house to atheism.

To Diderot man's conduct was dictated by nature, completely impersonal and subject only to its own laws - 'attraction and repulsion, the only truth'

Claiming to believe in a divine Architect of the universe Voltaire found such a concept to be irreconcilable with Christian belief and practice. He described Christianity as an 'absurd and sanguinary creed, supported by executions and surrounded by fiery faggots'. The Church was an infamous compound of superstition and intolerance which must be crushed. Voltaire's influence was not confined to his own country. Under the patronage of Frederick the Great, French writers, preeminently Voltaire himself, took to Germany the Gospel of Enlightenment and popularized further the Cult of Reason. But it was in France itself that the atheistic materialism of Voltaire's successors, Holbach, Diderot and the Encyclopaedists, reached its inevitable outcome in the irrational savagery of the French Revolution.

Until this triumph of unreason made nonsense of the claim that man could build the New Jerusalem on the ashes of an effete and discredited Faith, the temper of the eighteenth-century debate on religion had been on the whole mild and unimpassioned. Despite the fact that the authority of Church and Scripture were in dispute and the basic truth of the Christian revelation was being questioned, it seems never to have been to the contestants a matter of urgency, an issue of life or death. Although abuse was hurled by rationalism at Ortho-

235

doxy and vice versa, and legal action was taken against the more violent opponents of Christianity, the battle was on the whole fought in an urbane and civilized fashion befitting an age which prided itself on its elegance and good taste.

Protestant orthodoxy, despite its official allegiance to the faith once delivered to the saints and its defence of revealed religion, was prepared to concede that for sophisticated Europeans there was much that was unpalatable in traditional Christianity which must be allegorized, qualified or otherwise explained away. There was a deal of truth in Gibbon's sardonic comment that the upholders of the articles of faith 'subscribed with a sigh or a smile'. The kind of God who was worshipped in many churches and proclaimed from many pulpits was not so far removed from the abstract Architect of the Deists. In the chilly atmosphere of moral discourses which deprecated enthusiasm and distrusted the emotions, the *mysterium tremendum* which is of the essence of historical Christianity found no lodging.

The frontal attack on the Faith by Hume and Gibbon and above all the violence of the French Revolution put an end to polite exchanges. Orthodoxy took fright at the prospect of militant atheism being enthroned all over Europe. The Church of England might share with the Deists an abhorrence of popish superstition but it could not view with anything but dismay the spectacle of a Christian monarchy being supplanted by secularism and anarchy. Reaction set in and Church and State combined to safeguard the fabric of Christian civilization. On the part of the Church this meant an attempt to recover the badly shaken authority of creeds and scriptures by a more intransigent attitude to rational criticism and a more uncompromising assertion of the supremacy of revealed religion.

Massive support in this direction came from the Evangelical Revival. More than a century before in France, Blaise Pascal had maintained that 'the heart has its reasons which reason does not know' and his countryman Jean-Jacques Rousseau, despite his political extremism, was now preaching a religion of the heart. But while Voltaire was doing his utmost to discredit Christianity on the Continent, John and Charles Wesley and George Whitefield in England were clothing Rousseau's vague

The Wesleys and Whitefield led the Evangelical Revival, ending in the establishment of Methodism outside the Church of England. Here John Wesley is characteristically preaching in the open air

'religion of the heart' in the full dress of a gospel of salvation, and revitalizing the barren orthodoxy and general indifference which distinguished the established Church of their day.

To provide an antidote to the rising tide of philosophical scepticism, or to avert the outbreak of an English Revolution was far from their minds, although in effect they accomplished

237

both. What moved these loyal Anglicans was a deep concern for the souls of men and a profound anxiety over the empty parish churches and the cold morality that was preached in them. A Church which had lost its hold on the people had done so, they believed, because it had failed to proclaim the full-blooded Gospel message where men were confronted with heaven and hell, grace and damnation as the paramount issues of life, beside which dilettante discussions on the credibility of this or that Biblical incident or this or that article of faith were wholly irrelevant. The Scriptures were God's Word to man, and in face of the mighty evidences of the power of the Spirit, as throughout the length and breadth of England and Scotland the Revival brought men and women to their knees in penitence and new conviction, academic disputes as to what might constitute a 'reasonable' faith seemed to Wesley a monstrous underrating of the urgency of the situation.

Whitefield was said to have been able to pronounce the word 'Mesopotamia' with such effect as to bring tears to the eyes. Certainly John Wesley's herculean preaching tours drew thousands to hear him wherever he went, and the hymns of his brother Charles brought powerful aid to the oratory of the indefatigable evangelists. They were attacked by the rabble, resented by the settled clergy, and eventually, through a tragic conflict of legalism on the one side and obstinacy on the other, the Methodist movement which they had founded was declared to be no part of the Establishment and the Church of England suffered a grievous loss from which it has not yet recovered. Many who shared Wesley's zeal for the saving of souls and were as concerned as the Methodists that the religious life of England should be rescued from the plight into which it had fallen in the Age of Reason, nevertheless shrank from schism and formed the evangelical party within the Church of England.

Clearly, however, the Evangelical Revival was no more likely to produce a rebirth of Christian art than the arid rationalism which had preceded it. Painting and sculpture had no place in the thoughts of men who saw religion in terms of individual soul-saving by the preaching of the Word in the power of the Spirit. Emotion was channeled into fervent,

By the late 18th c. the architectural spirit exemplified by Wren's St Mary-le-Bow had died out, and most churches were dull or imitative

congregational praise - and the hymns of Wesley, Newton, Cowper and Toplady are no mean legacy.

It must be said, however, that the incredible ugliness of the Nonconformist chapels which were springing up at this time had little to do with the poverty of the worshippers. The genius of Christopher Wren and the opportunity for building new churches after the Great Fire of London in

1666 had studded the city with masterpieces of native Protestant art, and this tradition had lasted into the early years of the eighteenth century. At that time too, within the limitations imposed by post-Reformation worship, fine craftsmanship such as that of Grinling Gibbons found expression in the embellishment of church furnishings.

But the artistic achievements of the Age of Reason, which were considerable, were almost wholly secular. With the notable exception of church music, where Bach defied all the laws of logic by producing the supreme contribution of Protestantism in this field while the Deist controversy was at its height, the arts reflected the spirit of the age. Whether it was for the gay decoration of the salon and the boudoir in the Catholic France of Louis XV or for the construction of more sober but equally elegant stately homes and their adornment with the portraits of their owners in the Protestant England of the Hanoverians, architects, sculptors and painters employed their skills for purposes which were in harmony with a view of life in which religion provided little more than a framework for the exaltation of man in all his glory.

If we may take painters like Boucher and Fragonard as typifying the French preoccupation with the boudoir and the drawing-room, and Reynolds and Gainsborough as the founding-fathers of the fashionable English school of society portraiture, what are we to say of that eccentric and mysterious genius William Blake, who happens to fall within the period but has nothing in common with it or with anyone in it? He is the only English painter of the time who is passionately concerned with religious themes, yet he is professedly neither Catholic nor Protestant, perhaps not even 'Christian' in the technical sense at all. Nevertheless this strange and obscure mystic and visionary, who in a way created his own faith which he expressed in poems and paintings, communicates in them an intensity of religious insight and understanding which constitutes a major contribution to Christian art.

He claimed that at the age of four he 'saw God put his forehead to the window' and, as Eric Newton has already noted, that as a child of seven he saw a tree full of angels at Peckham Rye. He claimed to be on speaking terms with

240

Blake's etching of *Albion and the Crucified Christ*, done between 180
and 1818, illustrates the final dialogue in his long poem, *Jerusalem*

Moses, Homer and Virgil, and stated that his special technique of engraving had been revealed to him by his dead brother in a dream. His writing is often obscure and incoherent and sometimes unintelligible, and opinion in his day and since has been divided as to whether he was mentally unbalanced or whether what he saw and felt was beyond the power of words to express.

There is, however, no incoherence in his painting. The Bible was one of his favourite quarries for themes and his magnificent 'Illustrations of the Book of Job' show him at the summit of his creative power. Obviously a deeply religious man, he did not subscribe to conventional Christianity. His attempt to define his faith in 'The Everlasting Gospel' was never finished and it seems as if he somehow came to identify Christ with Art. Perhaps some of his own words take us nearest to an understanding of what that meant: 'I assert for myself that I do not behold the outward creation, and that to me it is hindrance and not action. "What!" it will be questioned, "when the sun rises, do you not see a disk of fire, somewhat like a guinea?" "O no no! I see an innumerable company of the heavenly host, crying Holy, Holy, Holy, is the Lord God Almighty." '

He communicates his own awe and exultation in face of divine transcendence, and moves us to a like humility and joy, yet it is perhaps on the darker side of religious experience that his work is most telling. It is not only his own life of hardship and bitter disappointment but his deeply sensitive spirit that speaks to us supremely in his engravings of Job and Ezekiel, of 'the burthen of the mystery, the heavy and the weary weight of this unintelligible world'. Unlike the gay courtiers of Louis XV or the apostles of Hanoverian urbanity, he grasped the profound religious truth that the knowledge of God is more likely to be won through tragedy and suffering than through laughter and logic. For Blake a religion worth having comes only when we recognize that life is

    'Heated hot with burning fears
    And dipt in baths of hissing tears
    And battered with the shocks of doom.'

VII

VII NINETEENTH CENTURY

The recovery of sincerity

ERIC NEWTON

Any attempt to define the temperament of the nineetenth century is bound to fail. It was too complex to be definable. It produced in its first half great artists: Ingres and Delacroix and Courbet in France, Turner and Constable in England; great poets: Wordsworth, Keats and Shelley, Browning and Tennyson, Victor Hugo; great scientists who, like Darwin, enlarged the frontiers of thought; great novelists, Tolstoi and Dickens, who made it clear that no previous century had been so obsessed by the study of human character, human motives, even human eccentricities. Yet, unlike the previous century whose arts seemed to be rooted in its own soil, the great men of the nineteenth century all give the impression of being rebels, men of startling independence who derived their vigour and their courage from the past and helped to lay the foundations for the future. One could even say that the century's great moments were isolated and magnificent acts of rebellion against itself, and that, to a lesser extent, its great men were rebellious against each other. Yet there was one mood that it developed in its first half, the mood of 'Romanticism'. It is true that Romanticism was an attitude of mind that can be traced back to the end of the eighteenth century. In the realm of literature German critics were aware, soon after the year 1774, that Goethe had tapped a new vein of inspiration, in *The Sorrows of Young Werther*, which somehow contradicted the neo-classic worship of serenity and beauty that had dominated the first half of the century. The notion was to develop more slowly with the visual arts than in literature, yet when, at last, the word 'Romanticism' became applicable to the arts of painting and sculpture, it seemed as though the nineteenth century had discovered its own means of expression. The old ideas of 'Beauty' as a set of simple, law-abiding formulae began to crumble. A heightened inten-

244

sity of emotion and a less disciplined system of form took their place. The Romantic Era was in full swing by 1825.

My reason for introducing this note on the Romantic Era of the early and mid-nineteenth century into a history of Christian art is that, contrary to expectation, nineteenth-century Romanticism itself proved a hindrance to the expression of religious emotion.

There seem to be two reasons for this, the first of which is that the Romantic Era drew much of its strength from a growing realization of the importance to humanity of man's environment and hence an increasing emphasis on landscape. In the later decades of the eighteenth century this realization had already begun with the discovery of 'the picturesque' and an obsession with dramatic effects of weather, ruined castles, precipices, and mountain torrents. One might have expected Romanticism to lead to a renewed feeling for the mystical or the visionary as an approach to the painting of religious experience as it had done with Blake; instead, at least in the first half of the century in England, it produced a frame of mind that could almost be described as pantheism - a worship not of God but of nature in all her aspects. What Wordsworth wrote in this exalted mood Turner painted. The devotion to nature of Turner's contemporary, Constable, had perhaps less exaltation in it but more genuine love of the meadows, the trees and the skies in his native country of East Anglia; but in the case of both these great painters, what happened was almost a turning away from Christianity as a paintable theme and a concentration on the marvels of nature ('there is room for a *natural* artist', said Constable) which in the end directed the attention of the nineteenth century towards the solution of the problems of translating nature into paint. That solution was finally achieved by the Barbizon School, and by the experiments of the Impressionists towards the end of the century. It needs no deep understanding of the visual arts to guess that Corot and Millet, Monet and Pissarro, Manet and Degas had neither the desire nor the temperament to tackle Christian themes.

The second effect of the Romantic Era as a positive hindrance to the religious element in the visual arts was the

cultivation of sentiment - sentimentality might be a more precise word - for its own sake. In England particularly, painting flourished that was based on scenes from everyday life,
but almost invariably backed by a kind of moralizing that
included pathos as one of its strongest weapons. Paintings
entitled 'The Proposal', 'The Love Letter', 'The Dissolute
Undergraduate', might be conceived with the highest motives,
but they could never have a more than superficial Christian
significance. They were little more than pictorial responses
to a set of social conventions which we, with a hardly disguised
sneer, agree to call 'Victorian'.

In England this wave of sentimental triviality might have
continued unchallenged and uninterrupted had it not been for
one painter, G. F. Watts, whose grasp of the grand manner
of the Venetian sixteenth century combined with an immense
seriousness of purpose enabled him to paint a few masterpieces on Biblical themes that rely neither on romantic pathos
nor on the purely literary background of texts they illustrate.
For Watts could invent gestures that explained their own
dramatic meanings. In 'Eve Tempted' in the Tate Gallery,
London, the naked body of Eve has a Venetian splendour
that is almost worthy of Titian, but it is memorable not because it is voluptuous but because of the urgent forward movement with which she buries her head in the mass of foliage
to reach the apple while the serpent writhes behind her to
whisper words of temptation into her ear. Even more memorable is 'For He Had Great Possessions' - a design of extraordinary simplicity. The back view, the heavy folds of drapery,
the bowed head, the concealed features of the man who
'went away sorrowfully' raise the commonplaces of Victorian
sentiment to the level of tragedy. Watts rarely rose to this
pitch of insight but when he did his powers of interpretation
cannot be ignored, and his use of Venetian opulence in no
way detracted from the poignancy of his best paintings.

But the English movement which proved, without recourse
to opulence or the grand manner but with an utterly single-
minded sincerity, that it could translate the fundamentals
of Christianity into painting by sheer intensity of feeling, was
that which originated in a group of young men who in 1848

246

G. F. Watts. '*For He Had Great Possessions*', 1894 (*left*), and *Eve Tempted*, c. 1892-96

decided to call themselves the Pre-Raphaelite Brotherhood. What enabled the members of the Brotherhood to formulate a creed that, in the best of their works, emerged as a kind of passionate, dedicated innocence, was their determination to organize a kind of artistic rebellion based on their own sincerity and a positive hatred (implied in the name they chose for themselves) of the Raphaelesque formula which in their eyes preferred grace and beauty to honesty and purposeful meaning. Victorian sentiment with all its shallowness could be

247

traced (so they thought) back as far as Raphael. They had to start again from the beginning, rather, since no one can start in a vacuum from some remote point in history, before Raphael had taken the fatal step of 'manufacturing' beauty, when art was honest and meaningful and unaffected by formulae or made trivial by convention. That point was difficult to find. They groped for it wherever they could discover the 'primitive'. It might be among the archaisms of the Gothic world or the tight diagrammatic style of Fra Angelico or Gozzoli or van Eyck. But it had to be stiffened by a close observation of fact, and it had to be made rich and passionate by a devotion to great poetry. Dante could supply that; so could Mallory and Keats and Tennyson and the story of the Annunciation and the legend of the Holy Grail.

Nothing could be more muddled, more 'Romantic' in the serious sense of the word, more full of contradictory enthusiasms and disgusts, than the Pre-Raphaelite creed. Yet nothing could be more dedicated to honesty of purpose or intensity of feeling. This is not the place to examine in detail the origins or the eventual sad decline and fall of the movement, but it certainly is the place to point out that the passion engendered by their beliefs did produce, whenever they chose Christianity as their theme, a few pictures of extraordinary, innocent power. Among them, and ranking high in any collection of truly Christian works of art, are Rossetti's 'Annunciation', Millais' 'Christ in the House of His Parents', Madox Brown's 'Christ Washing Peter's Feet'. Each of them has the hard, bright honesty of 'This is how it happened' and yet, behind the eye-witness is the pent-up effort to add 'And behind the happening was a meaning'.

I have already made much the same kind of comment on Rembrandt's religious paintings and drawings, and yet no two painters could be separated by a wider gulf than Rossetti and Rembrandt. Christina, Rossetti's sister, sits crumpled on The White Bed, her eyes full of childlike wonderment: one of Rossetti's friends acts the part of The Angel in the cramped little room. Yet the idea of a sister and a friend or of a part to be acted never occurs to us. We witness an unobtrusive miracle. Rossetti's strange gift at that moment in his life was

Rossetti.
The Annunciation,
1850

not to stage a miracle in a bedroom but to paint a simple bedroom so vividly that it was transformed into a miracle.

The same eye-witness point of view is the basis of Millais' 'Christ in the House of his Parents'. The carpenter's bench is the centre of activity. Not only are the tools and the wood shavings described in meticulous detail as they would have been in a Dutch genre painting, but each member of the family, including the child John, is concentrated on what he is doing. Behind the descriptive genre vision is a well invented moment of symbolism. The child Jesus has wounded the palm of his hand with a nail: Joseph pauses to inspect the damage, Mary kneels to get a closer view, young St John hurries in with a basin of water, St Anne leans over with grandmotherly concern. Jesus makes no fuss about the incident but seems to be the only member of the group who is aware of its meaning. All these careful fusions of symbolism and close observation, together with engaging hints of Gothic angularity and stiffness, remove the picture from the realm of prosaic genre art and link it up with the deeper humanity of Giotto.

Pre-Raphaelitism at this pitch of intensity lasted only a few years. Of the three pictures mentioned, two were painted in 1849, the third in 1851. Had the group belonged to an age when it was not necessary to be rebellious in order to be sincere, it would have slowly gathered force and would never have lacked patrons. As it was, it attempted to run counter to the mainstream of the age and the opposition of the age was too strong for it.

Already, in Germany, at the end of the first decade of the nineteenth century, a group of young artists whose aims, as described by themselves and under pressure from their supporters - especially Schlegel who had already detected the growing cult of Romanticism in literature - sound remarkably similar to those of the Pre-Raphaelites in England, had moved to Rome where they established themselves in a monastery and called themselves the 'Nazarenes'. Peter von Cornelius can be taken as typical of them. Yet the difference between what they professed as a creed and what they produced as artists is so lamentable that their connection with Pre-Raphaelitism is no more than superficial. To Rossetti and Millais

Peter von Cornelius. *The Wise and Foolish Virgins*, 1813

the painting of religious themes had been the result of intense
spiritual excitement. To the Nazarenes it was moral duty
and their professed admiration of the Middle Ages expressed
itself in a style based on the sweetness of the early Raphael
sweetened still further by the Romanticism of early nineteenth-
century sentiment. Meekness and piety were all they succeeded
in deriving from the past. Goethe found their misunderstood
imitations of primitivism sickly. For the art historian they
provide a strange example of high moral principles that result in meaningless devotional gestures. Yet they cannot
be omitted from a history of Christian art, for they spent
their lives in dedicated service to Christianity; it was a kind
of Christianity that had lost its strength because it had lost
its backbone.

One other nineteenth-century painter, Delacroix, must be
mentioned, for towards the end of his life he was seriously
engaged in two commissions that involved him in Christian
themes - the Chapelle de St Denis du Saint Sacrement and the
Chapelle des Saints-Anges at St Sulpice.

Eugène Delacroix is too well known for the part he played as the leader and the initiator of the Romantic movement in France to require any introduction here, and yet the very word 'Romantic' had connections in France which seem to have no relationship - at least in the visual arts - with those which gathered around it in England. The difference is not easy to define, but I think it would be true to say that its roots lie in a different attitude to the very purpose of art. In France, and particularly from the beginning of the nineteenth century, the French artist has been a professional, a man to whom the essence of the task he set himself was a complete control of the possibilities involved in the handling of his medium, whether in painting or sculpture. It followed that every French artist, whether it was an Ingres, dedicated to Classicism, a Delacroix exploring the meaning of Romanticism, or a Courbet limiting himself to the theory of Realism, became a disciple of a master of his craft. Ingres taking Raphael as his starting point, Delacroix acknowledging Rubens, Courbet refusing to interfere with appearances by idealizing or intensifying them, would have misunderstood the British Romantic artists' motives - the method of Blake which was to close his eyes to the material world and depend on his inner vision, or Rossetti and Millais who opened their eyes, but used their perception of the physical world as a stepping-stone towards visual adventure.

To the French, therefore, and particularly to Delacroix, Romanticism was an excuse for tackling a special kind of subject - the hectic situations of Byron's plays 'The Death of Sardanapalus', the colourful moments of history (the massacre of Chios), an allegory 'Liberty Guiding the People' or a scene of violence (a tiger hunt). What Delacroix attempted in each case was a masterpiece to be admired. To the English Romantic, what the artist attempted was not to produce masterpieces but to communicate; seen from the French point of view, this resulted too often in 'literary' painting. Delacroix's 'Sardanapalus' is a reinterpretation of Rubens. Rossetti's 'Annunciation' is a reinterpretation of the New Testament.

There was no reason why Delacroix should not have seriously attempted Christian themes, and his 'Crucifixion' at Van-

Delacroix. *Jacob wrestling with the Angel,* 1856-61, in St Sulpice, Paris

nes and his 'Jacob and the Angel' in the Church of St Sulpice
are both serious examples of such attempts. Yet they, too,
are a painter's efforts to bring Rubens up to date and not
an artist's to identify himself with the inner meaning of a
religious crisis. The St Sulpice picture could be entitled 'Athletes struggling in a Landscape'. Rossetti's picture could never
be mistaken for a description of a scene in a bedroom. The
very heroism of Delacroix's picturesquely struggling figures

253

Delacroix. *Christ crucified between Thieves,* 1835

robs them of their inner meaning and turns them into a great artist's essay, conceived in the studio, in the art of pictorial composition.

What applies to Delacroix as champion of the French Romantics is equally applicable to Ingres. It was typical of the French attitude to art that the two should be thought of as opponents and that the Classicism of Ingres and his followers

Ingres. Detail of *Les Voeux de Louis XIII*, 1824, in Montauban Cathedral

and the Romanticism of Delacroix should be regarded as incompatible or mutually contradictory. Yet both were products of the same professionalism. That Ingres was fundamentally a draughtsman who looked to Raphael for his inspiration while Delacroix, equally fundamentally a painter, drew his from Rubens, is relatively unimportant if we are in search of the quality that enables an artist to interpret Christianity. Both Ingres and Delacroix had the same end in view - to paint great and impressive pictures. Both succeeded, and the source of their success was also the source of their failure as painters of religious themes. Ingres, like Delacroix, attempted a masterpiece - the 'Voeux de Louis XIII' in the Cathedral of Montauban. It is a faultless performance as a painting and an empty one as a communication of emotion.

Evidently inspired by Raphael's Sistine Madonna, Ingres has given us a Virgin and Child, seated on clouds supported by angels and silhouetted against a luminous sky revealed by the drawing apart of a double curtain. As a painterly device it could hardly be improved upon. Ingres controls the main rhythms of his composition with a skill that Raphael himself might have envied, yet its classic perfection somehow empties it of meaning. When one compares it with a typical Byzantine icon of the Moscow School one realizes suddenly that the hieratic dignity, the symbolic divinity and tenderness which seemed to come so easily to a hundred anonymous Byzantine icon painters was utterly beyond the reach of Ingres. The smooth, expressionless perfection of the Madonna's head becomes an almost ludicrous stereotype: instead of the Mother of God proudly offering her divine Son to the world, she is, in essence, a pin-up girl of uncanny perfection constructed on a formula invented by Raphael.

The altar-piece was completed in 1824. It is odd to think that less than thirty years later, Rossetti, an immature youth and an amateur artist, painted his sister as the Virgin Annunciate and in doing so produced a symbol of divinity as compelling as the Virgin of the Magnificat by Botticelli. Perhaps the task of explaining how aesthetic perfection can result in spiritual emptiness is beyond the powers of the art critic. Ruskin, had he been minded to do so, would have discovered words to elucidate the mystery. He would certainly have written analytically about truth and falsehood - words that carry little weight in the vocabulary of the modern critic - and yet they would have been the only two words that could make clear the distinction, in Christian painting, between sincerity and sentimentality.

Yet Ruskin, in his insistence on truth - the kind of truth that he found in Giotto, in Tintoretto, Veronese and in Turner - surely missed one important step in the argument, namely that visual truth in any work of art that contains a spiritual or mystical message, whether it be part of the pantheism of Turner or the theism of the mediaeval world, can only be a means, never an end.

XIV GIAMBATTISTA TIEPOLO
The Adoration of the Magi (detail), *c.* 1753

An age of ferment and renewal

WILLIAM NEIL

When Joseph Butler, the philosopher-bishop, whose *Analogy of Religion* was the most effective reply to Deism and its apostles of 'religion without revelation', was offered the archbishopric of Canterbury in 1747 he is said to have declined it on the grounds that 'it was too late for him to try to support a falling Church'. Almost a century later, in 1832, Dr Arnold of Rugby sadly echoed Butler's words. 'The Church, as it now stands', he wrote, 'no human power can save'. In a sense both were right and both were wrong.

While Butler was interpreting correctly the bleak prospects of a Church whose spiritual temperature varied between lukewarm and freezing point, John Wesley and his followers were kindling the fires of revival, and Arnold's justifiable pessimism in 1832 was confounded almost immediately by the re-birth of the Catholic tradition which had been dormant in the Church of England since the Elizabethan Settlement. The Evangelical Revival, whether in Methodism or in the Establishment, added nothing, as we have seen, to the history of Christian art, but the Oxford Movement which may be said to have begun with a sermon by John Keble in 1833 was undoubtedly a factor in the emergence of the Pre-Raphaelite school of English painters, which flourished from the middle of the nineteenth century and which made one of the few contributions in that century to the subject of this book.

Well might earnest churchmen all over Europe, Catholic or Protestant, have shared the misgivings of Butler and Arnold as they felt the chill wind of eighteenth-century opposition to Christianity whipping up into gale force in the century that followed. No country was immune from the storms of industrial and social change, from the materialism consequent on the mechanical revolution, from the unsettling effects of

257

new scientific discoveries, from the increasingly hostile tone of philosophy. More and more men learned to master the forces of nature, and to exploit its resources; less and less, as Laplace said to Napoleon, did there seem to be any room for God as a hypothesis.

In the wave of optimism which followed the amassing of wealth through the industrial revolution, the conquest of disease and the prolongation of life by medical science, the expansion of new countries and the growth of colonial empires, belief in the progress of man to Utopia by his own unaided efforts became the public philosophy of the age. While the ruling classes saw the future in terms of the prosperity which would come from the operation of economic laws unchecked by any irrelevant factors such as consideration for the workers, the new proletariat turned more and more to Karl Marx and his disciples to free them from the bondage of laissez-faire capitalism. By allying itself with the bourgeoisie, partly through fear of anarchy and secularism, the Church largely lost the support of the working-classes and gave countenance to Marx's dictum that religion is opium for the people. On the Continent influential leaders of thought of the calibre of Schopenhauer, Feuerbach, Nietzsche and Haeckel were outspoken atheists and anti-Christian propagandists.

The prospects for the survival of Christianity in the nineteenth century were therefore not encouraging. Yet it is a mark of the innate vitality of both Catholicism and Protestantism that by the end of the century they were immeasurably stronger than they had been at the beginning. The concept of the Christian State had gone, if we mean by that the allegiance of a whole nation to one or other branch of the Church, but in its place had emerged a more tightly-knit Christian community within each state, better organized, better served by its clergy and better supported by its members.

In Roman Catholic countries the eighteenth century had been marked by the same forces of disintegration as in the Protestant world, if for different reasons. A series of mediocre Popes, who were regarded mostly as the temporal rulers of the Papal States rather than as the Fathers in God of Catholic peoples throughout the world, had been unable to stand up against powerful Catholic sovereigns, who insisted on the dissolution of the Jesuit Order, and generally curbed the rights and privileges of the Church. On the heels of the anti-clericalism of the French Revolution came the arrogance of Napoleon, whose contemptuous treatment of the Pope and whose exploitation of religion for his own purposes brought upon the Church such public humiliation as it had not known since the days of Constantine.

But the tide turned. Politically, the nineteenth century, appalled at the triumph of anarchy in the French Revolution, reacted in favour of an ancient and authoritarian institution like the Papacy. Spiritually, there was within the Catholic Church a revival of religious life. New monastic orders were founded, foreign missions became again a live concern, societies like that of St Vincent de Paul came into being for the relief of suffering and poverty. The Jesuits, restored to their privileges, resumed their traditional teaching function so that schools were multiplied and new universities were created.

In the congregational life of the Church, devotion to the Virgin Mary and to the Sacred Heart of Jesus, together with the perpetual adoration of the Blessed Sacrament, became intensified. Daily communion was encouraged, Lourdes became a centre for mass pilgrimages, and Catholic Action was founded to enlist the organized co-operation of the laity in renewing the life of society and making the Faith more vital at all levels. It was as a climax to this general upsurge of new life within the Roman Catholic Church, its increasingly efficient structural organization, and its expansion into a world-wide communion, that the Vatican Council in 1870 re-emphasized the supreme authority of the Pope and declared him to be the infallible custodian of Christian faith and morality. This was at once a refutation of the right of any secular state to control the Church, a challenge to divided Protestantism, and a safeguard against the infiltration of what were considered to be the heretical trends of the times.

Thus the reply of the Roman Church to the forces that militated against Christianity in the nineteenth century was to reassert its authority over the total life of its people, to develop the traditional pattern of Catholic faith and practice, to be cautious and conservative in accepting new ideas, and to set its face against the Renaissance principle that speculation and enquiry must be allowed to flourish unhampered by dogmatic or ecclesiastical restraints. Protestantism, on the other hand, by the very nature of its origins and ethos, was forced to ride the storm. At the Reformation it had insisted on the right of private judgment, and however much orthodox church-men might drag their feet, Protestantism had committed itself to the principle of freedom of enquiry in quest of truth, no matter how unpleasant and uncomfortable the results of that quest might at times prove to be.

Nowhere was this more evident in the nineteenth century than in Protestant Germany, which then assumed the role which it has maintained to the present day of being the source of most of the creative thinking in theological studies in the Christian world. There the view was taken that if attacks were being made on Christianity by atheistic philosophers they could be countered only by replies from equally able Christian philosophers and theologians, and not by withdrawal to the entrenched positions of an orthodoxy of a bygone age. Similarly, it was felt that the new knowledge that science was accumulating had somehow to find a place within a Christian view of the universe, although in the process many cherished preconceptions might become casualties. It was of the very essence of the Protestant position that risks had to be taken, avenues had to be explored which might prove to be blind alleys, and conclusions, often contradictory, had to be reached which would without doubt be painful for many of the faithful.

The intellectual ferment in German theology of the nine-teenth century may be traced to a variety of causes. There was firstly the reaction against the barren creed of Deism; yet the reply came by subjecting the Faith and the Scriptures to rational enquiry. There was also the conviction that Pietism, the German equivalent of the Bible faith of the Evangelical Revival in England, was not an adequate answer to the chal-lenge of secularism; yet without exception these theologians who were accused of destroying the simple beliefs of the faithful were themselves men of undoubted personal piety and

Christian conviction. The independence of the German universities, which unlike Oxford and Cambridge at that time were not tied to the apron-strings of the Church, offered opportunities for Christian thinkers to ventilate the most radical opinions without fear of clamorous accusations of heresy. Not least was the profound and lasting influence of Immanuel Kant, whose *Critique of Pure Reason* published in 1781, and subsequent works, had discomfited the Deists and at the same time drawn attention to the powerful arguments for Christianity to be drawn from the existence of 'the starry heavens above and the moral law within'.

Kant, unlike the Deists and orthodox Christians, held that ethics and metaphysics must be based on logic, rather than on revelation and dogma

University teachers of the outstanding intellectual calibre of Schleiermacher, Hegel, Ritschl and Troeltsch, critical of much that passed for orthodox Christianity, but stimulating their pupils and their readers to think about the old truths in new ways, seemed to many to be responding to the challenge of the times in restating Christianity as a valid and meaningful faith in an age of scientific progress.

Scientific methods were also applied to the study of the Bible. The honour of being the founder of the modern critical approach to the Bible, involving an examination of its component documents as literary and historical products of their time subject to the same vicissitudes as any other body of ancient writings, goes to Jean Astruc, physician to Louis XV in the middle of the eighteenth century. But it was in Germany that this Higher Criticism, as it came to be known, reached its apogee. Early pioneers in this field, such as Herder, Lessing, Reimarus and Eichhorn, broke new ground in various directions and paved the way for a radical approach to the study of the New Testament by a group of scholars in the University of Tübingen.

The chief spokesmen of what came to be known as the Tübingen School were D. F. Strauss and F. C. Baur. In the eighteenth century the conflict between rationalism and orthodoxy over the authority of the Bible had been based on the common premise that the Biblical narratives were factual records. Strauss was the first critic who saw that the Bible contained not only a record of what had happened, but also the interpretation put on these events by the writers or their

261

sources. On this basis he wrote a *Life of Jesus* in which he made allowance for legendary elements and pious accretions. Baur directed attention to the influence of the personal background and bias of the New Testament writers, and of their purpose in writing, upon the composition of the documents as we have them. The Tübingen School reached many false conclusions but it opened up the whole question of New Testament studies in a stimulating and fruitful way. The rest of the century was filled with the noise of academic battles but by the end of it German scholarship had put the world in its debt, and scholars of the quality of Wellhausen in Old Testament studies and Harnack in the field of the New Testament were the undisputed leaders of the Biblical criticism of the time.

It is in England, however, that the fascinating cross-currents of nineteenth-century Christianity can best be observed. This was undoubtedly England's century, the heyday of the British Empire on which the sun never set. England was at once the scene of the greatest triumphs and the greatest horrors of the Industrial Revolution, of the sharpest conflict between science and religion, of the most bitter last-ditch stand of orthodoxy against the new developments in Biblical scholarship, and of a remarkable Catholic revival within the Anglican Church. In the early days of the century the cold morality of the Age of Reason still dominated parish life and worship. A hundred years later, when Queen Victoria died in 1901, the Church could claim that despite considerable losses Christianity was far more firmly entrenched in the life of the nation and that never since the Reformation had the Church been held in such high esteem.

The losses had been sustained not only among the ranks of the intellectuals, many of whom had come to feel that Christianity had no longer any role in a world in which scientific progress was rapidly satisfying all men's needs, but also among the working classes in the new industrial areas, who were embittered by the failure of the Church to condemn the blatant iniquities of conditions in the factories, and who saw no hope in an organization that was concerned only for men's souls while allowing their bodies to starve.

A London slum known as Devil's Acre, drawn in the 1870's by Gustave Doré: traditional churches had little to say to the new urban poor

Indeed many of the bishops and clergy did not appear to care even about their souls.

When the Industrial Revolution changed the face of England, bringing great wealth to a few and poverty, malnutrition, slums and exploitation to the masses who flocked to the mills and mines, it found a Church better geared to minister to landed gentry, agricultural labourers and small town merchants than to the hordes of rootless wage-slaves whose numbers grew by leaps and bounds in the new centres of population. When the Church at last awoke to its responsibilities and tried to make amends, it was too late. Generations had sprung up which were untouched by the Church at any point save perhaps at baptism, marriage and burial. For many the only faith they had was in political action.

Yet on the positive side Christianity in England made considerable headway. First of all the Church put its own house in order. Its wealth was more equitably distributed among the clergy, and the holding of more than one living by a single parson was discontinued. But more important was the stimulus given to religious life by the Oxford Movement. The Church of England since the Reformation had tried

263

Cardinal Newman led the Anglo-Catholic Oxford Movement in the mid-19th c., then became one of the most eminent Victorian converts to the Church of Rome

to hold together two factions in uneasy association. There were on the one hand those who regarded the Church as Catholic in every respect except that it did not acknowledge the authority of the Pope and had repudiated certain peripheral beliefs and practices which at the Reformation were held to be wrong. For a variety of reasons they had been overshadowed and outnumbered by those who looked on the Reformation as virtually a new beginning, emphasized the supreme authority of the Bible and stressed the primacy of personal conversion. This was the view of the Puritans and the Evangelicals, and although many of them had left the Church of England to form various Nonconformist bodies, the temper of the Church was predominantly Protestant throughout the eighteenth and early nineteenth century.

It was in the 1830's under the influence of Keble, Pusey, and above all Newman, that the Church of England was made conscious of its Catholic heritage. Originating in Oxford, the Anglo-Catholic movement meant not only a rediscovery of the place of beauty and ceremonial in the worship of the Church, or a new sense of history and the continuity of tradition, but also a reawakening of slumbering bishops, clergy and laity who had been untouched by the Evangelical Revival. Although Newman and some others seceded to Rome, and bitter opposition was aroused both within the Church of England and in Nonconformist circles, the effect of the Oxford Movement was to introduce a new vitality into the religious life of the nation, a new devotional spirit, a new zeal for social service, and, by the recovery of Catholic faith and practice within the Reformed tradition, greatly to enhance the possibility of ultimate reunion between Catholic and Protestant churches everywhere.

It has already been noted that in Victorian England the Church was strangely indifferent to the plight of the masses in the urban centres and thereby lost their allegiance. It must have been difficult in the temper of the times for churchmen of any persuasion to believe anything other than that God had ordained some to privilege, most to humble acceptance of poverty but all alike to personal salvation. Honourable mention must be made, however, of the part played by Methodism in the early days of the Trade Union movement, of individual Evangelicals like Lord Shaftesbury who forced the Factory Act through Parliament in 1847, of Christian Socialists like Charles Kingsley and F. D. Maurice who saw, long before the rest of the Church realized it, that religion cannot be kept separate from politics, and of William Booth who took his Salvation Army lads and lasses with practical help and a message of hope into slum territory untouched by the Church. All of this good work, whether it added new members to congregational rolls or not, made the churchless feel that at least some Christians cared and that the Gospel was not wholly irrelevant.

General Booth created the Salvation Army to minister to the growing urban slums of 19th-c. England

There was indeed much need for the Church to do all that it could to commend itself to society, for the mid-nineteenth century saw it embroiled in a losing battle against the scientists. As we have seen, the reply of the Church to the attacks of eighteenth-century sceptical philosophy had been to take refuge in the doctrine of the verbal infallibility of Holy Scripture. It was possible to maintain this position in the first half of the nineteenth century even in face of new developments in physics and chemistry, but when geologists produced evidence which made it difficult to defend a six-day creation and the date of man's appearance on this planet as 4004 BC, it needed only the publication of Darwin's *Origin of Species* in 1859 to convince believers of all shades of opinion that not only was the authority of the Bible at stake, but the existence of God, the dignity of man and the whole Christian scheme of salvation.

The journalistic flair of T. H. Huxley, who constituted himself 'Darwin's bulldog', magnified the issue into a conflict between Science and Religion, Evolution and Moses, New Knowledge and Biblical Obscurantism. Most churchmen in their panic behaved, as Dean Church said at the time, 'more like old ladies than philosophers'. Even Prime Ministers Gladstone and Disraeli were moved to enter the fray, so great was public interest and concern. The battle was of course won by the scientists before it started. By the end of the century orthodoxy, except on the fringe, had come to realize that science was not engaged in a diabolical plot to overthrow the

Faith, that many scientists were themselves devout Christians, and that belief in the verbal infallibility of the Bible had been an obstacle to proper understanding and appreciation of the message of the Scriptures.

What had, however, led to this conclusion had been much more the patient researches of Anglican scholars, who had mediated the results of German Higher Criticism with characteristic moderation. The subjectiveness of the Tübingen School and their more erratic conclusions had been corrected, so that the sound results of Continental Biblical studies could now be seen in their proper perspective. In this fruitful field, in which men of letters like Coleridge also played a notable part, textual, literary and historical criticism of the Bible, using scientific methods, had at last made it plain, despite much opposition and various heresy hunts, that Christian orthodoxy had nothing to lose and everything to gain by subjecting the Biblical documents to the most rigorous examination, unhampered by dogmatic prejudices or ecclesiastical restraints.

Thus by the end of the Victorian era Christianity had weathered the storms of the century in a remarkable way. Scepticism among the intellectuals and indifference among the working classes were overshadowed by the fact that from the royal household downwards, through Parliament, the professions and the great middle class, Britain could have called itself a Christian country with more justice than at any time since the Reformation. It was not merely that churches of all denominations were well and regularly attended, or that churchgoing was a mark of respectability. Religion pervaded family life, Christian philanthropy and social service permeated the community, missionary efforts overseas were strongly supported, business ethics were on the whole of a creditable standard, and the administration of public affairs at home as well as of the Empire overseas was largely carried out with integrity and a high sense of duty.

It is easy enough now to hurl at the Victorian Church charges of hypocrisy, complacency, false optimism, lack of sensitivity, religiosity, stuffiness, censoriousness, and so on. Many of us would rather condone its failings for the sake of

Millais. *Christ in the House of His Parents*, 1850

its virtues. What is hardly in dispute, however, is that the nineteenth century was not one of the great ages of Christian art. That it produced some good hymn-writers and at least one great religious poet, Robert Browning - some would add Tennyson and Francis Thompson - is commonly accepted. Victorian Gothic in public buildings - St Pancras Station and the Albert Memorial are classic examples - and Victorian pretentiousness in domestic design and furnishings are perhaps too close to our own time and too alien to its spirit to enable us to pass fair judgment.

But one would not expect Christian art to flourish in a century which only eventually reached religious stability after decades of controversy and conflict during which the future of Christianity was in grave doubt, or in which empire-building, political and social reform and material progress were the main concerns that occupied men's minds. In Catholic Europe the Church was fighting for a place in the sun, and in Protestant countries the emphasis was on good works and personal salvation. Delacroix owed more to Romanticism than to French Catholicism and even G. F. Watts' sermons on canvas tend to reflect Victorian pulpit oratory.

267

The Pre-Raphaelite school of painters, however, who no doubt owed their inspiration to a variety of sources, such as the Gothic revival in architecture, the poetry of Keats, Swinburne and Tennyson, the precepts of John Ruskin and the example of William Morris, were in no small measure also the product of the Oxford Movement. It is difficult to imagine them flourishing in the climate of the Regency. But when the Brotherhood was formed in 1848 Keble, Pusey and Newman had left their mark on the Church of England and had given it a new sense of its mediaeval heritage. Thus when Rossetti went back to Dante and Giotto, he found a ready response and many followers. It was not a return to the Baroque of the Counter-Reformation, for England was a Protestant country and the realism and love of detail of the Pre-Raphaelites had more kinship with seventeenth-century Protestant Holland. But by combining the Catholic and Protestant traditions in this way, the Pre-Raphaelites not only reflected the comprehensiveness of the English Church but also brought a new breadth of vision into the religious life of the nation.

The Brotherhood had points of contact with the German school of the Nazarenes, as Eric Newton has pointed out. Both sprang out of a Protestant background but the Nazarenes were drawn to the Roman Church and painted from a specifically Roman Catholic angle. The Pre-Raphaelites, however, were not only better artists but their work had a far wider appeal. They recovered for Protestantism something of Blake's sense of the 'mystic harmonies that beat upon sense and sight', though unlike him they embedded it firmly within Catholic faith and tradition. Holman Hunt's 'Light of the World', Millais' 'Christ in the House of His Parents' and Rossetti's 'Ecce Ancilla Domini' (Annunciation) may not rank with Michelangelo's 'Creation of Adam' any more than Newman's 'Lead Kindly Light' can compare with Dante's *Paradiso,* but they are all genuine expressions of Christian insight and intensity of conviction which have brought to countless ordinary men and women a deeper sense of the wonder of the Gospel.

268

VIII TWENTIETH CENTURY

Christian art in a secular age

ERIC NEWTON

When Cézanne said of Monet 'He is only an eye' and added 'But what an eye' he summed up the whole purpose of Impressionist painting, its strength - which was to record with the utmost precision the appearance of the visible world in its most transient aspects - and its weakness - which was a comparative lack of interest in any other problem. When, for example, Monet painted a series of pictures of the western façade of Rouen Cathedral at different times of day and under different intensities and directions of light, he had no thought of expressing his emotional response to a masterpiece of Gothic architecture, still less of commenting on mediaeval ways of translating the Christian spirit into stone. He was painting the impact of light on a complex object.

The difference between Impressionism, the art of making a painterly record of appearances, and Expressionism, the art of discovering a visual equivalent for the emotions, is an important one and if we are attempting to find reasons for the nineteenth century's failure to tackle Christian themes with conviction, we can be sure that behind that failure lies an obsession with describing the exact 'look' of an isolated moment in time, the mist over the river, the splash of sunlight falling through foliage onto a meadow or a human body, or the gesture of a dancer as she prepares to execute a pirouette or stoops to adjust her shoe.

Manifestly such obsessions cannot be of any help to an art that is concerned with Christian themes. Before that can be achieved the Impressionist tradition must be replaced by a return to Expressionist ways of thinking and feeling and, in consequence, to an Expressionist habit of painting or making sculpture. And that return is precisely what happened when, towards the turn of the century, Impressionism began to swing over into Post-Impressionism. That swing, in its turn, led into a series of experiments none of which was concerned with the 'look' of phenomena and all of which, therefore, could, if necessary, be used to express moods or emotions. It became at last possible, if the artist wished to do so, to tackle the unseen or the supernatural, to work by symbol instead of description, to return, in fact, to the point where Blake had closed his eyes to the world of phenomena and drawn on his imagination to fill the gap, or where the early Pre-Raphaelites had used their eyes in order to select from what they saw only what would intensify the picture's meaning.

It is hardly surprising therefore to find, in England, in the early work of Paul Nash, echoes of both Pre-Raphaelitism and Blake, and in the etchings of Graham Sutherland (in the 1930's) undisguised derivations from Blake's romantic wood-cuts for Thornton's 'Vergil' or from the mood of Blake's disciples, Calvert and Samuel Palmer. The tradition that would make a revival of Christian art possible was establishing itself even though it was not until later in the century that it was used for a specific Christian purpose, and even then it was rather to a more adventurous policy of patronage than to a will or inclination on the part of the artist that one can trace the beginnings of Christian art in twentieth-century England.

In France, where the breakaway from Impressionism occurred a good deal earlier, one finds the same reluctance on the part of the ecclesiastical patron to utilize the new spirit in art. The appearance of Picasso's 'Demoiselles d'Avignon' in 1907 was a sudden signal that Impressionist realism had virtually ceased to be a valid means of communication. Picasso's picture struck those who first saw it - in particular, Braque and Guillaume Apollinaire - as a daring stylistic innovation to which they gradually accustomed themselves. What they did not realize was that here was a new visual language capable of communicating a new kind of message and that for many years two artists at least had already been experimenting with new stylistic modes for the very purpose of developing a new kind of content.

Van Gogh, from the moment early in 1888 when he left Paris for Provence, began to develop an Expressionist style,

271

Van Gogh.
The Good Samaritan,
after Delacroix, 1890

based, at first, on his early attempts to use the broken, vibrating brush stroke of the Impressionists, but eventually turning that brush stroke into a method for transmitting emotion rather than for making a factual record. Had he been given the opportunity to use the old Impressionist method and the new Expressionist content for religious purposes, there is hardly any doubt that we should now know him as a painter of religious subjects. As it was, he began (before his move to Paris) by painting dark, Rembrandtesque subjects full of Rembrandt's own human profundity, though they were not on specifically Biblical themes; and later, he did, in fact, paint a transcription of Delacroix's 'Good Samaritan' (1890) which is considerably more intense as an interpretation of a Christian parable than the original. It is a proof of the power of Post-Impressionism to convey emotions beyond the scope of any early nineteenth-century Romantic.

Gauguin, less tempestuous in temperament, chose the same escapist route in order to free himself from the bondage of Impressionist realism, and in doing so - even before his departure for the South Seas - painted, in Brittany, subjects that are fundamentally religious in inspiration, a Calvary that turns the old realism into the new symbolism, and a 'Jacob

272

XV GAUGUIN
The Yellow Christ (detail), 1889

Gauguin.
The Vision after the Sermon (Jacob Wrestling with the Angel), 1889

Wrestling with the Angel' that has none of Delacroix's heroic academicism or Rubens' vigorous materialism behind it. It is a frank return to the puritanism and innocence of mediaeval art and for that reason it leaps backwards at a single bound, across the gulf that had been gradually widening, ever since the beginning of the Renaissance.

Gauguin, like van Gogh, might have been an impressive painter of what we think of as religious pictures had he not discovered, in Tahiti, a new and entirely pagan environment - primitive but certainly not Christian - in the golden skins of the girls and in the hectic tropical landscape. Out of these he constructed what amounts to a new mythology. It was a rebellious gesture, not a rejection of the material in favour of the spiritual but an exchange of the old Hellenic ideals of physical beauty for a new and a more colourful kind of paganism. Although Gauguin's world, in his Tahitian paintings full of references to the kind of magic and ritual that connects primitive man with his gods, is certainly not Christian, it is equally certainly rooted in sympathetic understanding of religious beliefs.

It was this double adventure of the Post-Impressionism of van Gogh and Gauguin rather than the highly intellectual

273

Emil Nolde. *The Last Supper*, 1909

innovations of Picasso in the second decade of the twentieth century that led the way into a new kind of content. No 'school' of religious painting resulted from it, but that was because the demand rather than the supply was lacking. The visual vocabulary appropriate to Christian art was there; the need to use it had not yet arrived, nor could it arrive until the Church itself appealed for it in order to revive the old half-forgotten need for symbolism (and therefore for art) as an adjunct to ritual, whether it took the form of a chalice, a chasuble, an altar-piece or a statue - or even a building that expressed its function by means of its form.

'Expressed' is the inevitable word and though 'Expressionism' may be a vague term, it is a necessary one if Christian art is to exist at all, or is to be something more than an illustration of the superficial appearance of an event. 'Expressionism' is perhaps the key word in any serious analysis of the art of the twentieth century, just as 'reason' explains much of the eighteenth and 'Romanticism' the first half of the nineteenth century. It may be an accident, or it may be a corollary of something that Dr Neil can explain better than I, that could account for the fact that so little Christian art of importance has been produced during the past half-century in France (I shall refer later to Matisse's murals and vestments at Vence and to Rouault's passionate prints and paintings), while in England two artists of manifest imaginative sincerity have produced memorable instances of it.

What prompted Stanley Spencer to elaborate his own extremely personal interpretations of Christian themes was evidently a temperamental self-dedication, and at times a self-identification with the Gospel stories and their application to everyday life in our own century. Graham Sutherland, on the other hand, has been lucky enough to find the intelligent patrons who could and did offer him in the context of the Church itself the kind of opportunity that he is exceptionally fitted to grasp.

Spencer's upbringing in the Berkshire village of Cookham-on-Thames, which eventually provided him with a kind of topographical background for all his religious experiences, his exceptional powers as a draughtsman of immense precision, his intimate knowledge of the New Testament and his consequent ability both to visualize it as a narrative and to understand it as the prime basis of a religion, turned him, almost inevitably, into a painter of the Christian story. In his art the three elements - Cookham as a background, draughtsmanship as a method, the Bible as a theme to be described and intensified as the Pre-Raphaelites had done a century earlier - are fused together so intimately that they can hardly be separated. That fusion explains his strength and the authority behind his vision. It also explains the odd gaucheries that one finds in so many of his pictures, and especially in his religious pictures. For he had a strange streak of visual honesty which compelled him, when Pre-Raphaelite clarity of observation broke down, to invent. In his 'Last Supper' for example (painted in 1920) the setting is a barn in Cookham in which every brick is painted with an almost alarming realism, the disciples are formalized into a pattern that is positively Romanesque in its refusal to accept what the eye could see. These

275

men were a group of Cookham villagers whom Spencer could easily have taken as models and presented as portraits. They were the actors in a Christian drama and this was one of the critical moments in the action. Therefore the closed eyes of Blake had to take the place of the open eyes of Millais. But when Blake closed his eyes he saw something based on an engraving after Michelangelo; Spencer saw, perhaps, nothing at all but a chapter in the Bible. Consequently the heroic rhythms of Michelangelo disappeared. They were replaced by the utterly honest but oddly clumsy rhythms envisaged by Spencer himself. The marvel is that the photographic bricks and the Romanesque disciples could be persuaded to combine into one of the most moving Last Suppers ever painted.

Spencer's religious paintings are so single-hearted, so personal and so filled with these fusions of opposites which in the end do not contradict each other, that one is tempted here to upset the balance of a brief outline of Christian art by describing too many of them in too much detail. The temptation must be resisted though it is only fair to him to draw up a list of his major religious works with dates and the briefest of comments. The 'Centurion's Servant' (1915) is a translation into terms of the life of Cookham children of the story of healing by prayer (*Luke* 7), with the sick child tossing with fever on the bed and his friends praying round him. The big 'Resurrection' (a recurrent theme with Spencer) in the Tate Gallery (1923-26) is Spencer's most complete masterpiece. The graves that open in Cookham churchyard to give up their dead are so convincing that one is not even surprised at the scene. Spencer accepts the physical fact of the Resurrection as simply as Blake accepted the singing of the stars in his Job engravings. Christ carries the Cross (1920) through a street in Cookham while the villagers crowd round Him or watch Him from open windows. The Wise Men visit Mary (1940), in bed and exhausted by her travail, in a Cookham bedroom and extend their arms exultantly in gestures of praise. Towards the end of his life Spencer conceived and half completed a series of related pictures on the theme of Christ with His Disciples, preaching from a punt on the Thames during the

Stanley Spencer. *The Last Supper,* 1920

Cookham Regatta. Something of the crowded and confused complexity of Tintoretto's San Rocco Crucifixion turns the whole series into a kind of village epic, groups of visitors assemble to listen, to report or to partake of a picnic lunch. Each group is united by its own separate urgency yet the sermon firmly links each group to the central dominant theme. In 1939 Spencer painted a series of seven small panels each depicting Christ in the Wilderness, pondering compassionately on the destiny and the mysteries of nature; in one of them (a seated figure brooding over a scorpion) Spencer's whole attitude to the loneliness and humanity of Christ finds its intensest expression.

One could, of course, wish that Spencer's method of painting in series, as though he were engaged in a kind of auto-biography of his own spiritual life and experience, could have been utilized by providing the Cookham Regatta pictures with a building to house them as a single unit. Only by doing so could their cumulative effect have been given its full force and Cookham made the inevitable context for Spencer's interpretation of the urgent humanity of Christ's mission on earth.

277

The opportunity to combine a series of works in a single pictorial unit was, in fact, given to Spencer when, in 1933, his patrons, Mr and Mrs J. L. Behrend, built a memorial chapel at Burghclere near Newbury, in which Spencer could realize a series of drawings for a painted interior he had envisaged ten years earlier.

In the literal sense of the word the mural paintings that fill the side walls of the chapel are not Christian, yet they belong to a church and they sum up more completely than any of his other works, the meaning, as Spencer conceived it, of the underlying spirit of Christianity.

The theme is a simple one: what is depicted in these mural panels is the war of 1914-1918 in Macedonia, yet war, in the sense of acts of violence and hostility between groups of human beings whose purpose was to destroy each other, is never even indirectly referred to. The theme for Spencer is of brotherly love and companionship, of the incessant labour that soldiers have to face - marches, kit inspections, service in hospitals, fatigue, incidents involving effort and endurance. The sixteen panels, each describing a separate incident, yet each contributing to a central message, form one of the major works of twentieth-century English painting. And though the content is not Biblical the whole chapel is a dedicated effort to express the spirit of Christian mutual self-sacrifice.

The east wall, on the other hand, is conceived in a different mood, as though it were the climax to which the side walls had been an elaborate introduction. Again, Resurrection is the theme, but not the kind of Resurrection that Spencer had imagined in Cookham Graveyard ten years earlier. There the graves were giving up their dead in order to begin another existence in another world. At Burghclere there is no hint of a beginning. What Spencer had in mind was an ending - an ending of toil and suffering, a laying down of burdens. Each soldier brings with him the symbolic cross he has carried for so long and lays it down in a promised land. For once Cookham has been omitted as a background. The 'Resurrection' (the title hardly fits the content) occurs in an almost timeless landscape, a place that leads to a distant featureless horizon. The purpose of the whole crowded wall is to build up a sense of peace, a

Stanley Spencer. *The Resurrection,* in Burghclere Memorial Chapel, 1927-32

laying down of burdens, and a deliverance of earthly responsibilities into the hands of the Christ who, a diminutive figure in the middle distance, is symbolically important but makes no pictorial climax to the wall.

Patronage on this scale happens more rarely than one is apt to think. One has to go back to Giotto's Arena Chapel in Padua to discover a building constructed by a patron with an artist in mind. Scrovegni, like the Behrends, planned the building because he had a specific artist in mind, and the artist himself, in both cases, was enlarged and imaginatively enriched by the opportunity. In both cases it is the cumulative effect of a single mind at work on a commission that gave him the fullest scope that made the result so supremely satisfactory. Even Michelangelo in the Sistine Chapel and Tintoretto in the Scuola of San Rocco did not have the advantage of filling spaces that had been specifically created for them.

279

Three other instances of carefully planned patronage in England have produced examples of Christian art whose effect is to a great extent dependent on their architectural context.

It was in 1943 that Canon Hussey commissioned Henry Moore to carve the seated Madonna and Child in the south transept of the Church of St Matthew in Northampton, and a year later, his son, the present Dean of Chichester, asked Graham Sutherland to paint a Crucifixion on the wall of the transept opposite.

The Madonna by Henry Moore is an exceptional work by an artist who had spent his life solving problems of purely sculptural form unrelated to the kind of theme that could be dictated by a patron whose purpose was to relate a work of visual art to its specific content. And perhaps this is the appropriate moment to discuss this relationship in its application to the century in which we live.

It has become an accepted axiom that what the artist has to communicate is a kind of essence of himself rather than an interpretation of a theme dictated to him. And that consequently behind every commission to an artist is primarily a desire to possess an example of his work. Not a painting of the Montagne-Ste-Victoire but a Cézanne is what the patron has in mind: not an account of what happened at Guernica but a Picasso.

It is difficult to imagine that this situation was not always uppermost in the patron's mind. And certainly when Michelangelo signed the contract for the Sistine Chapel ceiling he must have been fully aware that Pope Julius II would rather have a good example of Michelangelo's work than a good interpretation of the 'Creation of Adam'. We know that Michelangelo signed the contract unwillingly, not because he hesitated to tackle the story of the Creation but because he preferred carving to painting. But we also know that Henry Moore hesitated to undertake a Madonna and Child, not because he doubted his own powers as a creator of sculptural form but because he had never seriously considered the deeper implications of the chosen theme.

As it turned out - and as it often does turn out - to impose a limitation, to ask an artist to conform to the rules of a game

Henry Moore.
Madonna and Child,
1945, in St Matthew's
Northampton

that is unfamiliar to him, may be a positive source of inspiration. The theme of maternity, the relationship between
protective motherhood and helpless immaturity, was one he
had often tackled. This was a specialized version of it in which
the mother-symbol was a primeval creature, half earth-goddess,
half peasant; and the child for all its helplessness faced the
world from his mother's knee with the consciousness of
divinity. There was sufficient difference in content between
this and any of his previous carvings to impose a difference of
form. This statue was personal in a way that no previous
mother-and-child sculpture of his had been personal. Yet it
contained none of the limitations of portraiture. It produced,
in Northampton, a mild shock of surprise when it was unveiled,

281

but that was the usual shock of stylistic unfamiliarity. What was left, after the shock subsided, was a marvellous impression of primeval dignity.

The 'Crucifixion' by Graham Sutherland, finished in 1946, was conceived in a different spirit but after a similar process of brooding on the implications of the theme. Sutherland's hesitation to come to grips with them was not, as with Moore, the result of unfamiliarity with the problem of using his aesthetic imagination in the service of religious imagery, but with the balance between all kinds of decisions about what mood should predominate in a generation which had abandoned the habit of making such decisions.

Hitherto, tradition had dictated its own terms. Between the sweetness of the early Raphael and the almost historical emphasis on suffering that is the keynote of Grünewald (both at Colmar and at Karlsruhe) almost any intermediate position was tenable. Sutherland, after a good deal of experimenting with the subject itself and with related subjects like studies of thorn-heads which would place the emotional emphasis on physical suffering and the Crown of Thorns, eventually decided on a painting that would retain the central theme of bodily martyrdom but would render it almost impersonal by refusing to turn it into an 'event' through any reference to the material world. The background is in no sense an 'environment'. It is a timeless abstraction based on vertical and horizontal rhythms, with a formal barrier at its base - a symbol of aloofness from the world of human affairs.

This, it seems to me, is a triumph of the Expressionist method, the fusion of fact with symbol, in which the fact has been sufficiently distorted to intensify its meaning and the symbol simplified so that its impact is direct and never obscure. Even the colour has its own emotional significance. The greygreen figure of the Crucified Christ, the deep, rather hot blue of the background, suggesting featureless space, and given a measurable rhythm by the black verticals and horizontals that traverse it, the sombre notes of red at the base of the picture, symbols of earthbound passion - these too are the evidence of an Expressionist determination to find the visual equivalents of the timeless meaning of the Crucifixion.

282

Sir Basil Spence's new Cathedral at Coventry, opened in 1962, lies at right angles to the 15th-c. Cathedral, whose ruins are reflected in its etched glass porch

But the most ambitious attempt hitherto made in any country in Europe to build up a massive sequence of Christian imagery in a single building is, of course, to be found in Sir Basil Spence's new Cathedral in Coventry.

What makes the building almost unique among cathedrals is the fact that it is an instance of a large-scale devotional building in which the architectural shell and its functional contents have been fused together as a single concept by a single controlling mind. It is not an interior whose form, however suitable to contain later additions, was intended from the first to make its own self-sufficient impact on the eye. What was intended, and was never lost sight of from start to finish, was the unity achieved by a chosen team of artists

283

working in collaboration under a single controlling mind. The choice of the artists was certainly important, but equally so was the team spirit which made the contribution of each a part of a foreseen total effect. In the ten great vertical stained glass windows that are concealed from the eye as one enters the west end of the Cathedral, the three artists who designed and executed them have worked to a controlling colour scheme and a controlling symbolic programme. The great Baptistry window by John Piper is visually self-contained by means of architectural devices which none the less ensure that it is still an important ingredient in a carefully thought out effect. The great tapestry by Graham Sutherland that covers the east wall is not an attempt to dominate the interior at the expense of what the other members of the team have contributed. It is true that - again by a series of deliberate architectural devices - it sets a mood for the whole and is designed as a climax, as is Bernini's gigantic baldacchino in St Peter's in Rome or Gaulli's visionary ceiling in the Church of St Gesù, but it neither suggests that the Cathedral has been built round it, as a play might be written as a vehicle for a character, nor does it look like an architect's after-thought, a trick to heighten the emotional effect of an interior. Indeed what is most worth saying about the Cathedral as a whole is that it shares with the best examples of Baroque architecture the notion that the whole is rather more than a sum of its parts, and that there is little justification for the criticism that it is an exhibition hall into which isolated works of art have been effectively fitted.

The window of the Baptistry, by John Piper, is a true and completely successful essay in the abstract symbolism of colour in a medium that produces colour at its intensest. The symbolism - a gradual progression of surrounding dark colour (earth and sky) changing, by a chromatic crescent, to a golden glow in the centre - is simple but instantly readable.

The ten windows that light the east end by virtue of the 'saw tooth' plan of the building are crowded with symbolism of a kind that is by no means easily readable, but is certainly not, for that reason, meaningless. Three artists, Lawrence Lee, Keith New and Geoffrey Clarke, collaborated in an iconographical programme and a colour scheme dictated by the

John Piper. Stained glass in the Baptistry of Coventry Cathedral

architect who, in addition to the symbolism of each separate window, decided that the series of five on the left were to be devoted to the religious development of man while those facing them on the right represented the nature and the power of God.

It would be hardly possible in so brief a history of Christian art to describe in detail how each of the three artists has worked out his own iconographical programme within the limits of the prescribed colour harmonies (green for innocence and childhood, red for growing maturity, multi-coloured for middle life, purple and gold for the wisdom of maturity and golden radiance for Life after Death). But I have never been in any doubt that in the complex relationship between content

285

and form, the artist who is aiming at a richness of decorative harmony is always stimulated to aesthetic inventiveness when compelled to work to a prescribed meaning. That the meanings should be decipherable or the symbols intelligible is of less importance than that there should be a close correspondence between content and design, between end and means. And in the ten great windows at Coventry this correspondence is traceable throughout. To put it in the simplest possible terms, the windows may not illustrate a story but they communicate a mood and in doing so reinforce the sense of a specific dedication to a specific faith.

Graham Sutherland's tapestry sets no such problem. The symbolism is both simple and, being founded on centuries of tradition, familiar. The dominant image of Christ enthroned in Glory, surrounded by the accepted symbols of the Four Evangelists, was common enough in the twelfth century. The artist's task was not so much to make the image powerful and convincing as to avoid the appearance of being a pastiche. What Sutherland had to do was both to create an overpowering presence in contemporary terms and to escape from the immense pressure of the long series of prototypes, themselves overpowering, that had been invented, developed and repeated with variations by a hundred Romanesque artists of the twelfth century, and always with the same end in view, that of imagining a presence whose effect should be at once radiant and powerful, compassionate yet awe-inspiring, gentle yet inescapable, and which, physically, should be gigantic without dwarfing the cathedral that contained it.

Sutherland has fully explained how he tackled this almost insoluble problem in *The Coventry Tapestry*, a book which is in itself a valuable contribution to the whole question of Christian art as seen through the mind of the artist himself, tracing each stage in the development from the first conception to the completion of the final image.

The Burghclere chapel and the interior of Coventry Cathedral are probably the most satisfying examples of Christian art done in England in this century. The former is the outpouring of an artist to whom religion was a personal experience and religious art a branch of autobiography: the latter is an example of a

Graham Sutherland. *Christ in Glory in the Tetramorph*, tapestry on the east wall of Coventry Cathedral, 1952-62

Ronchamp, when Le Corbusier built his chapel there in the early 1950s, had attracted pilgrims for over four hundred years: the porch on the right accommodates large groups of people at services in the open air

tradition centuries old brought up to date by contemporary minds working as a team. In both cases the fact that the buildings themselves are specifically related to the works they contain is of the greatest importance to the final effect. No isolated masterpiece in a museum can have quite the same hold over the imagination, and when one remembers that far more than half of the greatest examples of Christian art of the past are now to be found - admittedly well hung, well cared for and far better lit than they could have been in their original settings - in art galleries, one realizes that it is not always the artist's own imaginative power but his capacity to co-operate with his patron or architect that is the key to the story of Christian art. The mosaics of San Vitale, the stained-glass windows of Chartres or Bourges, the illuminated manuscripts of the thirteenth or fourteenth centuries are hardly detachable from their contexts.

Disillusionment and hope
WILLIAM NEIL

As the glittering splendour of the Imperial procession rolled along the Mall at Queen Victoria's Diamond Jubilee in 1897, or when the crowned heads of Europe assembled four years later for her funeral, it must have appeared to most spectators that though it was the end of an era there was no reason to suppose that the next one would be basically different. Europe still dominated the world, the British Empire maintained its supremacy over its far-flung possessions, stable monarchies and ancient aristocracies looked confidently into the future, prosperity and progress seemed assured. The theological counterpart of this optimistic view of the world was the current belief in the gradual realization of the Kingdom of God on earth by social reform at home and missionary enterprise abroad, by education and the increase of scientific knowledge, by the spread of democracy and the general improvement of the lot of mankind.

Sixty years later we may be inclined to echo Matthew Arnold's words: 'We stand between two worlds, one dead, the other powerless to be born'. The year 1914 ended a great chapter in human history, the bombing of Hiroshima in 1945 opened another. The Atomic Age has been announced and it is still far from clear whether the outcome will be one world or no world. What we *can* say is that there have been more radical alterations in the way of life for mankind in general over the past century than there have been in the whole history of Christianity. The early Victorians had more in common with the Romans at the time of Christ than we have with the early Victorians.

If we may take 1914 as the real beginning of the twentieth century its first half has been signally chaotic and confused. It has been a period of national and international upheavals on an unparalleled scale. There have been two World Wars, one international economic disaster, four major revolutions - in Russia, Italy, Germany and Spain - to say nothing of almost universal political eruptions. The United States has emerged as the greatest power in history, the Afro-Asian peoples have come of age or have thrown off their shackles, but to offset these advances the Iron Curtain and the Cold War have unhappily become painful features of the daily scene, with China like an active volcano rumbling uncomfortingly on the horizon.

It would be small wonder if twentieth-century man, unlike his Victorian predecessor, were to see little evidence of any providential order in world affairs, still less any signs of the uninterrupted march of man towards the Kingdom of God on earth. Yet in terms of material progress, which was to the Victorians part of the grounds for their buoyant optimism, twentieth-century man - at least in the Western hemisphere - has now at his disposal the fruits of an unprecedented technological revolution which provides him with his car, his television, his electric gadgets, his mastery of the air and other such benefits, most of which he takes for granted. He lives in a standard of comfort which was the exclusive preserve of the wealthy in the nineteenth century, though in his more reflective moments he might see the point of Hilaire Belloc's wry comment: 'When science has discovered something more, We'll all be happier than before'. He might even subscribe to Aldous Huxley's verdict that we have discovered improved means to an unimproved end.

The First World War was embarked on like a crusade. Men joined up and were sped on their way amid scenes of wild enthusiasm. No one then knew what modern war was really like. They came back in disillusionment and bitterness to find no land fit for heroes to live in and no world safe for democracy. They had come through a slaughter which seemed to have been the acme of pointlessness and their mood was well expressed by C. E. Montague in the title and substance of his book called: *Disenchantment*. So between the wars came the 'Debunking Age', characterized by what Lord Elton in *St George or the Dragon* called 'The Assault on Morale', meaning by 'morale' the military virtues of loyalty, courage and endurance; the philosophical virtues of beauty, goodness and truth;

294

Russian soldiers in World War I, before the Communist suppression of religion: on their flag is Veronica's Veil, and the motto 'God is with us'

the social virtues of freedom, justice and mercy; the theological virtues of faith, hope and charity. All of these were attacked between the wars as reactionary.

The first shot was fired by Lytton Strachey's *Eminent Victorians*, published in 1921. In it he set about dethroning the gods of the nineteenth century. These genuinely eminent and notable figures were depicted neither as heroes nor as villains but as merely slightly ridiculous. Everything that in Victoria's day counted as 'virtuous' was sneered at as bogus. From then on the fashion spread until, as Elton said, people were ready to 'titter at almost anything and admire almost nothing'. Religious orthodoxy, church-going and family religion, which were practised extensively by the Victorians, came in for their share of titters.

As a definite gain this led to the end of religious humbug of which there was plenty in Victorianism. It was a gain too that it was no longer profitable to be 'respectable' or to be a churchman. A friend who spent his boyhood in Eastbourne recalls that it was the done thing from twelve to one o'clock on Sundays to parade in front of the Grand Hotel with a Prayer Book under the arm. This showed that you were the

295

kind of person who went to church (whether you had been there or not), and, equally important, that you were the kind of person who did not need to cook his own dinner. This unholy alliance of religion with 'respectability' has now happily come to an end.

The cause of the debunking of morals and religion was partly the disillusionment and fatigue brought on by the First World War, partly the agnosticism which was fostered by popular peddlers of pseudo-science and pseudo-religion like Bernard Shaw and H. G. Wells, and partly the materialistic outlook which was the consequence of too rapid technical progress. Under the impact of these three antagonists it was difficult to feel intensely about anything. Moral values such as courage and loyalty were suspect. The new psychology of Freud and his disciples put large question marks against the nature and grounds of religious conviction. Self-expression rather than self-discipline provided a more attractive programme. Investigation of the sub-conscious was undoubtedly more entertaining than the cult of the supernatural.

So it came about in what have been called the Decadent Decades between the two World Wars that for large masses of the population in the Western world the traditional pattern of Christian belief and moral standards was shattered and discredited. There appeared to be no particular purpose or meaning in life, no faith to live by, no future to work for. This was reflected in the literature, art and music of the time. The literary world produced writers like James Joyce, the early T. S. Eliot and Gertrude Stein. Their writings made nonsense because they felt that the world was nonsense. In art the Surrealists painted three circles and a washtub and called it 'Sunset on the Underground' and the enigmatic Salvador Dali produced a composition which depicted the debris of an automobile giving birth to a blind horse biting a telephone. In music Hindemith clattered his brasses and tympani like hell let loose, and America introduced jungle culture on to the ballroom floor.

It is at this point that mention must be made of Søren Kierkegaard. Like William Blake whom he resembles in many respects he was one 'born out of due season'. Nothing could

XVI GRAHAM SUTHERLAND
The Crucifixion, 1946, in St Matthew's, Northampton

XVII STANLEY SPENCER
The Resurrection, Cookham (detail), 1923-26

have been more unlike the placid temper of the established Church of Denmark in the first half of the nineteenth century than the violent and revolutionary ideas of this stormy theological individualist. For him a Christian was a man who had seen through the bogus claims of philosophical, doctrinal and ecclesiastical systems: who saw himself to be a helpless creature trembling on the edge of an abyss or struggling for his life in an empty ocean. Only when out of the turmoil of his own experience he reached the point where he knew that there was no certainty but Christ and took the leap of faith could he find salvation.

Trained as a theologian, Kierkegaard rejected organized religion and held Christianity to be intensely personal

The otherness of God, the depravity of man, the reality of evil, the sense of guilt, the irrationality of life, Christianity as a religion of paradoxes which are beyond understanding, the Church and Christendom as travesties of New Testament teaching, the questioning of all authority, distrust of democracy, science and education, the key to life as an 'either-or' decision for Christ - these were the themes that dominated Kierkegaard's voluminous writings. He lived from 1813-1855 and it is not surprising that the nineteenth century felt that he had nothing of value to say to it. When the stir of his polemics had died down in Denmark he was largely forgotten. His contemporaries mostly regarded him as mentally unbalanced. It was left to the twentieth century, after the First World War, to rediscover him and to find that he spoke to its condition. He has been claimed as the father of existentialist philosophy and the 'theology of crisis', both of which came into prominence at that time. He is still venerated by some as a prophet and dismissed by others as a pathological neurotic.

But he matched the temper of the more thoughtful elements in a generation which had lost faith in the panaceas of politicians and preachers. The specious optimism which had looked forward to man's evolutionary progress by the exercise of his reason, by humanitarian idealism, by following the precepts of the Sermon on the Mount, had been exposed by the irrationality of the 1914-18 war as a caricature of the truth. Life, it had been found, meant tragedy, suffering, the clash of national interests, exploitation and self-assertiveness. Theologians like Johannes Weiss and Albert Schweitzer had looked

297

at the New Testament again and had found there no gentle Jesus promising a rose-strewn path to the Kingdom of God but a strange and cryptic figure who spoke in terms of crisis and judgment, of conflict and disaster.

The 'liberal' theology of nineteenth-century Europe had offered, in the words of Richard Niebuhr, 'a God without wrath who brought men without sin into a kingdom without judgment through the ministrations of a Christ without a cross'. This had filled the churches with docile and complacent believers who had not even begun to understand the depth and the mystery of the faith they professed to follow, who had neither come face to face with the sovereignty of God nor seen the need for their own redemption. What was wanted in the Decadent Decades was a new prophetic voice in the Church, powerful and arresting and radical enough to cut away the dead wood of conventional religion and proclaim the Faith to a generation that had lost its bearings.

It is not surprising that the voice spoke German, since it was in Germany that the post-war chaos was most acute, or that the prophetic fire of Karl Barth was kindled by his study of Kierkegaard, who seemed to him to have with uncanny prescience taken the measure of the hollow gospel of a brave new world. Significantly enough the first blast of his trumpet was a Commentary on the Epistle to the Romans, published in 1918, in which in the great succession of St Augustine and Luther he sought by returning to the mind of St Paul to reset the compass of the Church and correct its errors. Barth is of course a Protestant, with the limitations that the word implies, yet he would probably be acknowledged even by Catholics who differ from him at many points to be, *pace* Jacques Maritain, the greatest theologian of this century. His influence has certainly been enormous.

This is not to say by any means that his views have been generally accepted. Anglo-Saxons on the whole find his immense tomes indigestible and often incomprehensible. Many cannot subscribe to his denial of the possibility of knowing anything about God except through the Bible, his insistence on the total corruption of the intellect, his denigration of all human effort to shape the future, his definition of faith as 'a leap into the void'. Yet his re-emphasis of the Transcendence of God and the sinfulness of man, together with his reiterated claim that every human institution, including the Church, stands constantly under the Judgment of God and constantly in need of reform, have effectively counteracted the humanistic gradualism of the nineteenth century. Nor should it be forgotten that the splendid resistance of the German Confessional Movement to Hitler's attempt to make the Church a tool of the State was the product of Barthian theology.

By the end of the Second World War in 1945 the religious scene in Europe was vastly different from what it had been in 1914. Atheistic communism had suppressed the Church in what had once been Holy Mother Russia, and the Iron Curtain which was shortly to divide the East from the West brought to Orthodox, Catholics and Protestants beyond it heavy losses, deprivation of civil rights and persecution. In the West, communism had a powerful following even in Catholic Italy and had only with difficulty been driven underground in Catholic Spain. Lapsed masses were as much of a problem in traditionally Catholic countries as in Protestant lands. While nominal allegiance was still evidenced by Church baptisms and burials, it was generally estimated that by the middle of the twentieth century the average percentage of Europeans actively associated with any branch of the Christian Church was at the most ten per cent.

Prognostication is best left to the astrologers. But if one were to assess the present position of Christianity in relation to the past two thousand years one would be bound to say that the prospects are no more discouraging than the New Testament leads us to expect. This would still be true were the above-mentioned ten per cent to become one per cent. Obviously personal conviction cannot be eliminated in any such assessment. If it is felt that Christianity has simply been a necessary phase in mankind's development, to be superseded by something else - communism, scientific humanism, synthetic religion or religionless morality - then obviously there is no place in the future structure of civilization for a Church which bears any resemblance to the traditional pattern. If on the other hand the Church is believed to be the divinely

299

instituted instrument of the world's salvation its survival is beyond question.

Those who take the latter view will look back on Hiroshima not as the beginning of the end of the world but as the final warning to Western civilization. If the warning is unheeded it will mean the disappearance of Christian culture as it has taken shape over the past twenty centuries, and the next phase in the history of the Church, perhaps in Africa or Asia, may well be something more akin to its oriental origins. The beginnings of indigenous forms of worship and artistic expression can already be seen in the younger churches overseas, where the nineteenth-century fallacy of identifying Christianity with Western civilization is rapidly being corrected. A white Pope is no more essential to the survival of the Church than is capitalism or democracy.

There is good reason to hope, however, that the warning of Hiroshima may be heeded. If the combined efforts of statesmanship and a United Nations police force succeed in achieving a period of greater stability, the prospects for Christianity in the West are brighter than they would appear. For in a curious way the Second World War, which ought in theory to have completed the process of disillusionment and disintegration of faith which the First World War initiated, has on the contrary had a cathartic effect. The spectacle of Christian nations engaged in mutual slaughter, with each side claiming divine sanction and protection, which had for so many made Christianity meaningless in the 1914-18 War, was in the Second World War replaced by a purposeful effort by all who cared for humanity to destroy the power of evil incarnated in the Nazi war-machine.

However the issues were complicated by national interests, the gospel of Adolf Hitler judged by its fruits in anti-Semitism, slave-labour and concentration camps, compelled many who had been prepared to write off the Church as irrelevant, to take a fresh look at Christianity and to see new meaning in its doctrines of original sin, the reality of evil, the judgment of God and the sacredness of human personality. The Western world emerged from the Second World War with a wholesome fear of bringing about the total annihilation of its own civil-

The ruins of Coventry Cathedral, painted by John Piper after the 1940 bombing

ization, including its precious heritage of freedom and justice, and its legacy of art and literature. Combined with that was the determination to profit from past mistakes, to co-operate with men of goodwill anywhere whatever their religious beliefs or political convictions, to build a more just and equitable society at home and to grapple with the problems of poverty and ignorance abroad.

Political setbacks since 1945 have made it impossible to take this programme very far, yet it would be wrong to fail to recognize the contribution of Christianity to such recent

301

developments as the attack on the colour bar, the end of colonialism and the emergence of new nations, War on Want, the Welfare State, United Nations, the rehabilitation of Germany. No one could call these years the Decadent Decades. Tension, conflict, danger - yes! but disillusionment and despair - no! Christianity is at home in such a situation and thrives best when human foundations are most violently shaken. It cannot be said, however, that the Church has as yet risen to meet the challenge of the times. The innate conservatism of religious institutions, the unadventurous temper of clergy and laity, the drag of outworn denominational shibboleths are only too depressingly obvious.

Yet there are signs in plenty of a new stirring of the Spirit within the Church. There has never been a time when the Church has been so critical of itself and of its failure to fulfil its task. Concern to heal the divisions that make a mockery of the claim to be the Body of Christ has never been so acute. The beginning of a rapprochement between the Vatican and the Churches of the Reformation promises to heal the tragic schism of four centuries. The Liturgical Movement both in Catholicism and Protestantism seeks to find modes of worship more meaningful to twentieth-century men and women. Catholics and Protestants alike have also been led to a new discovery of the present relevance of the Bible, and the shared insights of scholars in all branches of the Church are gradually ensuring that the timeless message of the Scriptures is restated in terms of the present day.

There is a wind of change too among the theologians. The 'Honest to God' debate in England has drawn public attention to the stimulating ideas of Rudolf Bultmann, Paul Tillich and Dietrich Bonhoeffer, whose writings seek along various channels to come to grips with the problem of what we mean when we say 'God', what is the truth about Jesus of Nazareth, and indeed what is the nature of Christianity. Whatever emerges from this theological ferment there is clearly no lack today of the thinking and questioning which is the mark of a living Church. On the practical side experiments are being made with new forms of mission through house-churches and industrial chaplaincies, and with new approaches to religion through drama, music and television. The range and sale of popular paperback religious books is no sign of a dying Church. An evangelistic revival on the nineteenth-century pattern is neither likely nor desirable but the Spirit of God is undoubtedly at work in the Church today leading it to new insights and new ways of showing the relevance of the Faith in an atomic age.

The theme of this book has been a survey of Christian art in the first two thousand years of the Church's story and an attempt to show how the artistic expression of any particular period has been to a large extent conditioned by the theological climate. It is always more difficult to recognize trends and movements and to see events in proper perspective when we live in the midst of them. But by and large it would seem that so far the art and sculpture of the present century are what we should expect in a period which began with apparently solid foundations which proved to be shifting sands, which passed through a stage of disillusionment, and has now begun to reach towards a truer appraisal of the nature of Christian belief and worship and of the place of the Church in the world.

Eric Newton has asked why it is that so little of importance in the field of Christian art - apart from the work of Georges Rouault - has been produced in the last half-century in France compared with England. Part of the answer would seem to be that without the stimulus of inspired patronage England would have been as barren of creative religious art as France or for that matter the rest of Europe. Stanley Spencer would appear to be the exception who proves the rule, a child of his time who yet because of his deep personal faith refused to subscribe to its nihilistic philosphy. Graham Sutherland, on the other hand, may be said to reflect the beginning of the reawakening of a genuinely Catholic art in the modern idiom. It is fitting to end with the spotlight on Coventry Cathedral. All over Europe there are signs of a new consciousness on the part of the Church, in architecture and sculpture, in woodwork and silver, of the part that modern art forms can play in kindling the religious imagination, in teaching Christian doctrine, and in leading men's hearts and minds to make

303

the fullest possible response to the revelation of God in Jesus Christ. Nowhere is this more evident, however, than in Coventry where the adventurous and successful teamwork of architect and artists is matched by a dedicated staff of clergy and laymen who are alive to the present issues and are, like the artists, seeking new ways to communicate the traditional Faith. Here is surely a rediscovery of the proper relationship between art and evangelism which has been characteristic of the Church at its best. In the total world picture it is as yet a cloud no bigger than a man's hand, but it is rich in promise.

NOTES ON THE ILLUSTRATIONS

Numbers refer to pages

2 Christ in Glory, detail of an ivory bookcover; German, 7th C. *Staatliche Museen, Berlin-Dahlem*

5 Pectoral cross of St Cuthbert, of gold inlaid with garnets; English (Northumberland), 7th C. *Durham Cathedral*

9 Detail of the icon *Our Lady of Vladimir;* Russian, 12th C. with subsequent overpaintings. Tretyakov Gallery, Moscow. From Anisimov, *Our Lady of Vladimir*

19 The Werden Crucifix, of bronze, just over 3¹⁄₂ ft high; German (Hildesheim), *c.* 1070. Abbey Church, Werden. Photo *Marburg*

20 Ravenna: doves at a fountain, detail of a mosaic in the Mausoleum of Galla Placidia; mid-5th C. Photo *Mansell-Anderson*

21 Rome: head of Christ, detail of a fresco in the Catacomb of Peter and Marcellinus; *c.* 400. From Wilpert, *Le Pitture delle Catacombe*

22 Kwuzat Hefzibah, Israel: the Ark of the Covenant, mosaic in Beth-Alpha Synagogue; 6th C.

23 Reconstruction of Solomon's Temple at Jerusalem, after Stevens' drawing based on information from W. F. Allbright and G. E. Wright; 10th C. BC. After *The Biblical Archaeologist*, XVIII, 2

26 Fragment of the Isaiah Scroll, from the Dead Sea caves; between 4th C. BC and AD 135. *Palestine Archaeological Museum*

27 St Paul disputing with the Greeks, gilt copper plaque inset with *champlevé* enamel; English (Winchester), *c.* 1160. *Victoria and Albert Museum, London (Crown copyright)*

28 Kwuzat Hefzibah, Israel: the sacrifice of Isaac, mosaic in Beth-Alpha Synagogue; 6th C.

29 Rome: St Peter, detail of a fresco in the Catacomb of Peter and Marcellinus; late 3rd C. From Wilpert, *Le Pitture delle Catacombe*

30 Rome: a vine, fresco in the Catacomb of Domitilla; 1st C. AD. From Wilpert, *Le Pitture delle Catacombe*

31 Early Christian funerary stele carved with the fish and the anchor. Museo delle Terme, Rome. Photo *Pontificia Commissione di Archeologia Sacra*

33 Bronze cross in the form of the monogram of Christ, with the letters Alpha and Omega as pendants; perhaps from the Eastern Mediterranean, 5th C. *Kunsthistorisches Museum, Vienna*

35 Ravenna: exterior of S. Vitale from the south; 525-47. Photo *Mansell-Alinari*

39 Ravenna: mosaic panel showing the miracle of the loaves and fishes, in the nave of S. Apollinare Nuovo; from the time of Theodoric, early 6th C. Photo *Mansell-Alinari*

42 Ravenna: mosaic lunette in the Mausoleum of Galla Placidia showing St Lawrence with the grid on which he was martyred and, on the left, a cupboard containing the four Gospels; mid-5th C. Photo *Mansell-Alinari*

43 Ravenna: detail of the north wall of the nave of S. Apollinare Nuovo. In the two upper rows are scenes of the life and miracles of Christ, and figures of prophets; in the bottom row, a procession of virgins moving towards the east. The upper rows date from the time of Theodoric, early 6th C., while the bottom row is part of Justinian's scheme and dates from the mid-6th C. Photo *Mansell-Anderson*

44 Ravenna: mosaic in the conch of the apse of S. Vitale, showing Christ in Glory flanked by two angels, between S. Vitale and Bishop Ecclesius (founder of the church); mid-6th C. Photo *Hirmer*

45 Ravenna: mosaic on the north side of the chancel of S. Vitale, showing part of the story of Abraham; around it are the figures of Jeremiah and Moses, and the Israelites with Aaron at the foot of Mount Sinai; mid-6th C. Photo *Mansell-Alinari*

305

47 Ravenna: mosaic on the north wall of the chancel of S. Vitale, showing the Emperor Justinian, with bodyguards and courtiers, preceded by Archbishop Maximian and two priests; mid-6th C. Photo *Mansell-Alinari*

48 Rome: fresco of the three men in the fiery furnace, in the Catacomb of Priscilla; early 4th C. Photo *Hirmer*

49 Ivory throne of Maximian, Archbishop of Ravenna; probably made at Ravenna, mid-6th C. Archiepiscopal Museum, Ravenna. Photo *Hirmer*

51 The Harbaville ivory triptych; Byzantine (Constantinople), late 10th or early 11th C. Louvre, Paris. Photo *Hirmer*

52 David playing the harp, miniature from the *Paris Psalter*; Byzantine (Constantinople), mid-10th C. *Bibliothèque Nationale, Paris*

53 Metal book-cover decorated with pearls and *champlevé* enamel; Byzantine, 10th C. *Biblioteca Marciana, Venice*

54 Rome: mosaic of Abraham with the three angels, in Sta Maria Maggiore; mid-5th C. Photo *Mansell-Alinari*

55 Rome: two mosaics in Sta Prassede, showing the Virgin and Child *(left)*, and an angel of the Apocalypse; 9th C. Photo *Georgina Masson*

57 Venice: mosaic dome in the atrium of St Mark's, showing the Creation and the story of Adam and Eve; 12th C. Photo *Alinari*

59 Venice: mosaic in the atrium of St Mark's, showing Noah's drunken sleep during which his sons Shem and Japheth cover his nakedness, his reproof of his son Ham who had seen him naked, and his death; 12th C. Photo *Mansell-Alinari*

60-1 Torcello, near Venice: detail of the Last Judgment mosaic, on the west wall of the Cathedral. Christ sits in Glory between Mary and St John, surrounded by saints and angels, while below Him is the Book with the Seven Seals and, to the left, Hell; early 12th C. Photo *Mansell-Alinari*

62 Monreale, Sicily: interior of the Cathedral, looking east; late 12th C. Photo *Martin Hürlimann*

63 Palermo, Sicily: interior of the Cappella Palatina, looking west; 1132-89. Photo *Mansell-Alinari*

65 Rome: fresco of the Good Shepherd, in the Catacomb of Priscilla; first half of the 3rd C. Photo *Hirmer*

66 Roman marble bust of the Emperor Nero (54-68). *Trustees of the British Museum*

67 Roman mosaic showing bound Christians attacked by leopards. Tripoli Museum. Photo *Roger Wood*

69 Detail of ivory plaque showing the Forty Martyrs of Sebaste; Byzantine, 10th-11th C. *Staatliche Museen, Berlin-Dahlem*

70 God the Great Architect, frontispiece to a manuscript of the Old Testament; French, mid-13th C. *Österreichische Nationalbibliothek, Vienna*

71 Rome: interior of a catacomb. Photo *Mansell-Anderson*

73 Rome: fresco representing the miracle of the loaves and fishes, in the Catacomb of Calixtus; end of the 2nd C. From Wilpert, *Le Pitture delle Catacombe*

75 Rome: two frescoes in the Catacomb of Priscilla, showing Noah in the Ark *(above)*, and the sacrifice of Isaac *(below)*; early 2nd C. and late 3rd C. From Wilpert, *Le Pitture delle Catacombe*

77 Rome: detail of a mosaic showing the Baptism of Constantine, in the Church of the SS. Quattro Coronati; 12th C. Photo *Mansell-Alinari*

79 Medal commemorating the founding of the city of Constantinople in 330, bearing a bust of the personified city. British Museum. Photo *P. A. Clayton*

81 Cefalù, Sicily: east end of the Cathedral, showing the mosaics; 12th C. Photo *Jean Roubier*

83 Miniature from the *Vivian Bible*; French (Tours), 843-51. Count Vivian, lay-abbot of St Martin at Tours (in the centre at the extreme right), leads a delegation from his abbey to present the *Vivian Bible* to King Charles the Bald. *Bibliothèque Nationale, Paris*

84 St Jerome dictating to a scribe, detail of miniature from the *Cologne Gospel-Book*; German, mid-11th C. Staatsbibliothek, Bamberg. Photo *Hirmer*

85 St Augustine, miniature from a MS of Augustine's *De civitate Dei*; English, *c.* 1100. Biblioteca Medicea-Laurenziana, Florence. Photo *Sansoni*

86 Icon of St Simeon Stylites; Russian, 16th C. *Louvre, Paris*

87 Lincoln: detail of stained glass in the Cathedral showing the head of a haloed man, almost certainly Christ; 13th C. Photo *Alfred Lammer*

89 Vézelay: tympanum in the narthex of La Madeleine, *c.* 1125-30. The subject is the mission of the Apostles, combined with Pentecost: surrounding the central figures are vignettes of the peoples of the world, on the trumeau St John the Baptist prefigures the coming of Christ, and to the right SS. Peter and Paul descend to the unconverted peoples. Photo *Giraudon*

90 *Left.* St Mark, miniature from the *Lindisfarne Gospels*; Northumbrian, *c.* 700. *Trustees of the British Museum*

Right. St Luke, miniature from the *St Gall Gospels*; Irish, mid-8th C. *Stiftsbibliothek, St Gallen*

91 God admonishing Adam and Eve after the Fall, panel on the bronze doors made for the Benedictine church of St Michael at Hildesheim; German, 1015. Photo *Marburg*

92 Arles: tympanum of St Trophime, showing Christ in Glory; *c.* 1170-80. Photo *Giraudon*

93 Autun: capital by Gislebertus in St Lazare showing the Temptation of Christ; *c.* 1130. Photo *Jean Roubier*

95 Christ in Glory, miniature from the *Limoges Sacramentary*; French (from the Cathedral of St Etienne at Limoges), *c.* 1100. *Bibliothèque Nationale, Paris*

97 Berzé-la-Ville: wall-painting in the Cluniac grange, showing the martyrdom of St Lawrence; 11th C. Photo *Archives Photographiques*

98 *Left.* Souillac: Isaiah, on the jamb of the portal of the abbey church; *c.* 1110. Photo *Jean Roubier*

Centre. Virgin and Child of gilt and painted wood, from the priory of St-Martin-des-Champs in Paris; *c.* 1130. Abbey church of St Denis. Photo *Giraudon*

Right. Moissac: St Peter, on the jamb of the portal of the abbey of St Pierre; *c.* 1135. Photo *Archives Photographiques*

99 Benedetto Antelami: *The Crucifixion*, 1178, in Parma Cathedral. Photo *Mansell-Anderson*

101 Angoulême: detail of the façade of the Cathedral, *c.* 1140. Photo *Archives Photographiques*

102 Paris: air view of Notre Dame from the south-west; late 12th-early 13th C. Photo *Aerofilms*

103 Reims: west front of the Cathedral; *c.* 1255-90, towers early 15th C. Photo *Giraudon*

105 Bourges: tympanum of the central west portal of the Cathedral, showing the Last Judgment; *c.* 1270-80. Photo *Martin Hürlimann*

107 Beauvais: interior of the choir of the Cathedral; 1247-72. Photo *Bulloz*

108 *Left.* Lorenzo Maitani: one of the damned, detail of a marble plaque on the façade of Orvieto Cathedral, *c.* 1310-50. Photo *Mansell-Anderson*

Right. Naumburg: detail of the Betrayal, on the choir screen in the Cathedral, *c.* 1260. Photo *Martin Hürlimann*

109 Chartres: the Dormition of the Virgin, stained glass medallion in the south aisle of the Cathedral; 13th C.

110 *Left.* The Virgin and Child enthroned, adored by a clerical figure, miniature from the so-called *Missal of Henry of Chichester*; English, mid-13th C. *The John Rylands Library, Manchester*

Right. The Crucifixion, miniature from the *Psalter of Robert de Lisle (Arundel Psalter)*. English (East Anglia), early 14th C. *Trustees of the British Museum*

111 The fall of the rebel Angels, miniature by the Limbourg brothers from the *Très Riches Heures du duc de Berry*; French, 1413 16 Musée Condé, Chantilly. Photo *Giraudon*

113 The Mass of the Dead, detail of miniature from the *Milan Hours* (now destroyed); Flemish (attributed to Jan van Eyck), late 15th C. *Museo Civico, Turin*

115 Emperor Henry IV imploring Matilda of Tuscany and Abbot Hugh of Cluny, miniature, from the *Vita Matildis*; early 12th C *Bibliotheca Apostolica Vaticana*

116 *Left.* Francesco Traini: St Thomas Aquinas, from *The Apotheosis of St Thomas Aquinas*, fresco in Sta Caterina at Pisa, 1341. Photo *Mansell-Anderson*

Right. Statue of St Bernard, in the Church of the Assumption at Labussière-sur-Ouche, near Dijon; 15th C. Photo *André Fasquel*

118 St Francis preaching to the birds, drawing from Matthew Paris' *Chronica majora*; English (St Albans), mid-13th C. *By permission of the Master and Fellows of Corpus Christi College, Cambridge*

119 Subiaco: detail of a portrait of St Francis, from a fresco in the Chapel of St Gregory in the Lower Church of the Sacro Speco; *c.* 1220. St Francis, who was canonized in 1228, appears here without a halo: it is, according to Focillon, perhaps one of the few true portraits of the period. Photo *Mansell-Alinari*

120 The Two Witnesses of the Apocalypse shown as Dominican friars preaching the impending Judgment, in a miniature from the *Douce Apocalypse*; English, *c.* 1270. *Curators of the Bodleian Library, Oxford*

121 Domenico di Michelino: fresco in Florence Cathedral, showing Dante with a MS of *La Divina Commedia*, standing between Hell, Purgatory, and his native city of Florence; 1465. Photo *Mansell-Alinari*

123 Botticelli: head of the *Madonna with the Pomegranate*, 1487. Uffizi, Florence. Photo *Mansell-Alinari*

127 Giotto: *The Lamentation*, fresco in the Arena Chapel at Padua, *c.* 1306. Photo *Mansell-Alinari*

128 Giotto: detail of *The Betrayal*, fresco in the Arena Chapel at Padua, *c.* 1306. Photo *Mansell-Alinari*

129 Giotto: detail of *Joachim and the Shepherds*, fresco in the Arena Chapel at Padua, *c.* 1306. Photo *Mansell-Alinari*

131 Nicola Pisano: *The Adoration of the Magi*, panel of the hexagonal marble pulpit in the Baptistery at Pisa, 1259. Photo *Mansell-Alinari*

133 Fra Angelico (attrib.): *The Annunciation*, on the upper half of a painted tabernacle or altarpiece formerly in Sta Maria Novella in Florence, *c.* 1425-35. The painting is also attributed to Zanobi Strozzi. Museo S. Marco, Florence. Photo *Mansell-Alinari*

134 Fra Angelico: the Virgin and St Mary Magdalen, detail of *The Deposition*, fresco in S. Marco in Florence, *c.* 1440. Photo *Mansell-Alinari*

135 Benozzo Gozzoli: detail of the cavalcade from *The Journey of the Magi*, fresco in the Chapel of the Medici Palace in Florence, 1459. Photo *Mansell-Alinari*

137 Masaccio: fresco of *The Expulsion*, in the Brancacci Chapel of Sta Maria del Carmine in Florence, *c.* 1425-28. Photo *Alinari*

138 Piero della Francesca: *The Resurrection*, fresco in the Palazzo Communale at Borgo San Sepolcro, *c.* 1460. Photo *Anderson*

139 Antonio Pollaiuolo: *The Martyrdom of St Sebastian*, *c.* 1475. *By courtesy of the Trustees of the National Gallery, London*

141 Botticelli: detail of *Mystic Nativity*, 1500. *By courtesy of the Trustees of the National Gallery, London*

142 Leonardo da Vinci: *The Virgin of the Rocks*, formerly the central picture of an altarpiece, 1483. *By courtesy of the Trustees of the National Gallery, London*

143 Michelangelo: detail of *God separating the Earth from the sea*, on the frescoed ceiling of the Sistine Chapel in the Vatican, 1508-12. Photo *Mansell-Alinari*

144 Michelangelo: *Pietà*, *c.* 1500, in St Peter's, Rome. Photo *Mansell-Alinari*

145 Michelangelo: the *Rondanini Pietà*, unfinished in 1564. Castello Sforzesco, Milan. Photo *Mansell-Alinari*

147 *Left*. Raphael: *The Ansidei Madonna*, *c.* 1505-7. *By courtesy of the Trustees of the National Gallery, London*

Right. Raphael: *The Transfiguration*, begun in 1517. *Vatican Galleries*

149 Vittore Carpaccio: *St Ursula in Glory*, from a series begun in 1490 for the Scuola di Sta Orsola in Venice. Accademia, Venice. Photo *Mansell-Anderson*

150 Titian: detail of *The Assumption of the Virgin*, in Sta Maria dei Frari in Venice, 1516-18. Photo *Mansell-Anderson*

151 Tintoretto: *The Last Supper*, in S. Giorgio Maggiore in Venice, *c.* 1590-94. Photo *Mansell-Anderson*

152 Tintoretto: detail of *The Crucifixion*, in the Scuola di S. Rocco, Venice, 1565. Photo *Mansell-Anderson*

153 Avignon School: the *Villeneuve Pietà*, *c.* 1460, formerly in the Charterhouse of Val-de-Bénédiction at Villeneuve-lès-Avignon. Musée Calvet, Avignon. Photo *Bulloz*

154 Jan and Hubert van Eyck: detail of *The Adoration of the Lamb*, central panel of the Ghent Altarpiece, 1432. St Bavon, Ghent. Photo *ACL*

155 Tilman Riemenschneider: detail of *The Assumption of the Virgin* from the Creglingen Altarpiece, *c*. 1505-10. Parish Church, Creglingen. Photo *Georg Schaffert*

Veit Stoss: *The Dormition of the Virgin*, centre of the Cracow Altarpiece, 1477-88. St Mary's, Cracow. Photo *Kolowca Stanislaw (ZAIKS)*

156 Dürer: the Four Horsemen (Death, Famine, War, and Pestilence), woodcut from the *Apocalypse* series, 1498. *Trustees of the British Museum*

157 Grünewald: detail of *The Entombment*, panel of the Isenheim Altarpiece, from the abbey church of the Order of St Anthony at Isenheim, *c*. 1509-15; the Hermits of St Anthony maintained a hospital for sufferers from incurable diseases. Musée Unterlinden, Colmar. Photo *Thames and Hudson Archives*

159 Grünewald: *The Resurrection*, wing of the Isenheim Altarpiece, painted *c*. 1509-15 for the church of the Hermits of St Anthony at Isenheim. Musée Unterlinden, Colmar. Photo *Thames and Hudson Archives*

160 El Greco: detail of *The Burial of Count Orgaz*, *c*. 1585. S. Tomé, Toledo. Photo *Mas*

161 El Greco: *The Resurrection*, *c*. 1597-1604. Prado, Madrid. Photo *Mas*

163 Detail of the title-page of the Papal Bull of censure against Luther *(Exsurge Domine)*, bearing the Papal Insignia; 1520. British Museum. Photo *John Freeman*

165 Page of the Acts of the Apostles, from a manuscript of Wycliffe's English translation of the Bible; *c*. 1380. *Trustees of the British Museum*

166 Obverse of the *Baslerkonzilsbülle*, *c*. 1431. *Kunsthistorisches Museum, Vienna*

168 Raphael: head of Petrarch from the *Parnassus* fresco, commissioned by Pope Julius II for his private apartments *(stanze)* in the Vatican, 1509-14. Photo *Mansell-Anderson*

169 First page of Ariosto's *Orlando Furioso*, from the edition of 1542. British Museum. Photo *John Freeman*

171 Vatican, Rome: interior of the Sistine Chapel, looking toward the altar. The chapel was built in 1483 by Giovanni di Dolci; its paintings are of three periods: (1) 1481-82, walls painted by a team including Rosselli, Botticelli, Ghirlandaio and Perugino; (2) 1508-12, ceiling painted by Michelangelo; (3) 1536-41, altar wall painted by Michelangelo *(The Last Judgment)*. Photo *Mansell-Anderson*

172 Michelangelo: *God separating light from darkness*, detail of the frescoed ceiling of the Sistine Chapel in the Vatican, 1508-12. Photo *Mansell-Anderson*

173 Michelangelo: *The Creation of Adam*, detail of the frescoed ceiling of the Sistine Chapel in the Vatican, 1508-12. Photo *Mansell-Anderson*

174 Mantegna: *Christo Scorto (The Dead Christ)*, late 15th C. Brera, Milan. Photo *Mansell-Alinari*

175 Dürer: *The Virgin and Child with St Anne*, 1519. *The Metropolitan Museum of Art, New York*

176 Michael Ostendorfer: *Pilgrimage to the 'Schöne Maria' of Regensburg*, woodcut *c*. 1519-21. Staatliche Museen, Berlin-Dahlem. Photo *Walter Steinkopf*

177 Portrait of Savonarola, from a medal by Luca della Robbia, 1495. Bibliothèque Nationale, Paris. Photo *Jean Roubier*

178 Detail of a portrait of Erasmus by Hans Holbein the Younger, 1523. *Öffentliche Kunstsammlung, Basel*

179 Rubens: *The Holy Family under an Apple-Tree*, from the Ildefonso Altarpiece, 1630-32. *Kunsthistorisches Museum, Vienna*

183 Rubens: *The Great Last Judgment*, before 1618, commissioned for the Jesuit Church at Neuburg. Munich Pinakothek. Photo *Hanfstaengl*

185 Rubens: *The Assumption of the Virgin*, 1620. Kunstmuseum, Düsseldorf. Photo *Carlfred Halbach*

187 Rubens: *The Deposition*, central picture of an altarpiece for Antwerp Cathedral painted between 1611 and 1614. Koninklijk Museum voor Schone Kunsten, Antwerp. Photo *ACL*

188 Bernini: monument to Pope Alexander VII, 1671-78. St Peter's, Rome. Photo *Mansell-Anderson*

189 Gaulli (also called Baccicia): *The Adoration of the Name of Jesus*, painted ceiling of Il Gesù in Rome, 1668-85. Photo *Mansell-Alinari*

191 Rembrandt: detail of *The Adoration of the Shepherds*, 1646. Munich Pinakothek. Photo *Bayerische Staatsgemäldesammlung*

193 Rembrandt: *The Deposition*, c. 1637-45. By courtesy of the Trustees of the National Gallery, London

194 Caravaggio: *The Supper at Emmaus*, c. 1598. *By courtesy of the Trustees of the National Gallery, London*

195 Rembrandt: detail of *The Pilgrims of Emmaus*, 1648. Louvre, Paris. Photo *Giraudon*

196 Rembrandt: *The Raising of the Cross*, chalk drawing c. 1627-28. *Museum Boymans-van Beunigen, Rotterdam*

197 Rembrandt: *The Good Samaritan arriving at the Inn*, pen and wash drawing c. 1648. *Trustees of the British Museum*

198 Ribera: *The Lamentation over the Dead Christ*, c. 1645. By courtesy of the Trustees of the National Gallery, London

199 Zurbarán: *The Death of St Bonaventure*, one of a series of paintings of the saint for the Franciscan church of S. Buenaventura in Seville, 1629. Louvre, Paris Photo *Mansell-Giraudon*

200 Rembrandt: *The Annunciation*, pen drawing c. 1635. *Musée Communal, Besançon*

201 Detail of a woodcut of the Peasants' Revolt, from a German translation of Petrarch's *De Remediis utriusque Fortunae* printed at Augsburg in 1532. *Kupferstichkabinett, Berlin-Dahlem*

202 Woodcut showing the ship of the Church foundering, from Johann Lichtenberger's *Prenostication*, printed in Germany in 1526. British Museum. Photo *John Freeman*

204 Portrait of Luther by Lucas Cranach the Elder, 1520. Lutherhalle, Wittenberg. Photo *Marburg*

205 Detail of a portrait of Pope Leo X by Raphael, c. 1518. Palazzo Pitti, Florence. Photo *Mansell-Alinari*

206 Portrait of Calvin by an unknown French painter, c. 1550. *Museum Boymans-van Beuningen, Rotterdam*

208 Two woodcuts by Lucas Cranach the Elder from his *Passional of Christ and Anti-Christ*, printed at Wittenberg in 1521,

showing Christ ascending to Heaven and the Pope cast into Hell. British Museum. Photo *John Freeman*

209 Woodcut by Jörg Breu the Elder showing the sale of Indulgences in the early 16th C.

212 Titian (attrib.): *The Council of Trent*, shown in its final session in Trent Cathedral in 1564. Louvre, Paris. Photo *Giraudon*

213 Rubens: detail of *The Miracle of St Ignatius of Loyola*, from an altarpiece begun in 1620 for the Jesuit church in Antwerp. *Kunsthistorisches Museum, Vienna*

215 G. B. Tiepolo: *Sta Maria del Carmelo with St Simeon Stock*, detail of the ceiling of the Scuola dei Carmini in Venice, 1740-43. Photo *Mansell-Alinari*

217 Rubens: *The Adoration of the Magi*, c. 1624. Koninklijk Museum voor Schone Kunsten, Antwerp. Photo *ACL*

219 Wies: interior of the Wallfahrtskirche (pilgrimage church) by Dominikus Zimmermann, 1745-54. Photo *Hirmer*

222 Melk: interior of the Benedictine abbey church by Jakob Prandtauer, early 18th C. Photo *Marburg*

223 G. B. Tiepolo: *The Last Supper*, c. 1745. Louvre, Paris. Photo *Giraudon*

225 *Left*. G. B. Tiepolo: *The Adoration of the Magi*, c. 1745. Munich Pinakothek. Photo *Bayerische Staatsgemäldesammlung*

Right. Goya: detail of *The Taking of Christ*, 1798. Toledo Cathedral. Photo *Mas*

227 Blake: *The Ancient of Days*, from 'Europe', before 1795. Colour-print by means of millboard (a technique invented by Blake), touched up with watercolour. *Whitworth Art Gallery, Manchester*

228 Blake: *God creating Adam*, 1795, colour-print touched up with watercolour. *Tate Gallery, London*

229 Blake: '*Then the Lord answered Job out of the Whirlwind*', illustration on a page engraved for *The Book of Job* between 1820 and 1826. *Trustees of the British Museum*

231 Head of a bust of Voltaire by Houdon, 1778. *Gotha Museum*

235 Detail of a portrait of Diderot by L. M. von Loo, 1767. Louvre, Paris. Photo *Archives Photographiques*

COLOUR PLATES

INDEX

Numbers in italics refer to illustrations